Walkers

By the same author

THE THAMES VALLEY HERITAGE WALK (1980)
A GUIDE TO THE SOUTH DOWNS WAY (1984)

WALKERS

MILES JEBB

CONSTABLE · LONDON

First published in Great Britain 1986
by Constable and Company Limited
10 Orange Street, London WC2H 7EG
Copyright © 1986 by Miles Jebb
Set in Linotron Plantin 10pt by
Rowland Phototypesetting Limited
Bury St Edmunds, Suffolk
Printed in Great Britain by
St Edmundsbury Press Limited
Bury St Edmunds, Suffolk

British Library CIP data
Jebb, Miles
Walkers.
1. Walking – History
I. Title
796.5'1'09   GV199.5

ISBN 0 09 467430 2

Contents

Acknowledgements

Two earlier studies of walking have provided me with inspiration for this book: Geoffrey Murray's _The Gentle Art of Walking_ (Blackie, 1939), and Morris Marples' _Shanks's Pony_ (Dent, 1959). Other books which have been of special assistance in particular aspects of my study have been: Ronald Clark's _The Victorian Mountaineers_ (Batsford, 1953); Colin Fletcher's _The Complete Walker III_ (Knopf, 1984); Gunther Rothenburg's _The Art of Warfare in the age of Napoleon_ (Batsford, 1977); Jonathan Sumption's _Pilgrimage, an image of Medieval Religion_ (Faber, 1975); and Kim Taplin's _The English Path_ (Boydell Press, 1979).

I wish to make acknowledgement to the following for extracts quoted from their books: to Hodder & Stoughton and Sebastian Snow for _The Rucksack Man_; to Chatto & Windus and John Merrill for _Walking my Way_; to Longman and Sir George Trevelyan for _Clio, a Muse_; to the Bodley Head and John Buchan for _Scholar Gypsies_; to George Allen and Hilaire Belloc for _The Path to Rome_; to Jonathan Cape and W. H. Davies for _The Autobiography of a Super-Tramp_; to John Murray and Walter Starkie for _Raggle-Taggle_ and _Raggle-Taggle in Spain_; to R. Holden and Stephen Graham for _The Gentle Art of Tramping_; to Andre Deutsch and Laurie Lee for _As I walked out one Midsummer Morning_; to John Murray and Patrick Leigh Fermor for _A Time of Gifts_; to Jonathan Cape and Ramsay MacDonald for _Wanderings and Excursions_; to Holt, Rinehart & Winston and Patrick McManus for _A Fine and Pleasant Misery_; to Rodale Press, James

Acknowledgements

R. Hare and Andrew Giger for *Hiking the Appalachian Trail*; to
Constable and John Hillaby for *Journey through Love*; to Elkin
Mathews and John Masefield for the poetry from *Salt Water Ballads*
on page 132; to G. H. B. Ward and the *Sheffield Clarion Ramblers'
Handbooks*, including the poetry on page 163; to the Ramblers'
Association for the Southern Federation *Ramblers' Handbooks*, in-
cluding the poetry on page 158; to Michael Tobias for his article in
Climbing; and to Richard Wilson for his article in *The Great Outdoors*.
I am also grateful to the Cooper-Bridgeman Library for permission to
reproduce Gustave Courbet's 'The Meeting' on the jacket.

My thanks go to my excellent editors, Miles Huddleston and
Prudence Fay; and to Kevin Maddison, who has illustrated the
chapter headings.

M.J.
1986

Introduction

WALKING is natural and universal and people have walked for innumerable reasons and in countless ways. But, because we are all practitioners, we each tend to think our own style the central one. This is a restrictive view. For instance, the hill walker of today is no more or less a walker than the pedestrian tourer of the past; and the casual though habitual walker complements the marathon walker. Even to maintain that the only true walkers are those who have walked for pleasure would be to ignore several important insights into the experience of walking. For there were many who were obliged to walk and yet made creative use of it – pilgrims, peasants, poets, scientists and explorers among them. Besides, among those who did walk for 'pleasure' some did so as a means to other things and not just for walking's sake, such as climbers on long walks of approach to the mountains, or tramps who walked so as to live rough, or writers seeking copy for books, or athletes determined to break records of endurance. As I see it, the main criterion of the true walker is that he makes something of it and does not consider it merely as drudgery. So I have chosen ten themes – of course, they overlap and mix – which demonstrate the wide diversity of sensation that has sprung from the same simple ingredient. Throughout I have tried to focus as much as possible on the physical and mental experiences engendered by the walk itself, examining blisters and peeping into backpacks and probing morale. An appendix deals with military marching.

Two hundred years ago when the young German, Karl Moritz,

attempted a walking tour in England, he was refused admission at pubs as being 'some poor travelling creature': and twenty years ago John Hillaby in his walk through Britain often suffered the same rejection. For walkers, whether needy or not, have always had to be prepared to put up with insult and disdain. Even today, with walking generally recognised as a desirable leisure activity, there are many who despise walkers: most motorists when they are actually at the wheel, for a start. The very fact that walking costs nothing looks suspicious to those who pay a lot of money for their recreation; that it is uncompetitive, to those who watch sport. Social status has always gone with riding, and anyone walking is declaring an affinity with ordinary humanity; indeed, with the simpler, harder life of past millennia. The walker is moving in the most natural possible way, except that he is wearing shoes. And although footwear is one of the major comforts of civilised life and few would wish to revert to going barefoot, it is a fact that good walking can nowhere be better seen than by observation of primitive people, hunters and gatherers, often semi-naked and still barefooted, who walk with such dignity and grace. It is they who provide our tenuous link with the origins of human walking, from when over a million years ago man evolved from the shuffling gaits or jog-trots of early hominoids and established his smooth, easy, confident, rhythmical stride.

In surveying scores of remarkable walkers one is struck by the wealth of character which so distinguishes them from, say, a selection of leading sportsmen. Sports champions are by definition people notable for physical rather than cerebral skills. Their sporting prowess has dominated their lives. But many of the great walkers have made use of walking as a background physical activity, a therapy which served to assuage their often very fertile minds, minds which tended to flourish on intellectual rather than practical or commercial matters. What also differentiates them from sportsmen is that many came to walking through not being very good at games involving a good eye and co-ordination: a certain clumsiness and gaucheness is a recurring feature. So is a certain introspection, which often impeded them in worldly affairs and made some of them frustrated in terms of ambition, inhibited in terms of sex, or outsiders in terms of society. Another factor which accounts for their diversity is that walkers vary enormously in age, from teenagers to the very old. On either side of middle age, it seems, people often feel the need to test themselves. They want to prove something, the youths that they can do it and the old that they can still do it: and, in walking, the amazing thing is that many of them still can. This appeal to all ages is one of the most attractive features in the story of walking.

Though experience of walking is found in many forms, pride of place attaches to those who have been for long walking expeditions alone, the great soloists of the craft. Ultimately, all had to come up against the fundamentals of their own individual temperaments, which made their external tests relatively easier or harder. At one extreme one feels that people like Hutton, Cooper, Giger or Merrill shared an imperturbability which was more than a match for any setback; a stolid single-mindedness which precluded imaginative mind-wanderings or gloomy broodings. A tough persona and a thick skin also served to protect the likes of Shaw, Borrow, Graham and Hillaby; though lurking behind their masks were wilder and more passionate natures. Charm was another form of protection, much used by Muir, Lee and Leigh Fermor: and a quaint and perky humour another, employed to good effect by Coryate, Taylor, Starkie and Snow. I would place Warner, Stevenson, Thomas and Belloc among those who suffered most from their more susceptible natures.

In describing their walking several of these have contributed memorable phrases. Some, particularly among the earlier walkers, who were usually reticent about their pains, are remarkable for their blandness: for example, the near-octogenarian Hutton's description of his last 139 miles in six days as 'easy marches'; or Borrow's reference to his pace towards the end of a long day as being a 'bounding and elastic step'. A passing admission of foot trouble, quickly brushed aside, is the most that is conceded by Muir, with his 'my feet were sore, but oh! I am paid for all my toil a thousand times over'; and Cooper dismissed his aches as 'Mere spots on the sun, mere thorns on the rose'. The reality of physical suffering is exposed more clearly by Stevenson with his stated desire to 'find the globe granite underfoot and strewn with cutting flints'; a tribulation crisply turned by Giger – 'Bend, twist, wrench, turn; your feet keep step on the rocks by slipping, arching, squeezing, sliding forward, sideways, back-ways, and around them.' Also by Lee – 'treading the rim of a burning wheel'. To this is added the more serious mental suffering of walking, as expressed by Snow when he says that for three weeks 'every bloody step I took became an individual act of will'; by Thomas with his 'constant struggle between impatient mind and dull tired body'; and by Hillaby with 'All the pleasure of pioneering had drained away; I wanted nothing more than to conserve what little energy and enthusiasm I had . . .' Taylor precedes them all with his cry from the heart three and a half centuries ago: 'since I was born, I never was so weary, or so near being dead with extreme travel.' But Belloc puts it most poignantly of all: 'I still went forward a little, because when I sat down my loneliness oppressed me like a misfortune; and because my feet, going painfully and slowly, yet gave a little balance and rhythm to the movement of my mind.' Here is the authentic expression of the will that drove all these men forward at their darkest moments, without which their stories would have been of failure not success and, for all their talents as writers, merely amusing travellers' tales instead of heroic sagas.

Throughout we find that walking is not merely a natural motion that calls for physical skills in terms of stance, stride, pace and, above all, rhythm. It is also associated with mental attitudes such as independence, sense of purpose, determination and unpretentiousness. What is more, it induces states of mind ranging from acute thinking to suspension of thought, from inner calm to ecstasy, which serve to purge the walker from inner conflicts and heighten appreciation of all that is encountered. But this only happens to those who make an effort to walk properly and sustain to the upper levels of individual capability through energy or endurance. For one basic element in walking is its graduality. It is the antithesis of instancy. Its appeal is meaningless to spectators. It is anti-climactic. It is a big spender of time. But it is time very well spent.

Pilgrims

ALONG the roads of England five hundred years ago there moved a slow procession of foot-travellers, sometimes a constant stream, sometimes a solitary figure, all making their way purposefully and all resigned to be walking, not riding. Most were engaged in basic trades or dealings: drug sellers, pedlars and chapmen, who bought and sold and bartered; jobbing workmen such as stone-masons or joiners; and entertainers – perambulating minstrels, singers, buffons and glee-men. A special breed were the messengers, bearers of letters or packets or verbal tidings, often the fastest of the foot-travellers and, though themselves of humble status, protected by the authority of those who had sent them. To these were added the religious, the preachers, pardoners, mendicant friars and pilgrims. And finally

1

there were the people on the fringe of society, some utterly ignored by it – beggars, poachers, escaped peasants, robbers, bandits and general down-and-outs. On they went through the hours, keeping to the sides and out of the way of the horses and palfries and axle-creaking wagons on which rode the more fortunate; and for the purpose of the journey there were but two classes, those who walked and those who rode.

Only in imagination can we picture this tableau of humanity through half a millennium, but imagination can be assisted by the description given by Rudyard Kipling of a similar and more recent scene in India, the 'river of life' flowing along the Grand Trunk Road. Among the pedestrians seen by young Kim as he walked beside the holy man were a troop of 'long-haired, strong-scented' Sansis, moving 'at a quick, furtive jog-trot'; a man recently released from prison, 'walking wide and stiffly across the strong shadows, the memory of his leg-irons still on him'; a Sikh who 'stalked past'; whole groups of villagers, 'the women, with their babes on their hips, walking behind the men'; a gang of female earth-carriers, 'flat-footed, big-bosomed, strong-limbed', who 'walked with squared elbows, swinging hips, and heads on high, as suits women who carry heavy weights'; a strolling juggler; soldiers on leave; and 'Brahmins and chumars, bankers and tinkers, barbers and bunnias, pilgrims and potters – all the world going and coming'.

But for the fifteenth-century English there was no Grand Trunk Road, not even an ordinary trunk road. The highways connecting even the largest cities were in an appalling condition. Royal authority had weakened; civil war was endemic; and besides, for many journeys it was quicker and smoother to go by sea or river. So the main roads were peppered with pot-holes and scarred with ruts, cut by brooks and streams and often flooded, and in soft sections completely impassable in winter. To avoid bad patches people deviated in loops and sometimes walked along the edge of the adjoining fields, so that the route became a series of separate tracks. Bridges were exceptional rather than the rule; gangs of bandits attacked wayfarers, especially those who strayed. Small wonder that throughout medieval Europe travel was seen as something to avoid, especially if on foot. Petrarch was quite exceptional when he took long rambles in the hills north of Rome or in Vaucluse, on one occasion – 26 April 1336 – actually ascending Mont Ventoux. Aimless wanderings like this were regarded with deep suspicion; and optional walking in the Middle Ages occurred in an utterly different manifestation, namely in pilgrimage.

2

In its purest form pilgrimage was voluntary journey to worship at some holy shrine, and the journey itself was expected to be hard and fraught with difficulties, a form of penance. But to private penance was added public penance, imposed as penalty for misbehaviour. Further, there were 'testamentary' pilgrims, people who had been left a bequest on condition that they went (or got someone else to go) on pilgrimage. So altogether there were many reluctant as well as enthusiastic pilgrims marching to the promised land through the night of doubt and sorrow. Central to the concept of pilgrimage was that it should be undertaken on foot. Not only did the extra effort increase the element of penance, but it endowed the pilgrim with an aura of poverty and humility, and hence with Christian virtues. A long tradition of the Church held that walking was the most virtuous method of travelling. In the process of the establishment of the Church in the West during the Dark Ages the Christian missionaries, especially the Irish, had been notable in foregoing the use of horses, and many were the stories of saints that included lengthy walks. Among the English saints we find St Cuthman, who walked from the West Country into Sussex to preach the gospel, pulling his disabled mother, Frippa, along behind him in a cart: and later St Godric who, when a boy, trudged the roads as a chapman and, according to his hagiographer, 'walked with simplicity; and, in so far as he yet knew how, it was ever his pleasure to follow in the footsteps of the truth.' Several walked to Rome so as to impress the papacy with the justice of their cause in cases which were under appeal: St Wilfrid, for one.

Pilgrims were *meant* to be on foot, and were shown as such in sculpture or painting; as were the pilgrim saints such as St Roch, in contrast to the more triumphalist saints such as St George, St James Matamoros and St Martin. And even St Martin, though depicted on a horse when cutting his cloak to share with the beggar, expressed his contempt for priests who went mounted in the course of their duties. The rule of St Francis specifically stated that friars were not to ride unless some manifest necessity or infirmity obliged them. Even more virtuous was to walk barefoot; this was frequently done and, when by some grandee, duly noted and applauded. Joinville, historian of the First Crusade, after receiving his blessing at the abbey of Chaminon, made his way without shoes or coat to the embarkation point at Marseilles. And Robert, Duke of Normandy (the father of William the Conqueror), under strong suspicion of murdering his brother, travelled barefoot to Jerusalem in 1035. Some centuries later the

3

Countess of Clare threw away her shoes as she started on a pilgrimage. Sometimes, especially when approaching the shrine, pilgrims crawled on their knees: but the notion that any walked with pebbles in their shoes is probably a later invention. For example Peter Pindar, who wrote satirical poems in the eighteenth century, tells the tale of two pilgrims to Loretto who set off with peas in their shoes. One of them strides ahead while the other hobbles along in agony: he eventually encounters his companion who is now on his return journey, and accosts him:

> 'How is't that you can like a greyhound go,
> Merry, as if that nought had happened, burn ye!'
> 'Why,' cried the other, grinning, 'you must know
> That just before I ventured on my journey,
> To walk a little more at ease,
> I took the liberty to boil my peas.'

Though millions went on medieval pilgrimages we have few accounts of actual travel experiences, particularly of walking. The first reference I have to foot-soreness on pilgrimage is as late as 1726, when one Manier from Picardy started out towards Compostella from Paris. Near Tours he found he couldn't walk any further: at which a passing horseman recommended a remedy which was either a sick joke or else confined to rich people – 'candle-grease mingled with brandy and olive-oil' which is reminiscent of Kipling's simpler recipe:

> An' if your 'eels are blistered an' they feels to 'urt like 'ell,
> You drop some tallow in your socks an' that will make 'em well.

The fact is that in the Middle Ages people simply were not interested in such mundane matters. Physical exhaustion, injury, hunger, discomfort, these were all common things: and descriptions of distant lands were beyond comprehension to those who were confined to feudal villages. What really fascinated them was the operation of the miraculous, and pilgrims who returned with some example of it, particularly if they had been the beneficiary, could be assured of much more respect and attention than if they had merely told of mileages or blisters or strange sights. Still, we are able to patch together some semblance of what it was like to undertake the long-distance walk that constituted a major pilgrimage in its prime.

4

At the initiation ceremony the pilgrim was given an all-purpose coarse tunic, instantly recognisable, which was a sort of walking equivalent of the ankle-length habits worn by the friars, and stamped him as a member of a quasi-religious order himself. With it went his staff, a tough six-foot wooden stick with a knob at one end and a metal toe at the other; and his scrip, a soft leather pouch, strapped to his waist, in which he kept basic items such as food, mess-can and money. His hat was broad-brimmed, his footwear usually sandals. Thus arrayed, he set off into the unknown towards a series of gathering points. They travelled in groups for protection and convenience, though in earlier centuries solitary pilgrims were more usual, and it was always considered praiseworthy to travel alone. Once on the main pilgrimage route progress was regulated by the staging-posts provided by the great hospices. These were situated basically at one full day's march from each other, on the average about 25 miles apart. This was the distance that healthy people could cover without difficulty in good conditions, and there is no doubt that many of the pilgrims were young and healthy and capable of great endurance. Those who were not healthy, or who were caught in storm or rain, had to spend intermediate nights crouching beside the track; and since the big organised pilgrim convoys must have marched at the speed of the slowest, it is probable that they covered only about 10–15 miles a day on the average. At the hospices they received the most basic sustenance, such as bread and soup, and shelter to lie down under. Elsewhere the poor pilgrims had to live rough and hope for alms from begging: those with cash (or sometimes promissory notes and bills of exchange) could go to inns. Their journey was beset with perils such as plagues and wars, or wild uninhabited areas where they might get lost or perish in the cold or be savaged by wild animals or, most likely, attacked by brigands – brigands who sometimes attached themselves to the group, disguised as pilgrims themselves, before they struck.

Undoubtedly a trance-like state of mind impelled the pilgrims forward: a resignation, an asceticism, an indifference to chance. They sublimated themselves above the dirt, the grime, the sweaty clothes, the sores and aches, by prayers and invocations to the saints who they felt to be like spirits all around them, and whose deeds were as familiar to them as those of leading pop heroes are to millions today, whose glittering shrines were as marvellous as any television spectacular. Endlessly they repeated catch-phrases and chants, such as the Languedocian triplet (each phrase to two paces, a left and a right foot): '*E ultreia, E sus eia, Deus aia nos,*' which means 'Above our head, Below our feet, God be our hope.' But behind all this there lies one further basic aspect of the medieval pilgrimages. For, quite apart from religion there existed a wanderlust which had been inherited from the era of the great tribal migrations of the Dark Ages not so many centuries before, when the ancestors of the pilgrims, as yet unsettled and more pastoral, wandered with their flocks and herds along the ancient ridgeways. The recently established feudal system had confined people to tight prison-like villages, and just as modern man longs to escape from the town to the countryside, so did feudal man yearn in an unspoken way for the lost liberties of the open spaces. In the subconscious perhaps there still lurked folk memories of the old Nordic gods and of Wotan, the chief of the gods, who was wont to walk the world disguised as a wanderer, clad in a long dark-blue mantle and brown broad-brimmed hat, and bearing an ash-plant inscribed with ancient runes, fixing you with his single beady eye. And then again, although the feudal system had clamped everyone into a tight framework, there was as yet no concept of nationalism or state frontiers, so that the English found it quite natural to join a crowd of French pilgrims to Jerusalem, or Germans to walk with Flemings to Santiago.

There were three main pilgrimage routes in Europe: to Jerusalem, to Rome, and to Compostella; and those who took them were called respectively Palmiers, Romées and Jacquets (from which comes our word 'jacket'). That to Jerusalem was the longest but, though there was a land route via Vienna, Belgrade, Constantinople, Cilicia and Antioch, it was usually done with large stretches by sea. The route to Rome was the shortest but all overland and not without great hazards at times, whether from the Alpine passes, Saracen bands in the Midi, or German outlaws in the central Apennines: and this despite Rome being the centre of Christendom. Pilgrimage to Rome was boosted by the institution of Jubilee years, and in 1300 some three hundred thousand pilgrims arrived there in the summer at the rate of around three thousand each day. But the most interesting of the major pilgrimages was that to Santiago de Compostella, the remote shrine of St James the Great at the north-western extremity of Spain. In the twelfth century it was the pre-eminent pilgrimage, associated with the Christian reconquest of the peninsula. There were four routes through France (from Orléans, Vezelay, Le Puy and St Giles) which converged at the Pyrenees and then led through Spain along the great

Camino de Santiago, sometimes making use of ancient Roman roads. The return journey from, say, Paris was some 2000 miles and was usually walked over about six months through the summer. Of course, besides these three great pilgrim routes there were many more local ones, of which the principal in England were to the shrines of St Thomas at Canterbury, King Edward the Confessor at Westminster, Our Lady at Walsingham, St Swithun at Winchester, and St Cuthbert at Durham.

The three main pilgrimages were closely associated with the Crusades, of which two are notable as being utterly chaotic affairs much more like pilgrimages than military operations. The People's Crusade under Peter the Hermit left Cologne on 20 April 1096 and met its horrible end in massacre at Civetot on the shores of the Bosporus on 21 October. Peter in his itinerant preaching had usually walked barefoot; but he set out on his Crusade mounted on a donkey, to which, with his long lean face, he bore a strange resemblance. The few knights who had joined him were of course mounted on their warhorses. But, these apart, the whole motley collection of some twenty thousand enthusiasts – consisting mainly of under-employed peasants together with numbers of townsfolk as well as brigands and criminals – walked. Their route led along roads up the Rhine valley and then all the way down the line of the Danube and, since they reached Semlin (Malavilla) near its mouth on 20 June, they must have covered 25 miles a day when conditions were good: quite an achievement for such a large and disorderly group, which also included some women and children. At Semlin they had the first of many clashes with the civic authorities along their way, and it is not surprising to learn that the riot which started it had begun over a dispute about the sale of a pair of shoes! Even worse rows, with full-scale fighting, took place at Belgrade and Nish, after which things grew quieter as they proceeded under armed escort to the Imperial City of Constantinople, covering this last 400 miles at an average rate of 20 miles a day.

The pathetic disorganisation of the People's Crusade was exceeded by that of the Children's Crusade over a century later in 1212. An hysterical twelve-year-old called Stephen, a shepherd boy from Orléanais, preached at the entrance of the Abbey of St Denis to such effect that, despite the disapproval of the authorities, he succeeded in persuading several thousand children (some of them girls) to head off with him on foot to Marseilles. Here, they believed, the waters would part to enable them to continue their walk along the seabed to the East

7

where the Infidels would be so impressed by their innocent eloquence that they would embrace Christianity and everyone would live happily ever after. Alas, reality was different, and the children mostly got captured by pirates and sold as slaves, which was also the fate of Nicholas and a group of slightly older German children from the Rhineland who walked south in the same year, some to Genoa and some to Ancona.

But, as with all other human institutions, pilgrimage in time fell into decline. Kings and princes were less willing to let their economically active subjects enjoy a year off, and the whole impetus of the Crusades was spent. The flow of pilgrims was sharply reduced, and those that went were more likely to be the ill seeking cures and the curious seeking change. Neither of these types was so prone to walk and, as the roads gradually improved, more horses, litters and wagons were seen along the routes. Magnates such as John of Gaunt and William of Aquitaine travelled as pilgrims with liveried retainers who nightly erected gorgeous tents hung with silk in which they ate off gold and silver plate which was carried behind them on long trains of packhorses. Chaucer's Canterbury Pilgrims all left on horseback as a matter of course, with no mention of foot-pilgrims in any of their tales. Women, who earlier had hardly been seen on the pilgrimages, now travelled much more freely. The shrines became increasingly commercialised and cynicism spread among the more thoughtful. What now captured general attention were tales of travel to strange countries. Of these the most well-known was *Mandeville's Travels*, purporting to be the journeys of one 'Sir John Mandeville' though in fact a clever compilation from the – often fictional – works of earlier writers, written in French in the fourteenth century. Ironically, it was accepted as fact whereas the travels of Marco Polo, which appeared about the same time, were derided as the wildest fiction. It was in the spirit of Mandeville and with the veracity of Marco Polo that William Lithgow wrote his *Totall Discourse of the Rare Adventures and Painefull Peregrinations of Nineteene Yeares Travayles from Scotland to the most famous Kingdomes in Europe, Asia and Affrica*, first published in 1632.

Though a 'peregrination' meant the action of travelling in foreign lands, especially on foot, it was of the same root source as 'pilgrimage'; and Lithgow certainly saw himself as 'the wandering pilgrim', and not merely because he made the pilgrimage to Jerusalem. He was a Protestant pilgrim, determined to denounce idolatry and prepared to undergo terrible hardships in the course of his travels. In fact, what

8

ended them was that he was arrested in Malaga as a spy and was severely tortured before being released through the intervention of the English ambassador. But, whether pilgrim or wanderer, he was emphatically a foot-traveller, doubtless mainly for reasons of economy. Born in Lanark in about 1582, he would probably have remained there as a tailor had it not been for a romantic misadventure. The four brothers of a certain Miss Lockhart, finding their sister with Lithgow, set upon him and cut off his ears, from which he was locally nicknamed 'Cutlugged' Will. It seems that this 'undeserved wrong' was the original motive for his wandering first to the Orkneys and Shetlands and then, in 1609, on the first of his three great journeys. In the *Totall Discourse* he claims that his 'paynefull feet traced over (besides my passages of Seas and Rivers) thirty-six thousand and odde miles, which draweth neare to twice the circumference of the whole Earth': but actually by far the greater part of this was by sea. In the course of his three journeys he says he visited all the European countries except for Scandinavia and Russia: though his accounts of his progression through some of them – for example Hungary, Poland and Portugal – are so cursory as to induce a twinge of doubt. He also went to Constantinople, Cyprus, the Lebanon and Mesopotamia, as well as Tunis and Algiers, and travelled (on a donkey mostly) with a pilgrim caravan from Aleppo to Jerusalem and then on to Cairo. In Syria he took an eleven-day walk, escorted by a hired Janissary.

In his book he quotes several instances of purely pedestrian adventures. We find him walking towards the shrine of Loretto in Italy and overtaking a coach carrying two young unmarried couples. These were so impressed by his pilgrim spirit that they got out of their coach and walked the remaining miles with him, and later after supper 'each youth led captive his dearest Darling to an unsanctified bed, and left me to my accostomed repose'. In the Peloponnese he experienced exhaustion in wandering over the hills but continued on his march, camping en route at night, where 'I had the ground to be a pillow, and the world-wide fields to be a chamber, the whirling windy-skys, to be a roofe to my Winter-blasted lodging, and the humide vapours of cold Nocturna, to accompany the unwished-for-bed of my repose'. In Crete, in the course of one day when he walked 37 miles, he was set upon by brigands who stripped him naked and took his small change (fortunately, he had deposited most of his money at Lanerke, now Kasteli); but after some special pleading they 'restored back again my Pilgrime clothes, and Letters, but my blew gowns and Bagantines they kept'. At a later stage in his first journey, on his return through France, he was again attacked as he walked along the coast road between Nice and Antibes. Perhaps he looked fair game to his attackers, for he was dressed in a long Turkish gown, but when he had identified himself as a penniless pilgrim by showing his Jerusalem certificate, they laid off. At the start of his second journey William Lithgow tells us that 'I measured all the Netherlands with my feete in two moneths space'; and then he walked all the way south to Sicily, for some time in company with another Englishman.

Though his pedestrian achievements were all his own, Lithgow's mention of and pride in them were undoubtedly due to the influence of an account of a journey to Venice made in 1608, under the title of *Coryat's Crudities*: and it may be said that Thomas Coryate was the first person to glorify in walking as such and encourage pedestrians to walk tall rather than feel themselves to be inferior beings. It needed a man of originality, indeed eccentricity, to make this point, and Coryate was both these things. What is more, he was recognised as such by the Jacobean nobility: for at the time he set out he was in some position in the household of Prince Henry, the eldest son of James I, seemingly as a sort of unofficial court jester. The impecunious son of the rector of Odcombe, near Yeovil in Somerset, Thomas had small hope of advancement since his main attribute was his mordant wit and talent for joking and ridiculous disputation. Thomas Fuller in *The Worthies of England* wrote that 'sweetmeats and Coryate made up the last course at all court entertainments. Indeed he was the courtiers' anvil to try their wits upon; and sometimes this anvil returned the hammers as hard knocks as it received, his bluntness repaying their abusiveness.' These attributes would have condemned him to a life of bitterness, like Rigoletto, had he not at the age of thirty-two had the inspiration to make use of them in conjunction with some amazingly courageous and independent travelling. The result was his *Crudities*, a marvellously vivid and perceptive account of his journey to Venice, full of descriptions and observations not previously recorded in English. As in most travel books, Coryate made extensive use of existing sources; but the greater part of the *Crudities* is his own personal story, far cleverer and funnier than Lithgow's later effort, with the recently expanded English language larded with exaggerated rhetorical tricks as a means of amusing and impressing his readers.

There are moments in European history when a lull appears between the spasms of wars and fighting, and the first decade of the seventeenth century was one of these. France was recovering from the wars of religion under the policy of toleration imposed by Henry IV; Spain was at peace with England and the Netherlands; and in Germany the Thirty Years War had not begun. A trickle of English noblemen began to filter down to Italy, and it would have been natural for Coryate to attach himself to one of them. Instead he set off all alone and unprotected, prepared to walk if necessary. On his way out to Venice through France and Savoy he did in fact walk about 150 miles, though he covered more than this on post-horses as well as in such novelties as a Picardy cart (two wheels) and a coach. When crossing the frontier to Savoy at the Pont de Beauvoisin, Coryate decided to dismount from his horse and instead walk up the steep slope to the col, but getting lost among the rocks he was obliged to make use of a chair carried on poles by two chairmen, which cost him eighteen pence for just half a mile's ride. However, it was on his return journey that his principal walking took place, for not only was it through the central Alps but also he had evidently decided to forego the use of post-horses when he could perfectly well walk instead. As a result he walked all the way from Venice to Mainz, that is, apart from using boats on the Venetian canal, on Lake Zurich and down the Rhine from Basle to Strasbourg.

The initial mileages made for dull walking because towards Vicenza the straight road had been denuded of avenues and the countryside of trees as a precaution against surprise attacks on Padua. The cultivated land was largely arable, though with cattle-pastures and many vineyards. The custom was for travellers to pick bunches of grapes from the roadside unhindered, which gave Coryate a perpetual supply of fruit. There were also ancient milestones and inscribed pillars. More sinister was the fact that most of the mounted men were armed with muskets already charged with gunpowder, tinder boxes at the ready for instant ignition at the sight of a bandit. But Thomas Coryate was unarmed, partly because by appearing as a man without means he would be less liable to attack, and partly because of the expensive firearm controls at the towns. Refreshed by two nights in Verona he continued at his usual 3 miles to the hour to Brescia. The day after that was a long one – 30 miles to Bergamo – and there were many others on the road. They were attending the week-long St Bartholomew's Fair, and as a result all the inns were full and he could get in nowhere even though he was prepared to offer three ducats, an enormous sum, for a comfortable bed. Thanks to a helpful priest who had also been on the road he eventually got leave to lie on a pallet of straw in a stable, and was so tired that he slept as soundly as on a feather bed. The friendly priest had promised to come to Coryate next morning and show him the antiquities of Bergamo; but when he failed to turn up Coryate on enquiring was told he had been murdered in his lodging by a man who bore him 'an old grudge'. However, this may have been just a blind for the priest to avoid further contact with the heretical Englishman, and indeed Coryate was warned (by a friendly Dominican friar) not to take the obvious route up into the Grisons because of a Spanish garrison on the shores of Lake Como who would be keen to seize him and pass him to the Inquisition, but to take a more northerly route. Soon he was in hilly country on rough tracks with hard stones against which his pumps gave no protection, and was reduced to about a mile an hour. There was talk of bandits who had attacked travellers only a few days before. On the third day out of Bergamo he crossed the Pass of St Mark and the delimitation of Venetian territory and entered the Grisons, a group of tiny, virtually independent republics. Now accompanied by an English-speaking Swiss, he walked down the Valtellina, in which delectable valley he noticed, besides the vines and sheep, a 'marvellous abundance' of frogs. The Swiss left him at Chiavenna, the first of the Protestant towns, and Coryate continued alone over the Splugen Pass into German-speaking lands and so on to Zurich. He was enchanted by the Alpine valleys and their inhabitants, so peaceable and honest that a traveller could pass through with a 'thousand crowns' without fear of robbery, the wooden houses stocked with good fresh food – and pickled beef – eaten on wooden trenchers at least an inch thick, the abundance of fruit, the green meadows, the tree-trunks used for bridges across tumbling streams.

The second stage of Coryate's walk was from Zurich to Basle and included visits to the sulphur baths at Baden and the monastery of Kiningsfelden. Coryate was a poor linguist and got by largely in Latin with a strong English accent. This was all right for conversing with educated men but not so good for simple problems like finding the way, so he wandered about for some time before discovering the baths. Apart from learning of the curative effects of the sulphur springs he was intrigued to see that mixed bathing was very much the order of the day. 'Here also I saw many passing faire yong Ladies and Gentlewomen naked in the bathes with their wooers and favorites in the same. For at this time of the year many woers come thither to solace themselves with their beautiful mistresses. Many of these yong

Ladies had the haire of their head very curiously plaited in locks, & they wore certaine pretty garlands upon their heads made of fragrant and odiferous flowers. A spectacle exceeding amorous.' Resuming his walk at Strasbourg, he crossed to the right bank of the Rhine at Lichtenau by what was in those days the lowest bridge across the river: it was 'a thousand four score and sixe paces long. For I paced it. The longest bridge that ever I passed. But it is nothing faire. For the boordes and plankes are verie rudely compacted together.' Now his way led through the Black Forest to Baden Baden, taking him nine hours to cover 16 miles, due to getting lost. More serious was an encounter with a couple of 'Ragged Boors', armed rogues whom he saw approaching along the road. Although his clothes 'being but a thread-bare fustian case were so meane (my cloake onely excepted) that the Boores could not have made an ordinary supper with the money for which they should have sold them', he had gold coins quilted into his jerkin, and was unarmed except for a short knife. Quick as a flash

> I put off my hat very curteously unto them, holding it a pretty while in my hand, and very humbly (like a Mendicant Frier) begged some money of them in a language that they did but poorely understand, even the Latin, expressing my mind unto them by such gestures and signes, that they well knew what I craved of them: and so by this begging insinuation I bothe preserved my selfe secure & free from the violence of the clownes, and withall obtained that of them which I neither wanted or expected. For they gave me so much of their tinne money called fennies (as poore as they were) as paid for halfe my supper that night at Baden, even foure pence half-penny.

After a reviving draught of good Rhenish wine at the entrance to a friary, he entered Baden Baden. Here he naturally inspected the baths, more extensive though less communal than at the Swiss Baden, and used as a cure for all sorts of complaints, from none of which, fortunately, was Coryate suffering. The country was fat with vegetables such as cabbages, turnips and radishes, as well as fruit, particularly pears. No one objected to travellers gleaning near the roadside. There were large cornfields, and hemp was being beaten by the women: there were frogs and red snails. Durlach was hard to enter because of strict control at the gate; but Coryate had his letters of

13

recommendation and was received in audience by the Prefect of the Margrave's Court. Then, at Heidelberg, where he arrived wet to the skin in a heavy shower, he was given a private tour of the Palatine library and the castle cellar, which contained the Great Tun which held some 25,000 gallons of wine.

From Heidelberg he walked back to the Rhine, passing through 'a great wood, which by reason of the manifold turnings of the way like a company of voluminous Meanders, did so exceedingly purplexe me, that I got out of the same with no small difficulty'. After a couple of days at the Imperial City of Speyer he set off for Worms. A mile or two short of it he decided to pick a bunch of grapes, just as he had in Italy: but

> there came a German Boore upon me (for so are the clownes of the country commonly called) with a halbert in his hand, & in a great fury pulled off very violently my hat from my head, looked very fiercely upon me with eyes sparkling fire in a manner, and with his Almanne wordes which I understood not, swaggered most insolently with me, holding up his halbert in that threatening manner at me, that I continualy expected a blow, and was in deadly feare lest he would have made me a prey for the wormes before I should ever put my foote in the gallant city of Wormes.

There followed a mutually incomprehensible slanging match, the Boor in German, Coryate in Latin, and peace only came with the arrival of others on the scene: for a payment of twelve pfennigs his hat was restored to him. Two days later he fell in with a woodman who did speak some Latin, but instead of praising this, Coryate ridiculed it to his readers, employing a most remarkable adjective: 'The Latin which he did speake was such incongruall and disjoynted stuffe, such antipriscianisticall eloquence, that I thinke were grave Cato alive he should have more cause to laugh if he should heare this fellow deliver his minde in Latin, than when he saw an Asse eate thistles.' From Mainz, apart from a visit to Frankfurt, partly walked, Thomas Coryate's journey home was entirely by water. After a short rest in London he returned to Odcombe, where he later hung his shoes up in the church. By his own calculations he had covered in all 1975 miles on his journey. Of these, 397 were walked between Padua and Mainz on his return route in twenty-seven walking days, making 15 miles each day on average.

Thomas Coryate now became the butt of much attention, both affectionate and malicious. Despite financial entanglements resulting from a failed debtor, he managed to publish his *Crudities* himself, and used some unusual methods to promote its sale. He was constrained to include in it an extraordinary selection of mock panegyric verses, preceded by a 'Character of the Author' by Ben Jonson which begins 'He is an Engine, wholly consisting of extremes, a Head, Fingers, and Toes. For what his industrious toes have trod, his ready Fingers have written, his subtle head dictating.' Jonson also wrote:

How well and how often his shoes too were mended,
That sacred to Odcombe are now there suspended,
I meane that one paire, wherewith he so hobled
From Venice to Flushing, were not they well cobled?

The self-styled Peregrine of Odcombe and Odcombian Legge-stretcher still had itchy feet and now decided to travel to the East, to Constantinople and the Holy Land. After making his pilgrimage to Jerusalem in 1613–14 (in the same manner as William Lithgow had done in only the previous year) Coryate determined on a far more ambitious journey – to travel overland to India on foot. Though this decision to walk was probably mainly due to lack of money, he also wanted to establish his reputation as the greatest walker the world had ever seen. Amazingly he succeeded in this venture, setting out from Aleppo in September 1614 and arriving at Ajmer at the court of the Great Mogul in July 1615, having covered some 3300 miles 'all which way I traversed afoot, but with divers paire of shooes, having become such a propateticke . . . that is, a walker forward on foote, as I doubt whether you ever heard of the like in your life.' Alas, we have no full account of his experiences on this mammoth walk (apart from a few letters and references to them in the writings of Samuel Purchas) since Coryate died soon after in India and his manuscripts were never found. But we have glimpses of him, as for instance being robbed of his money by one of the Spahis (horseguards) of the caravan at Diarbekr in Kurdestan, or resting two months in Isphahan, or encountering Robert Shirley and his train of attendants somewhere near the frontier of Persia and India, or walking along the main road between Lahore and Agra and admiring the countryside. It seems that on the whole journey from Aleppo he spent only fifty shillings 'yet fared reasonably well everie daie; victuals being so cheape in some countries where I travelled, that I often times lived competentlie for a penny sterling a day'.

In the summer of 1619 two men were independently making their way on foot from London to Edinburgh. One was the author and playwright Ben Jonson, now aged forty-five and corpulent. The reasons why this literary man should have decided to make this walk are uncertain. It is known that he intended writing an account of it, so maybe literary copy was the motive, especially after the impact of Coryate's *Crudities*: or possibly he wanted to lose weight. All we know for certain is that he walked up the Great North Road and got new shoes at Darlington. The other was John Taylor, who has left us his experiences in *Taylor's Penniless Pilgrimage*. It must have riled Ben Jonson that this second-rate versifier and odd-ball should have matched his achievement and one must suspect that Taylor may have done so on purpose to make fun of the man of letters. But evidently they met when in Edinburgh and Jonson gave Taylor twenty-two shillings, so such cheekiness was not obviously expressed. Be this as it may, it is to Taylor we must turn for an account, written in his horrible doggerel as far as the border and thereafter in prose. The title page reads:

> *The Pennyless Pilgrimage, or the Money-lesse perambulation, of John Taylor, alias the Kings Majesties Water-Poet. How he travailed on foot from London to Edenborough in Scotland, not carrying any Money to or fro, neither Begging, Borrowing, or Asking Meate, drinke or Lodging. With his description of his Entertainment in all places of his Journey, and a true Report of the unmatchable Hunting in the Brea of Marre and Badenoch in Scotland. With other Observations, some serious and worthy of Memory, and some merry and not hurtfull to be remembered. Lastly that (which is Rare in a Travailler) all is true.*

He called himself the 'Water-Poet' because he held a position as a Thames waterman, and had already established a reputation for eccentric travel by rowing and sailing his wherry around the coast and up to York, and on another occasion around the south coast and up to Salisbury. These stunts were performed for reward, with subscribers undertaking to pay him on their successful completion. This was the basis of his walk to Edinburgh, though eventually it backfired because more than half the backers refused to pay on the grounds that he had not walked entirely alone but was accompanied by a mounted servant with provisions, and also had paved the way by arranging for hospitality from friends en route. Still, he made it, and walked every yard – including fording the Esk rather than making use of the horse to avoid getting wet – and then went on to attend the great annual deerhunt at Braemar. John Taylor, like so many other famous pedestrians since, having had the idea of a walking-tour, could not put it down later in life, and in 1649 when seventy years old wandered to Land's End, walking for most of the way there and back; four years later he walked to Wales. Of the former journey he wrote:

> Six hundred miles, I (very neere) have footed,
> And all that time was neither sho'd or booted;
> But in light buskins I perform'd this travell
> O're hill and dale, through dust, dirt, flint, or gravell.

Of his walk to Edinburgh the facts briefly are that he covered the 400-odd miles over a period of twenty-six days, of which sixteen were walking days, so averaging 25 miles each walking day, quite a bit more than Coryate had achieved in Europe: his longest day was from Carlisle to Moffat, 40 miles. After being given free accommodation at the Bell Inn in Aldersgate, the Saracen's Head at St Albans, and the Queen's Arms at Stony Stratford, he failed to get it at the Horse Shoe at Daventry, where he arrived feeling pretty tired after a day of stony roads and blistering weather: what is more, the people at the inn had helped themselves to a jug of beer which a friendly rider had ordered for him. Inwardly cursing, he had to hobble on as far as Dunsmoor Heath, where he and his servant slept out on rushes and bracken which they cut, occasioning a few lines of respectably good verse:

> My bed was curtained with good wholesome airs,
> And being weary, I went up no stairs:
> The sky my canopy, bright Phoebe shined
> Sweet bawling Zephyrus breathed gentle wind,
> In heaven's star-chamber I did lodge that night,
> Ten thousand stars, me to my bed did light.

There followed convivial stops in private houses at Coventry, Newhall and Lichfield; but then, failing to get any free meal, let alone a bed, along the road past Stone, he and his servant had to crouch in the long-grass under a makeshift bivouac of broom and endure six hours of steady rain through the night. After this the Water-Poet gets really fed up and breaks from verse into prose to tell us how he lost his temper with a passing ostler and, not finding any inn for a second day, had to 'breakfast in the sun': though this cannot have been too much of a hardship since the horse was laden with provisions such as bacon, biscuits, tongue, cheese, jam, vinegar, oil and liquor in the form of 'Aqua Vitae' and 'Ambrosia'. Things seemed much better that night when he arrived at the hospitable house of a 'complete gentleman', Sir Urian Leigh, of Adlington, who gets a whole page of adulation (now in verse again) and who gave him good contacts for his next stop at Manchester. Then it was to Preston (Master Hind), Lancaster (Master Covill), Sedburgh (Master Branthwaite) and Carlisle (Sir John Dalston). Taylor must have been amusing company for all these people to be prepared to put him up and put up with him. Finally it was across the lowlands, and here John Taylor endears himself to us because he gives one of the earliest admissions of exhaustion through walking, of a sort that neither Lithgow nor Coryate bothered with or thought it right to do. He describes how on the day after leaving Moffat he arrived 21 miles on at the small village of Blythe, 'but I was blithe myself to come to any place of harbour or succour, for since I was born, I never was so weary, or so near being dead with extreme travel'. After a night in a cottage, 'I mounted upon my ten toes, and began first to hobble, and after by degrees to amble, and so being warm, I fell to pace by degrees'; and so eventually to Edinburgh.

Taylor called his walk a 'pilgrimage' in the sense that one might say he was 'martyrising' his feet. The word was used outside its religious meaning to describe a self-imposed journey on foot. Meanwhile, in religious terms, the word 'pilgrimage' had been transformed into denoting a spiritual journey. Erasmus, a century before, had poured scorn on the late medieval journeys to the shrines, and had said that a far better pilgrimage was that of a housewife who went about her house doing the chores in the right frame of mind. By the same count, the word 'walk' had spiritual connotations. The English Bible was full of its use in the context of how people should conduct themselves in life – 'the way wherein they must walk': they were to walk out of darkness and walk into the light and under the divine law. From this there came various allegories which described aspects of life as seen in the form of a pilgrimage or walk. Of these the most beautiful and original is John Bunyan's *Pilgrim's Progress*, written in the rich English of the Bible leavened with the homeliness of the Bedfordshire vernacular. Bunyan, like many nonconformist preachers, such as George Fox, was obliged to 'walk cheerfully over the world' in pursuit of his calling (and it is interesting to note that a century later Charles Wesley elected to walk rather than ride so as to save funds for the Methodist cause). He is said to have had his first spiritual experiences when walking between Elstow and Bedford. And so, since my subject is walking, I hope I may be excused for turning the allegory on its head and summarising *Pilgrim's Progress* merely in the mundane terms of Christian's walk as he faces his big challenges along the way.

On foot, and weighed down with a heavy burden on his back, Christian falls in with Mr Worldly Wise and together 'they drew near to a very Miry Slough that was in the midst of the Plain, and they being heedless, did both fall suddenly into the bog.' After taking a wrong direction he is told: 'Strive to enter in at the straight gate: for straight is the gate that leadeth unto life, and few there be that find it', and with this he 'went like one that was all the while treading on forbidden ground, and could by no means think himself safe, till again he got into the way.' Later, in company with Formalist and Hypocrisy, he approaches the Hill Difficulty where the narrow way leads right up the hill and paths to left and right are ways of Danger and Destruction: 'I looked then after Christian, to see him go up the Hill, where I perceived he fell from running to going, and from going to clambering upon his hands and his knees, because of the steepness of the place.' From the Palace Beautiful he beholds at a great distance 'a most pleasant Mountainous Country, beautified with Woods, Vineyards, Fruits of all sorts; Flowers also, with Springs and Fountains, very delectable to behold': but before reaching it he has to descend into the Valley of the Shadow of Death, dark as pitch and with a continual howling and yelling, and tread an 'exceeding narrow' pathway between a very deep ditch ('into which the blind have led the blind in all Ages and have both miserably perished') and a very dangerous quagmire. After passing through the snares and traps of the town of Vanity Fair, Christian goes on, now joined by Hopeful. Byends and his three friends walk behind and discuss them: 'Why they after their headstrong manner, conclude that it is duty to rush on their Journey all weathers, and I am waiting for Wind and Tide.' After resting by a river they walk on, the way now rough 'and their feet tender by reason of their travels'. They decide to take a path to the left across a stile into By-Path-Meadow: 'But behold the night came on, and it grew very dark, so that they that were behind lost sight of him that went before';

and 'it began to rain, and thunder, and lighten in a very dreadful manner.' Then, having escaped from the grips of Doubting Castle and Giant Despair, they reach the Delectable Mountains, with gardens and orchards and vineyards and fountains. They meet some shepherds 'leaning upon their staves (as is common with weary Pilgrims, when they stand to talk with any by the way)' who ask them 'Whence come you? and How got you into the way? and By what means have you so persevered therein?' Down from the mountains by the crooked lane to the Country of Conceit they are misled by Ignorance who says 'I hope well, for I am always full of good motions that come into my mind to comfort me as I walk.' Finally, in the Country of Beulah where the sun shines night and day, they rest; and then face the final ordeal, the River of Death. His head held up by Hopeful as he swims, Christian 'presently found firm ground to stand upon'.

Tourers

As part of the general increase in travel which took place from the latter part of the eighteenth century, pedestrian tourers began to be an accepted part of the scene. These were men who wanted to travel but decided to go on foot partly for reasons of efficiency and economy but also partly for the sheer pleasure of walking. They differed from the likes of Coryate or Taylor in not being stunt men, and they tended to be educated and keen to observe the curiosities of the different localities through which they passed. The settled times of the Age of Reason had greatly facilitated travel both to neighbouring countries and to the remoter corners of one's own, and the construction of trunk roads had made that travel much easier in many places. In England the turnpike roads now offered at least the possibility of a firm surface all year round, artificially constructed of small pebbles and gravel on a convex surface; and in France the magnificent highways were cobbled in great measure and lined with fine avenues which served the double purpose of providing timber for the state and shade for the horses and men who toiled along them. The English turnpikes were financed by tolls, which were high; but pedestrians were not charged, so no wonder they felt they were saving money as they passed through the little gates to the side of the barriers, quite apart from what they were saving by not having a horse.

This easing of travel for pedestrians was even greater from the early years of the nineteenth century when roads began to be macadamised. This involved proper drainage and the use of small angular stones not bound by clay or earth or chalk and so not subject to cracks or buckling. At first these were set loosely, which was agonising for walkers, but very soon they were covered with pitch, which was beneficial. Real smoothness, such as we have on roads nowadays, was not possible until the invention of asphalt, and anyway would not have been best suited for the iron-shod hoof of the horse or the iron-tyred narrow wheel of the carriage. Consequently macadamised roads were slightly irregular, and the hoof and the foot could find a firm hold and slight yielding on the surface. This was perfect for walking on as it did not give that jarring to the body that is caused by really hard pavements or road surfaces. Along the roads in towns and villages more inns opened to cope with the needs of travellers and coaching inns kept post-horses at regular stages, which was important also for the pedestrian tourers, who expected to find some sort of accommodation and a hot meal to be cooked for them at the end of each day. Brigands and highwaymen were becoming scarcer and foreigners treated less suspiciously, at least in times of peace.

An early pioneer on the road was Thomas Ellwood, the Quaker son of an Oxfordshire squire, who in 1661 decided to dismiss his horse and groom at Beaconsfield and walk to London. He was very soon arrested as a 'sturdy beggar' and would have been put in the lock-up had not an old woman recognised and vouched for him. More ambitious was the plan of a Lutheran pastor from Berlin, Karl Moritz, who made a visit to England in 1782. Deciding to see something of the country, he took the stage-coach to Richmond and from there proceeded to walk, a method of travel which did not seem to him unusual, since in Germany respectable foot-travellers were fully accepted (even though pedestrian tourism, of the sort described in this chapter, remained a largely English phenomenon). He soon found that 'a traveller on foot in this country seems to be considered as a sort of wild man or an out-of-the-way being who is stared at, pitied, suspected, and shunned by everybody that meets him.' Along the road towards Windsor over Hounslow Heath he was constantly being offered lifts in coaches by people who simply could not understand when he politely declined. At the inn at Eton where he dined the staff looked down their noses at him as a beggar but made him pay through the nose as a gentleman. At Windsor where he spent the night they gazumped him out of his room and made him share with another, telling him to be off next morning – all this because he had arrived on foot and without any baggage. Careful to keep to the roads, what with notices warning of steel traps and spring guns, he went on through Maidenhead and Henley as far as Nettlebed, where he got a carpeted room. Beyond Dorchester, at Nuneham, he was refused not only a bed but even food and had to walk on to Oxford, arriving at midnight.

After a few days in the university city Karl Moritz pursued his journey onwards to Birmingham by coach. In the coach he asked a young man why the English didn't walk if they could possibly avoid it, and got the reply, 'Oh, we are too rich, too lazy, and too proud', which sums it up perfectly. Despite this Moritz took to his feet again from Birmingham north into Derbyshire. At Sutton he was addressed as 'master' and not 'sir' and shown into the kitchen not the parlour, in company with a female chimney-sweep and her children. Not daring to receive more snubs he walked through Lichfield to Barton, but when recognised as a foreigner he was hissed at so much that he walked on into the night. As he sat exhausted by a turnpike gate, a passing farmer took pity on him and introduced him into a neighbouring inn. At Matlock he caused ill-will by failing to drink a toast to the landlord or the others in the room, and at Tideswell by rejecting the toasted cheese, ale and brandy. There followed another total rejection at a pub on the usual grounds that since he had come on foot he could not be a gentleman but only 'some poor travelling creature', and then a night in a colliers' pub near Nottingham. At Leicester he took to the coach again and rode uncomfortably on the outside back to London. From these experiences it is evident that Karl Moritz was a young man of shy disposition who was constantly muddling his relationships with people and letting himself be bullied, not the best recipe for a pedestrian tourer. It is a pity that he had such a bad time because his account of the English scene in 1782 is most interesting, and he admired the countryside immensely: 'Any of the least beautiful of any of these views that I have seen in England, would anywhere in Germany be deemed a paradise.'

By the turn of the century more walking tourers were on the roads and were penetrating into the hilly country of the north and west – the Lake District, Wales and Cornwall. They were encouraged into these areas by a spate of guidebooks which gave accounts of varying accuracy about the ancient monuments – great houses, castles, churches, ruins – to be seen, and also remarkable natural sights such as grottoes, hot springs and strange rock formations. Thomas Pennant was foremost as a writer of such travel books, and was emulated by, for instance, Skrine with his *Tours through Wales* in 1795 and Shaw with *Tour of the West of England* in 1788.

These were followed by accounts of walks, or walking guides, of which Richard Warner's can serve as an example. *Mr Warner's Walks through Wales* appeared in 1798, followed in 1800 by his *Walk through the Western Counties of England*. This takes the form of a series of letters from Richard Warner sent at intervals to a friend during a journey starting from Bath, where he was curate of St James's Church. He walked through Somerset and along the north coast of Devon into Cornwall, then back via Okehampton and Exeter, 386 miles done in the first three weeks of September. Though his style is verbose and his attitude bland and he cannot resist quoting from Gray's 'Elegy' at every opportunity, he does try to give a balanced impression of all he sees, churches and houses as well as such curiosities as the chasm of the Lid, the cove at Culborne, the Valley of Stones near Lynmouth, or the Spinster Rock near Teignmouth. Near Radstock he prudently made a detour up a hill behind a village to avoid a band of carousing coal miners. Between Minehead and Ilfracombe he several times got lost in the maze of country tracks. Around Barnstaple he had to pick his way through the large stones with which the turnpike road was so roughly paved and which proved almost fatal for the small pony he had with him at this stage to carry his belongings. In Bideford, confined to the inn by a day of pouring rain, he was overcome by a sense of loneliness and decided to shorten his tour, originally intended to extend to Land's End, an admission of human frailty which gains him our sympathy. He also dropped his plan to walk across the centre of Dartmoor on hearing that the emaciated body of a sailor, probably making a short cut home on leave, had recently been discovered on it. In Newton Bushel he was laughed at by the local populace and on his returning stages to Bath he suffered from freak weather with much rain and thunder. These apart, the Reverend Richard Warner clearly enjoyed his walking tour and, encouraged by the success of his travel books, embarked upon a history of Bath.

In the very next year a man old enough to be Warner's grandfather undertook a walk from Birmingham to Newcastle and back. William Hutton was a Birmingham businessman who had started in his father's trade as a stocking maker but had spread his interests into real estate as well as owning a bookshop and a paper warehouse and, at one stage, making musical instruments such as bell-harps and dulcimers. As his affairs prospered and his son began to take his place in running them, Hutton devoted more of his time to what he would call 'antiquarian' interests, which nowadays would be termed amateur activity in the fields of history and archaeology – at a time when there were no professionals in either. As one of the city fathers he wrote a history of Birmingham. It is a recurring feature in the story of people who walk for pleasure that many only come to do so later in life, but surely none have left it as late as William Hutton who first saw the light at the age of sixty-four. It happened in the following way. In 1787 he took a holiday in Wales with his wife and daughter, mainly for the sake of his wife's health. In Aberystwyth he decided at short notice to return to Birmingham for reasons of business whilst the two ladies stayed on. There was no coach leaving that day and he was told that the only way to get to Birmingham was to hire a horse at the rate of sixpence a mile as far as Shrewsbury and from there to catch the stage-coach. Annoyed at this inconvenience, he resolved to walk the 75 miles to Shrewsbury, which he did in two and a half days despite very hot weather and dusty roads.

Perhaps because he felt ill for some weeks after this he didn't properly catch the walking bug for some years more: in 1797 we find him touring Wales again, his wife now dead and with only his daughter for company, by means of two coach horses, he on one and the daughter riding pillion behind a servant on the other. However, in March 1798, now aged seventy-five, on being asked to dinner at Heath, 43 miles from his home at Saltley, he got up early and walked there, arriving at 5 p.m. just as the others were finishing their meal. He couldn't resist repeating this performance in September and making the return journey on foot too a day or two later, though on this occasion he injured his tendon. Expeditions to Wales, during which he sometimes walked 30 miles a day, continued till 1803: he made the ascent of Snowdon in 1799. In 1801 he decided to travel north and inspect the Roman Wall, accompanied by his daughter and a servant. The extraordinary part of the plan was that though the daughter (a woman of forty-five) was to ride pillion behind the servant, William Hutton, now aged seventy-eight, was to walk the whole way there – and back. 'I procured for myself the exclusive privilege of *walking*; which, of all the modes of travelling, I prefer.' The idea was for the daughter and servant to go ahead each day and obtain lodging for the night. Next morning Hutton would rise early and put in some mileage before breakfast, by which time the others would have caught up with him. This supremely practical man had given much thought to the details of his walk. He decided to dress in black, which in those days implied that he was a clergyman or maybe a law official. A black pouch contained maps of Cumberland and Northumberland and the wall, and various notes as well as pen and ink. Fastened to the pouch by a strap was an umbrella in a green case. Thus equipped, he set out from Saltley on 4 July.

In terms of adventure the journey was uneventful. What impresses is not the unexpected but the dogged persistence of this old man plodding along the roads at a steady 2½ miles to the hour and averaging 20 miles a day, meticulously recording his progress and observations which were duly published in his *History of the Roman Wall*. From the start his notes display his benign humour, as when a grocer at Sutton asked him to procure a good wife for him; his anticlericalism, in his dislike of ostentatious worship in Lichfield Cathedral; and his practicality, in remarking on the healthy appearance of the girls at the Preston market, who displayed more of themselves than was customary because they had tucked their skirts up against the wet, exhibiting 'limbs of a giant size, well adapted for working, running, or kicking'. He allowed himself two days' rest at the newly established bathing resorts of Heysham and Hest Bank, and then to be driven 8 miles across the sands of Morecombe Bay – the only bit of his entire journey that he didn't walk. In the Lake District, Hutton showed scant appreciation of the hills in describing the Shap fells as 'a most barren and solitary desert, without the sight of a human being, a house, cottage, tree, or even an acre of cultivated ground'. At Penrith he insisted that his daughter, servant and horse should remain in the Lake District while he continued alone towards his 'long-wished-for Wall' through the hot unclouded days.

Never a man to cut corners, Hutton began his tour of inspection by walking first to the western extremity of the wall at Bowness on the Solway Firth, then eastwards along its line to Newcastle. All the way he was noting down exactly what he could see of it – the remaining sections of stonework, the turrets, as well as the wall ditch to the north and the separated vallum to the south. These notes have been of great value in showing what has since been lost or reduced, though thanks to recent excavations there are many things now uncovered which Hutton never saw and which have increased our knowledge of the origins and purposes of the wall. He punctuates his account with scene-setting statements just like a television documentary: 'I am now at the twenty-third mile stone. I still have Severus' Trench, and what remains of the Wall, on my right, and Hadrian's works on my left.' He was infuriated at constant evidence that the wall was being used as a convenient quarry by farmers and landowners, and found time to call at the house of one of the desecrators. He was not at home, but Hutton told his servant 'to give my compliments to Mr Tulip, and request him to desist, or he would wound the whole body of Antiquaries. As he was putting an end to the most noble monument of Antiquity in the whole Island, they would feel every stroke.' But such was the respect for private property in those days that he did not question Tulip's right to pull down the wall if he wished to. Hutton's book eventually shamed many farmers into ceasing their raids and is one reason why, of the original 73½ miles of the wall, there are still approximately 10 left standing today. It is tragic that this awakening conscience did not come a few decades earlier, for the worst of this vandalism (an appropriate word here) had taken place in the late eighteenth century.

No one could make him out. A passing farmer took him for a doctor who might cure his sick brother; but Hutton, with little love for the wall-raiding farmers, curtly told him that in his opinion his brother was dying. Others, seeing him with pen in hand and ink-bottle suspended from chest, were convinced he was an exciseman: in fact, in one of the pubs he sat next to a supervisor of excise who was sure that Hutton was one of his colleagues but was too intimidated by the great man's personality to ask any direct questions. On another occasion, after a couple of hours' chat with three fat gentlemen in a pub, one of them said: 'You are the most agreeable companion I have met with; but, I do assure you, when you first entered, I took you for a spy employed by the government.' Meanwhile he had to endure all sorts of discomforts and snubs. At Stanwix the landlady was a fine figure of a woman who had evidently once been a beauty 'and yet showed as much of that valuable commodity as could be expected from forty-five': (he learnt later that she had been the mistress of a duke). She refused to admit him, giving as one of her reasons that she was a single woman, to which he retorted, 'Did you ever hear of a woman losing her character by a man of seventy-eight!' Eventually he got a bed in a pub where he got badly bitten by fleas, 'the dancing gentry of the night'. Elsewhere he had to do without any dinner, and to lie on a damp mattress on an earth floor. But the most striking scene was at the lonely pub called the Twice Brewed, near Haltwhistle, where he was told that a group of carriers had booked all the rooms. Hutton persisted: 'You must be so kind as to indulge me with a bed. I will be satisfied with anything.' No, all they could offer was for him to share a bed either with 'a poor sick traveller who had fallen ill upon the road', or with a boy of ten. Soon the fifteen carriers arrived, and Hutton watched them eat gargantuan helpings of beef and pudding – 'every piece went down as if there was no barricade in the throat', and the tankard emptied 'like a bowl of lading water out of the mill'. In the end he got a bed to himself.

Trifles such as having no dinner didn't deter William Hutton, nor did rough patches along his walk, as when he had to cross a river by rolling stones into it, to zig-zag up a hill through brambles, and to clamber up rocks and over stone walls, at one point stumbling and cutting his hand in a hawthorn hedge. Nor did his pace slacken on his return journey, for he got from Newcastle to beyond Carlisle in only three days, on the third clocking up his greatest mileage – 26 miles. After this there were still another eight days of hard walking to Birmingham (broken by a few days recuperating at Hest Bank where he was reunited with his daughter). These, though averaging 23 miles daily, are referred to by him as 'easy marches', and in his account he omits to mention that at Aston in Lancashire he was bitten by a dog which, according to his daughter, caused 'a wound the size of a sixpence'. When he got home on Friday 7 August this indomitable man had walked 601 miles in just over a month. He had lost a stone in weight. He had worn the same pair of shoes throughout and there was hardly a hole in his stockings. He had worn his coat and waistcoat all the time, his only concession to the heatwave being to unbutton his waistcoat. The total cost of his journey had been forty pounds. 'As so long and solitary a journey on foot was, perhaps, never wantonly performed by a man of seventy-eight, it excited the curiosity of the town; which caused me frequently to be stopped in the street to ascertain the fact.'

After his famous walk to the Roman Wall he increasingly tended to demonstrate his walking prowess as proof that he was in completely good health, which was ultimately rather a mistake. Watched by anxious relatives he daily walked the 4½-mile return journey to the offices of the family firm: towards the end of his life he not infrequently stumbled on the way. He plodded round and round his garden to keep his mileage up and the last entry in his autobiographical notes reads: '1812. This day, October 11th, is my birthday. I enter upon my ninetieth year, and have walked ten miles.' This grand old man of walking died in 1815 aged ninety-two. As he said, 'Every man has his hobby horse, and I ride mine when I walk on foot.' Antiquary he may have been, but he was never antiquated, since he displayed a distinctly modern and scientific approach in all his interests, and his pedestrian achievements must be an inspiration to many people of his age today who are so scornfully and ungrammatically dismissed as 'geriatrics'.

When Hutton on his journey south from the wall stopped the night in Wigan he lay only 3 miles from the village of Up Holland, whose twenty-five-year-old schoolmistress, Ellen Weeton, was later to become a remarkable walker. Though she had regularly walked for local visits or exercise, she was driven towards compulsive walking by the stings and arrows of outrageous fortune in a life where everything seemed to conspire against her. Ellen's father had been a privateer captain who soon got his come-uppance in an action with an American man-o'-war. He left no money, so his widow opened the village school helped by young Ellen, who took over when she died. A selfish brother and a dictatorial aunt then made things so unpleasant for her that she left the school to become a governess, for some time to a family where the father had an uncontrollable temper and the epileptic daughter was burnt in a fire. But worse was to come when she was persuaded by her brother (who stood to gain from it) to marry a terrible man called Aaron Stock who was bankrupt and merely after her for what little money she had. His main aim soon became to make life so awful for her – beatings, confinements in a room with only bread and water, abuse, a mocking mistress, even imprisonment on a false suspicion of arson – that she would lose her nerve and flee, leaving him in full possession of their baby. Eventually she gained her freedom and a miserably small income by a deed of separation.

For many years her time was largely taken up by two occupations:

writing Journals, or long letters which she carefully copied into Letter Books; or going for long walks. She had her first taste of the pleasure of testing her strength in length of walk when she visited the Isle of Man a few months before her marriage in 1812. After a couple of test-runs, in walks of 13 and 16 miles, she set out from Douglas for the big one, a walk to the south end of the island and back via Peel, totalling 35 miles. She wore a small slouch straw hat, and a grey worsted jacket and skirt: in one hand she held a parasol and in the other a white net bag which contained her map, notebook, three boiled eggs and a crust of bread. It was a glorious day and at the higher points she could see England, Wales, Ireland and Scotland. She passed some turf-cutters who at the sight of her 'ceased working, and stood to gaze; others sat down'. It took her twelve hours and when she got back to her lodgings she collapsed into bed and all she had for supper was tea and bread and butter. Several other long walks followed, including an ascent of Snaefell, and when she left the Isle of Man after a month Ellen reckoned she had walked 203 miles in all.

Twelve years later, after her release from Aaron Stock, Ellen spent a couple of months in London averaging around 10 miles a day. But it is in her tour of North Wales in 1825 that she is best seen as a walker. Although her tour was not consecutive from place to place, as she set out every day from her lodgings in Bangor and then Caernarvon, her achievement is comparable to those of the other pedestrian tourers in this chapter. By now forty-eight years old and with white hair, she was delighted to note that she retained the elasticity of youth. She presented an unusual figure, tall and thin and long-legged, such as the Welsh peasants hardly recognised as that of a female. She walked up the hills and along the rocks every day and in all weathers, on one occasion soused by driving rain: 'the wind had blown in my face furiously, and yet when I got dry clothes on, I was very little fatigued with a 15 miles walk.' Her culminating achievement was an ascent of Snowdon, up from Beddgelert, down to Llanberis and on to Caernarvon, a 25-mile hike. At the summit 'I stood, perched on a ridge like a crow at the point of a pinnacle.' On the ascent she astonished a gentleman and his guide on their way down, by being a woman and alone. Indeed the story of Ellen Weeton is of a brave attempt by an intelligent and independent woman to resist the inhibiting restraints on female rights that pertained in her time. With bitter personal experience she could write: 'What numbers of men murder their wives; and that, by the most cruel of all means – slow torture.' She is our first example of a female walker (though not the first in time, for Dorothy Wordsworth preceded her) and of someone who walked therapeutically to retain sanity in a misunderstood life.

The urge to travel on foot in order to observe the natural and social scene in a matter-of-fact way was not the sole prerogative of clergymen such as Richard Warner or antiquaries such as William Hutton, and it is not surprising that military men were also on the march. One such was Charles Shaw, late of the 52nd Light Infantry. Being an eminently practical man Charles Shaw precedes his account with some basic hints for pedestrians. He begins, sensibly, with the feet, and recommends English leather boots, with an additional sole added and nails inserted. As for stockings, they should be woollen and 'the stockings made by old women on wires are the best, and the finer the wool the better.' The pedestrian should wear trousers of twilled cloth and a coat but not a waistcoat. Against rain, an oilskin cape and hat; and against mud, leather gaiters up to the knee. Attention must be given to having the best kind of knapsack: it should also be of oilskin and should have broad leather straps. Inside the knapsack should be carried a spare shirt and trousers, a waistcoat for evening wear, and an ankle-length cotton nightshirt, useful when beds are not clean. Other tips are to rub the feet with soap before putting the socks on, and to start the day early: 'As the hour of dinner abroad is about twelve, endeavour to clear fifteen miles before ten o'clock, and rest quietly for two hours, so as to be cool on sitting down to dinner; between two and three again begin your journey, and then you can easily finish another fifteen miles, and be ready to sit down cool to supper at eight o'clock.'

In March 1831 he set out for Tours from where his initial walk was to be some 200 miles across country to the Saône at Chalon. He was constantly stopped at check-points by gendarmes, or local home guards, busy watching out for spies and counter-revolutionaries who might plot against the new liberal Orleanist regime. Near Villefranche two shifty characters started to trail him. He drew aside from the path to let them pass and take a good look at them. Sure enough, they waited for him just beyond: so, clutching in one hand his stick and in the other his fishing rod which in its metal case bore some resemblance to a large pistol, he marched determinedly at them, and his general unshaven and mud-spattered appearance was so wild that they let him pass unchallenged. Then it was on via Bourges to Nevers through a wild and barren *maquis* in which grazed flocks of scraggy sheep tended by ugly and half-witted shepherdesses, quite the opposite of the

Chloes or Phyllises of romantic notion. At Baugy the village was full of conscripts heading for enrolment, and Shaw was interested to note that their sticks were of different shapes and sizes. The differences were regional, dependent on tradition and prevalent types of wood: also some were thicker at the base, and this was because their owners came from areas of heavy clay soil where pointed sticks would just stick in the mud. Next day was an extremely long one and he was on the move for eighteen hours before reaching Nevers at midnight. From here he went across the Morvan hills, stopping to catch the odd trout and feeling more at home among the blossoming hawthorn hedges.

The second part of his walk began at Avignon and led him across Vaucluse and up the valley of the Durance. In his description he gives instances of that tough and authoritative approach so essential to the success of a pedestrian tour, an approach which Karl Moritz so obviously lacked. Shaw explains: 'I contrived always to get on well by determining to keep my temper; and if there was a want of attention, to make a noise and find fault with what was really good, with a view to make them believe that I would not act so if I could not pay.' He demonstrated this sang-froid at Sisteron where he arrived 'excessively fatigued' having walked more than 40 miles during the day. Going straight into the best hotel he entered the dining-room, an apparition which brought the hum of conversation to an abrupt silence. 'I had neither waistcoat nor neckcloth, while my face and throat were covered with red bristly hair. I was, moreover, sun-burnt and not particularly clean from perspiration and dust. My coat was tolerably decent, but the best part of it was hidden by the knapsack. My trowsers were of black shining camlet, with the lower part covered with a stout pair of gaiters up to the knees, of a deep yellow colour.' The landlady questioned him. Why had he walked? Why hadn't he come by the diligence? Promptly, and in passably good French, he asked her, was she married?; and, on the affirmative, why had she married? 'Because it was my pleasure.' To which he replied: 'That is the reason why I walk.' Laughter all round, and he was duly bidden to eat his supper with the landlady and her husband. In his walk along the roads through the Maritime Alps via Gap, Shaw admired the fertile valleys and snowy mountains but found some of the human scenes less attractive – the goitre and the xenophobia (he was hooted out of one village as a spy). He made a diversion to see the Grande Chartreuse, and found his way to Lyons.

32

Now began the longest and most impressive part of his walk, for, joined by his brother, he walked from Lyons to Geneva and then, after a diversion to Chamonix, north via Basle to Strasbourg, east via Ulm to Munich, and south through Tyrol to Italy. In Italy he found it impossible to walk; the heat was too great and the Italians simply couldn't accept that Englishmen should travel on foot. What is interesting about his walk through the Alps is his lack of interest in the mountains and his timidity on their slopes. From Chamonix he grandly records: 'After I had eaten a capital breakfast, a guide appeared: and supplying myself with a long staff tipped with iron, I began the ascent of Mont Blanc.' But it transpires that he is merely going to the spot where tourists could tread on the Mer de Glace. Later, nearing the top of the Stelvio pass in South Tyrol, he and his brother decided to take a short cut, avoiding the zig-zagging road. A peasant led them for a mile, 'a single false step being certain death', where to rest 'it was necessary to lie down at full length, and even then it was difficult to avoid slipping.' From this path Shaw attempted to regain the road, now above: 'I was forced to lie down, holding on with stick and umbrella fixed in the earth, as well as chin and toes. Still I felt slipping and breathless, either with fear or the rarity of the atmosphere, or a mixture of both.' Charles Shaw returned to Edinburgh by non-pedestrian means, and in the following year joined the mercenary force recruited by the legitimists in Portugal to fight the usurper, Don Miguel.

There are some long-distance walkers who are not altogether honest in their accounts of mileage covered or days walked, or forgetful to inform us of those bits in between which were covered on wheels, especially if they feel that they cannot be found out. Deliberate deception or exaggeration is indeed a common ingredient in travel books, though sometimes the alchemy for some fine imaginative writing; but if we want to discover what really happened we have to be careful to read between the lines. Few great writers wrote more mysteriously about themselves than did George Borrow, the author of *Lavengro* and *Romany Rye*. How long did he live with the gypsies and was he truly accepted as one of their brotherhood? What happened to him during the veiled period of his life, of which we know nothing? What is the truth of his experiences in Russia and Spain where he travelled on behalf of the Bible Society? And what were the real characters of such larger than life types as the Flaming Tinman, Blazing Bosville, Tawno Chikno, Benedict Moll and Abarbanel the Jew? Life for George Borrow was one large drama, peopled by gypsies, jockeys, horses, wild men of many lands, and several murderers. No matter, the books tell us of Borrow's character and mind by indirect means. The philosophy of Lavengro is best expressed in the lines attributed to his gypsy blood-brother Jasper Petulengro, who is of the opinion that death is final but life is sweet: 'There's night and day, brother, both sweet things; sun, moon, and stars, brother, all sweet things; there's likewise a wind on the heath. Life is very sweet, brother; who would wish to die?' That this magician should in later life have embarked on a series of walking tours and written about them should immediately put us on our guard. However, the older George Borrow was no longer the elusive Lavengro of his youth but a stern seeker after truth and investigator of manners and morals, and he records his pedestrian progresses with an exactitude which is far more impressive than if he had romanticised about them. It is true that at the age of twenty-nine he walked the 120 miles from Norwich to London for reasons of economy, expending only fivepence ha'penny on a pint of ale, half a pint of milk, a roll of bread and two apples during the journey, which took him twenty-seven hours. But his passion for horses kept him mounted for most of his wanderings, and it was not till over twenty years later, when staying with relatives in Cornwall, that he discovered the pleasures of pedestrianism by spending several days in walking from their house near Liskeard to Land's End and back.

Encouraged by this experience he spent the summer and autumn of 1854 in Wales. He began with a number of one-day walks, based on Llangollen, and then came his expedition to Anglesey, starting with two days to cover the 52 miles to Bangor. His account of them is full of energy: 'quickening my pace I soon left the Llangollen valley', or 'I walked on briskly over a flat uninteresting country', or, in the approaches to Bangor, when another man started walking beside him, 'I quickened my pace, but he was a tremendous walker, and kept up with me. On we went side by side for more than a mile without speaking a word. At length, putting out my legs in genuine Barclay fashion, I got before him about ten yards, then turning round laughed and spoke to him in English. He too laughed and spoke, but in Welsh. We now went on like brothers, conversing, but always walking at great speed.' He ascended Snowdon with his step-daughter Henrietta Clarke, who, with his wife, had come to Bangor by train to join him. Driving to Nant y Glyn, they walked up the mountain escorted by a local boy, much of the time arm in arm and with Borrow 'singing at the stretch of my voice a celebrated Welsh stanza', which must have startled the other tourists who were walking up or down the path. Nearer the summit the path became steeper and the wind blew strong. 'I was at one time apprehensive that my gentle companion would be obliged to give over the attempt; the gallant girl, however, persevered, and in little more than twenty minutes from the time when we rose from our resting-place under the crags, we stood, safe and sound, though panting, upon the very top of Snowdon, the far-famed Wyddfa.' At the hut at the top there was coffee for Henrietta and ale for George Borrow. They got back to Nant y Glyn within four hours from setting out.

He pursued his journey alone into Anglesey, first to the north of the island to visit the birthplace of the poet Goronwy Owen, and then to the western extremity at Holyhead. As he stomped into the station hotel at Holyhead the 'boots' observed his dusty shoes and clothes and asked if he had walked from the railway station. '"Confound the railroad!" said I. "I came walking from Bangor. I would have you know that I have money in my pocket, and can afford to walk. I am fond of the beauties of nature; now it is impossible to see much of the beauties of nature unless you walk."' All the same, he did condescend to ride by railway back to Bangor. From there it was 68 miles over four days back to Llangollen via Caernarvon, Beddgelert, Festiniog and Bala. By now he was in tip-top form as he sped along the road 'at a round pace'. Like Charles Shaw, he was not so adept on rougher ground, and at one point took a short cut up a rugged path amid rocks, thickets and precipices where he was 'scorched by the sun, which was insufferably hot, and my feet were bleeding from the sharp points of the rocks which cut through my boots like razors.' He met the Snowdon Ranger who slightly disparaged road walking, to which Borrow defensively replied that 'to be able to move at a good swinging pace over level ground is not something to be sneezed at'. But he scored better at a pub near Beddgelert where the local postman spoke to Borrow in English in a fawning and sycophantic way, but then turned to the others and in Welsh began to ridicule him. 'Going up to the man I put my right forefinger very near to his nose and said "*Dwy o iaith dwy o wyneb*, two languages, two faces, friend!" Then after leering at him for a moment I wished the people of the house good-evening and departed.'

Now October was coming to its close. It was time to return to East

Anglia. But Borrow, elated by all he had seen and heard in North Wales, decided to take the long way out. While wife and daughter were to depart by coach and then the trains which he so despised, he would walk right through Central and South Wales before he condescended to board the iron monster. All that was needed was a little preparation. 'I bought a small leather satchel with a lock and key, in which I placed a white linen shirt, a pair of worsted stockings, a razor and a prayer-book. Along with it I bought a leather strap with which to sling it over my shoulder. I got my boots new soled, my umbrella, which was rather dilapidated, mended; put twenty sovereigns into my purse, and then said I am all right for the Deheubarth' (South Wales). Wearing his customary black frock coat and gaiter-trousers, he left Llangollen: up he went through Llansanfaid, down into the vale of Ceiriog, then southwards through lumpy hills. He heard the brooks murmuring, the men singing in the fields, the mills grinding, the pigs grunting. At some point he took a wrong turning and had to retrace his steps. The road got horribly muddy and he was in it up to the knees. It was already dark when he came down the steep descent into Llan Rhyadr and knocked on the door of the Wynstay Arms.

Two days later, to get himself across the hills to Bala lake, he hired a guide. They went up across a moorland and between hillocks of gorse and whin. They crossed several streams. Where the road led down to Bala the guide left him. Borrow looked back at the hills he had crossed: 'There they stood, darkly blue, a rain cloud, like ink, hanging over their summits. Oh, the wild hills of Wales, the land of old renown and of wonder, the land of Arthur and Merlin!' On the way down his thoughts turned to his umbrella, which for him was an instrument of many purposes. Besides the obvious function of protection against rain – for the upper part of the body at least – it was equally helpful as a parasol against the heat of the sun. Apart from this it was an excellent weapon of defence against dogs or bulls: opened suddenly against the attacking brute it would utterly confuse him and maybe turn him away. Even footpads could be warded off in this way. Finally, in mid-nineteenth-century Wales the umbrella argued a certain respectability and its possessor would be treated with deference. In short, the umbrella was the pedestrian's best friend. With these thoughts George Borrow arrived that evening at the White Lion at Bala, at the end of 18 miles.

This inn produced the most superb breakfasts. When Borrow stayed there on his return from Anglesey they offered eggs, mutton chops, broiled salmon, fried trout and potted shrimps. This time there was hare, trout, sardines and beefsteak, as well as eggs and shrimps. And the usual bread, muffins, butter, tea or coffee. It being a Sunday, Borrow did not walk but attended the services. (Actually, he had broken this rule some weeks earlier and got ticked off by a cottager. When Borrow protested that 'the Son of Man walked through the fields on the Sabbath-day, why should I not walk along the roads?' he got the reply, 'He who called himself the Son of Man was God and could do what he pleased, but you are not God.'). Monday found him striding along the banks of Bala and then up into the hills to the south, to Mallwyd, and next day to Machynlleth. From here he decided against advice to head south towards Devil's Bridge by a direct but rough route over the hills. Eventually he got lost, but at a mining camp was provided with a guide who led him through the rain and mist. From Devil's Bridge he struck back to climb Plynlimmon. Though not so high as Cader Idris, this mountain was renowned as being the source of three rivers – Severn, Wye and Rheidol. But it was not enough for him to be pointed out the sources of the three rivers. He insisted on getting right up to each (or rather, thought he did, for a recent study has demonstrated that his guide probably misled him about the source of the Severn), and drinking from the spring and reciting Welsh poetry. On the homeward trail Borrow had difficulty in keeping up with the guide over the rough ground, but once back on the road, soon in darkness, 'I walked along with a bounding and elastic step, and never remember to have felt more happy and cheerful.' At the end of 18 miles, some of them really tough, he could say 'How one enjoys one's supper at one's inn after a good day's walk.'

Through dreary country under a dull grey sky George Borrow continued his walk to the south 'at a great rate' by way of Tregaron, Pumsaint and Llandovery. November was at its most gloomy when he set out to cross the Black Mountains into the Deheubarth, with lowering rain and hail showers, and by the time he reached Gutter Vawr at the end of 20 miles it was dark (he was never an early starter) and he was drenched. After dinner in the parlour (veal cutlets, fried bacon, potatoes, jug of ale) he repaired to the kitchen and managed to charm a crowd of suspicious miners by addressing them in Welsh and calling them 'gentlemen', and telling them tales of Russia and Spain. Then to a bed, vacated by one of the maids; flinging off all his clothes, by now 'steaming like a boiling tea-kettle', he got between the blankets and in a minute was fast asleep. Next morning he dressed in clothes still damp, took a look over the local iron foundry, and then continued his walk to Swansea and strode into the best hotel, the Mackworth Arms. After attending divine service – it was now a Sunday again – George Borrow left Swansea in the afternoon for the last section of his walk, through the valleys of South Wales. No longer was he amid scenes of unspoilt nature, but nature alternating with industry, a 'mixture of nature and art, of the voices of birds and the clanking of chains, of the mists of heaven and the smoke of furnaces', as for instance at his approach to Merthyr Tydfil, where the sky was lit by lurid colours, and glowing masses of dross emerged from the iron forges. Eventually he came to Chepstow. Ceremonially he descended to the bank of the Wye and drank from it here at its mouth as he had done at its source eleven days before. A hearty dinner was rounded off with a bottle of port as he sang more Welsh songs to himself in front of the fire, his legs which had served him so well now propped up on either side of the fireplace. Then it was a first-class ticket on the night train, arriving at Paddington at 4 a.m. In eighteen walking days this fifty-one-year-old man had walked 269 miles besides conducting all sorts of interviews, visiting ancient monuments, and doing a bit of hill climbing. In his journey he had acquired a wealth of experience about Wales such as very few Welsh obtained throughout the whole of their lives.

By now properly hooked on walking, Borrow next summer visited the Isle of Man and travelled over the island for seven weeks, returning from time to time to his wife and daughter at Douglas. In 1857 he was again in South Wales, walking some 400 miles through Dyfed, Powys and Shropshire. The next year it was Scotland, all over the Highlands and to the Orkneys and Shetlands, and in ensuing years the west of Ireland and Scotland again. By 1868 he had lowered his sights to an autumn walk through Sussex and Hampshire, and though he lived till 1881 we hear no more of walking. George Borrow was the perfect pedestrian tourer. It brought out the best in him. Privately he was an irritable and cantankerous man, and when unable to exercise himself well he fell prey to moods of apocalyptic gloom. But with 10 miles behind him and 10 more ahead he felt completely refreshed. His powerful presence (he stood over six foot high) and authoritative manner may have frightened some, but all were impressed; he never bullied or pulled class but on the contrary was always studiously polite and treated the down-and-outs as if they were gentlemen. As a result he was seldom downtrodden or hounded by local people as he wandered through the country, and besides he was not too particular about his personal comforts and didn't mind getting wet. He made full use of his walks to further his absorbing interest in people, their languages and customs, and in *Wild Wales* produced the best travel book of the principality that has ever been written.

Very much in the mould of Borrow was Elihu Burritt – linguist, reformer, pacifist and internationalist; and in the 1860s residing in England in the capacity of United States Commercial Consul in Birmingham. In order to learn more about British society and agriculture he undertook a number of pedestrian tours of which the longest was from London to John o'Groats in 1863. Although in his accounts he saw fit to obscure his actual walking progressions (confining himself to phrases such as 'I resumed my walk . . .'), there is little doubt that he did cover them entirely on foot. On this particular walk he started from Essex, where he had gone to inspect an experimental farm at Tiptree. In heading across the country towards the Great North Road he suffered the disturbing experience of walking for 6 miles by small lanes only to find himself back at his starting point, the village of Great Bardfield. But thereafter this sturdy fifty-three-year-old headed steadily north at the rate of 20 miles a day, enjoying the happy sensation of improving health. 'When I left London, about the middle of July, I was slowly recovering from a severe indisposition and hardly expected to be able to make more than a few miles of my projected walk. But I had gathered strength daily, and when I brought up at this little inn at the very jumping-off end of Scotland, I was fresher and more vigorous on foot than at any previous stage of the journey.'

By now pedestrian tours, or walking tours as they had come to be called, were more generally accepted among the professional classes, at any rate by the serious-minded. In *Hints for Pedestrians* published in 1862, G. C. Watson has plenty of practical advice about clothes and equipment, including an interesting point about shoes, stressing the superiority of 'rights and lefts', as we now know them, as against the old style 'straight shoes' which could be worn on either foot: also of laces as against the old-fashioned leather wellington boots. He is something of a cissy when it comes to minor comforts. The cravat 'may be taken off with impunity whilst in the act of walking, but it should be readjusted on stopping', to prevent a sore throat. And 'a silk night-cap is no bad addition to this slender stock of usefuls, for those, especially, who are fond of lying down to take their siesta on the inviting fresh grass, under the shade of some, perhaps, "far-spreading beech".' And he is at his wettest in his advice on how to avoid damp beds. 'If there is any suspicion of such . . . request the servant to take up a warming pan and to warm the bed as usual for a few minutes; then take a tumbler, wipe it very dry with a silk handkerchief, within and without, and put it upside down, mouth downward that is, in the middle of the bed, between the sheets; take it out for a minute or two, and if the bed is damp, there will be a dew formed on the sides of the tumbler, inside, of course.'

This type of emphasis on healthy living appealed to the Victorians and persuaded some of them that walking would be good for their children also. This idea was boosted by the delightful accounts by Rudolph Topffer, the art master of a school in Geneva, who in the 1830s and 40s took groups of pupils on a series of summer rambles through the Alps, accompanied also by his wife and a servant to see to the heavy baggage. The boys were kitted up in trousers, smocks and caps and had satchels on their backs, and their walks across the lower Alpine passes often involved unexpectedly long days, and nights on the hay in barns: but inspired by their light-hearted pedagogue they clearly had a tremendously enjoyable time, which he has recorded in words and pictures. At Martigny as they sat at the inn they observed the different types of pedestrian tourers toiling up the hill. There was the thickset type, encased in heavy broad-shouldered clothing, with his head appearing like the cork of a large amphora; the hairy type, looking like a dromedary escaped from the zoo; and the stripped type, with his garments stowed in his backpack, looking as if he had been robbed of his clothes.

Not surprisingly it occurred to the eminently serious-minded Prince Consort that it would be good for his rather truculent and wayward elder son to take some walking tours, and accordingly on 25 September 1856 the fourteen-year-old Prince of Wales, travelling incognito as Baron Renfrew and accompanied by his tutor Frederick Gibbs, put up at the Crown in Wimborne in Dorset. Next day they walked to Swanage, ferrying across the mouth of Poole harbour. Though arrangements were made for their baggage to be sent from place to place by carrier, strangely they did not make hotel reservations, and at the Royal Victoria Hotel the landlord said that 'the young gentleman must put up with the sofa in the corridor'. Then it was on via Wareham to Dorchester and Bridport, after which the tour had to be cut short because the royal walker had been spotted by the press. However, the press reports were highly complimentary and gave out that 'the young Prince walked the streets with the jaunty independent air of an Englishman and chatted without the smallest restraint or without the slightest show of formal condescension with the poorest of the inhabitants.' Commenting that 'Bertie has manifestly profited by his tour', the Prince Consort sent him off on two further tours the following year, this time accompanied by four carefully selected Etonians. In the spring they walked in the Lake District, where they incurred some local trouble from chasing a flock of sheep into water. In the summer, as part of a tour of the Continent, they walked across the Glacier des Bossons at the foot of Mont Blanc and also over the Grosse Scheidegg pass. Though he probably made the best of it at the time it can hardly be supposed that the Prince of Wales enjoyed his walking experience; for the rest of his life he studiously avoided any sort of walking and his outdoor exercise was largely confined to shooting gamebirds in enormous quantities, being conveyed from drive to drive in a shooting-brake.

The zenith of pure road-walking tourism may be seen in the achievements of Arthur Cooper, vicar of Filey in North Yorkshire, and widely known as the Walking Parson. From when he had been a curate up in Durham he had formed the habit of walking rather than riding in the course of his duties; and soon after he had secured the living at Filey he conceived the idea of walking all the way to Rome, not for any theological reasons such as leaving the Church of England and becoming a Roman Catholic, but for the sake of the walk itself and because he considered it the best way to see Europe and the Eternal City. A highly practical man, like Charles Shaw, he preceded his expedition with a test walk to London. This he did over a week, between Sunday services. His night-stops on this 200-mile walk were Bridlington, Brigg, Grantham, Peterborough, St Neots and Hatfield; and he reached London early on the Saturday afternoon. Nothing happened in terms of adventure but he felt tremendously well and ready for his big project. 'I would show with money and a pair of strong boots you can get to Rome. Good-bye, all ye vampires of modern travel. Good-bye, insolent cab men and tip-loving porters. Good-bye misdirected luggage and dusty railway carriages.'

He now set about his preparation. His walking costume was a 'short coat, knickerbockers, putties, and a black tie'. He was never afraid of getting wet: 'I have tempted Providence in a hundred different ways: I have let my clothes dry upon me; I have flung myself down to rest on damp grass, and taken no harm; I have gone to bed in wet socks to allay the irritation of my feet – indeed, I have never known the process described as taking care of oneself, and I attribute my immunity from aches and pains to my partiality for the open air and cold water.' On arrival at a hotel he would wash, in a hip bath if he could, otherwise from the basin, and wash his clothes himself, hanging them out of the window to dry and not caring what people said about it. He sewed up his banknotes in the waistband of his trousers 'which, by the way, I always put under the pillow at night'. A passport, Prayer Book, toothbrush, a packet of Fuller's Earth and some Vaseline completed his necessities. He ate heartily but was a total abstainer from alcohol, though he had one curious use for whisky. When fully shod and on a long walk he would enter a pub and order a large whisky which he then poured gently into his boots: it 'makes foot and sock and shoe all pliable together, and prevents alike sores and chilblains'. Finally, he made arrangements for someone else to look after the spiritual needs of the church-people of Filey and on the day after Easter 1887 he was off.

The Walking Parson first strode south to Hull and then embarked for Rotterdam. Walking through the Dutch *polders* he came to a point where there should have been a ferry but bad weather had stopped it. So he clambered up on to a railway bridge and the angry remonstrations were soon silenced by the magical effect of an English silver coin. Holland had no milestones or signposts, but Belgium had markers every tenth of a kilometre. He walked along the straight road to Antwerp. 'I tried every means to break the monotony of the journey. I took off my boots and walked in my stockings; I took off my stockings, and walked in my bare feet.' On the third day out he reached Brussels where he rested next day, it being a Sunday. Observing the Sabbath in this way was both practical and religious. Expressed in terms of Sundays, on the second Sunday he reached Trier; on the third, Basle; on the fourth, Milan, from where it was about two weeks more to Rome via Bologna and Florence. At times he felt extremely footsore: 'every one of my ten toes seemed determined to remind me of its existence. And when the toes ended, the heels began, accompanied by a running fire of blisters along the soles.' His face peeled in the sun and his ears were sore. 'But after all these were only bagatelles compared to the splendid health I was otherwise enjoying. Mere spots on the sun, mere thorns on the rose.' He kept his mileages up, on one day covering 40 miles, and made the 743 walking miles in seven weeks. This achievement was followed by others to even more distant parts, and the places he subsequently walked to included Copenhagen, Stockholm, Vienna, Budapest, Berlin, Lourdes, Madrid and Monte Carlo. He always walked alone and was extremely self-contained, and was not particularly enthralled when once, taking refuge from heavy rain in a brick-kiln in the Morvan in Burgundy, a man said: 'Why, Cooper, is that you? I don't wonder you don't recognise me, but my name is Bellot, and I was with you at the House.' Arthur Cooper wrote several books about his walks, and gave lectures on the subject. Though considered a crank he undoubtedly persuaded many others to walk, even if not quite in the manner of his long-distance tours. For by the time he died in 1920, at the age of ninety-three, cars had taken over on the roads and the English gentleman-walker could no longer lord it along the highways of Europe.

But from the point of view of sheer enjoyment rather than exceptional achievement the apogee of pedestrian tourism in its classical form is to be found not so much in the walks of A. N. Cooper of Filey as in those of E. W. Fox of Harrogate. Fox was of much the same mould as the Walking Parson but less concerned with distances and more with appreciation, especially for France: and fortunately his walks in France in 1902–6 coincided with the thawing of relations between the two ancient enemies, as manifested in the *Entente Cordiale*. Ever receptive to chance encounters, of a direct and self-confident disposition, and in command of reasonable French, Fox was able to savour the pleasant side-effects of tour-walking far better than Cooper. Certainly his appearance and equipment were very similar: he wore 'a strong tweed suit, with breeches and stockings, and for a change an extra couple of pairs of stockings, a woollen sleeping suit, strong slippers, collars, razor, brushes etc', in a knapsack (carried sometimes on both shoulders, sometimes on one) that weighed under 15 lb. In 1902 he carried an umbrella but in the next year this was discarded in favour of a stick and a Burberry. His boots were strong, roomy and well sewn. But unlike Cooper he avoided main roads and wound his way through the villages of Normandy, Burgundy and Brittany, content to walk some shorter stages (and occasionally take a ride in a cart) although quite capable of doing 35 miles and averaging 15–20 miles a day.

He made friends and studiously avoided quarrels, especially with those who tediously trotted out their anti-English prejudices, and the French responded warmly to him. He dilated on the gastronomic pleasures out-turning from the healthy appetite engendered by long-distance walking. In Normandy he enjoyed a succession of excellent meals, such as 'a princely lunch of soles, omelettes and sparkling cyder, all clean and well served'. At Sens for six francs (then worth four shillings and ninepence) he got dinner, bed and breakfast, and dinner was 'soup, fish done up with eggs, beef and green vegetables, partridge on toast, salad, sweets, peaches, and a bottle of excellent burgundy'. In Brittany he was so persuasive about the joys of walking that an Austrian Archduke joined him for a couple of days. On another occasion, in Scotland on his way to John o'Groats, he came to the house of Andrew Carnegie and that great capitalist, in between telling him of the reforms that should be made in the economic system, confided to Fox that he thoroughly approved of walking and had indeed 'walked with his knapsack in France and Germany when he was younger'. Fox was aware that the age of pedestrian tourism along roads was coming to an end in the face of cars and bicycles but was convinced that walking was the best method of travel so long as it remained possible. Like Cooper and Borrow and the others he was not afraid of getting wet and quotes one of the advantages of road-walking as being that it can be enjoyed in rain or other bad weather when horsemen and cyclists can only suffer. It is this combination of hardness and humanity, of keeping going whilst also being prepared to stop and talk, of enjoying the walking for its own sake but also using it as a means for other pleasures and discoveries, that makes Edward Fox an appropriate subject on which to end this chapter on pedestrian touring.

Romantics

THE use of walking as a key to the admiration of nature and a stimulus to thought may be said to have originated with Jean Jacques Rousseau, the prophet of the Romantic movement. As early as 1728, when a sixteen-year-old boy, he escaped from Geneva and walked into the big wide world, and in the first instance walking was in his mind associated with the ability to wander through the countryside outside the city walls and drawbridges, and in fact 'to enjoy all the freedom a man is capable of having'. After walking for three days to Annecy, revelling in this sentiment, he put himself under the protection and the spell of Mme de Warens, and would have ceased his wandering there and then had he not been obliged to go to Turin to further his Catholic education and his prospects. He accompanied a lively couple also travelling to Turin and they spent nearly three weeks in reaching it on foot. They shared a room each night, where Mme Sabran's 'noisy spells of sleeplessness frequently woke me up, and they would have woken me up even more often if I had known the reason for them'.

Jean Jacques basked in the Alpine scenery, its grandeur, variety and beauty. The memory of this journey left him with the strongest taste for travelling on foot, in which he indulged again three years later when he went from Neuchatel to Paris, taking two weeks in a combination of hiking and hitch-hiking. 'I spent a fortnight on this trip, which I count among the happy days of my life. I was young and in good health; I had enough money and plenty of hopes; I was travelling on foot, and travelling alone.' Sadly, for neither this nor his journey south soon afterwards does he give us any detailed description apart from one solitary scene where, after getting lost while making a detour, he came to a peasant's house and was given an excellent dinner as soon as they were assured that he was not an exciseman; he also tells us that when approaching Chambéry on foot he was particularly struck by the wild scenery. Instead Rousseau says this:

> In thinking over the details of my life which are lost to my memory, what I most regret is that I did not keep diaries of my travels. Never did I think so much, exist so vividly, and experience so much, never have I been so much myself – if I may use that expression – as in the journeys I have taken alone and on foot. There is something about walking which stimulates and enlivens my thoughts. When I stay in one place I can hardly think at all; my body has to be on the move to set my mind going. The sight of the countryside, the succession of pleasant views, the open air, a sound appetite, and the good health I gain by walking, the easy atmosphere of an inn, the absence of everything that makes me feel my dependence, of everything that recalls me to my situation – all these serve to free my spirit, to lend a greater boldness to my thinking, to throw me, so to speak, into the vastness of things, so that I can combine them, select them, and make them mine as I will, without fear or restraint.

In later years he toyed with the idea of making a pedestrian tour and tried to persuade the savants Diderot and Grimm to accompany him, 'each willing to contribute fifty louis from his purse and a year of his time for a joint tour of Italy on foot, with no other attendant than a lad to come with us and carry a knapsack;' – but it came to nothing. All the same Jean Jacques walked constantly throughout this life, taking long afternoon strolls, whether in the gardens of Paris, the forest of Montmorency, the hillsides of Val-de-Travers, the park of Wooton, or the woods of Ermenonville; even, when travelling in slow coaches, getting out and walking for a stretch. It was in these walks that he used walking as an inspiration: 'I can only meditate when I am walking. When I stop I cease to think; my mind only works with my legs.' But never did he experience such ecstasies of pleasure as when he walked with Mme de Warens amid the periwinkles, half in love with love and half, one suspects, with himself.

Not until one or even two generations later did anyone else express such sentiments about walking, and in England the man who first took up the theme and put on the mantle of high priest of walking was William Wordsworth. What is more, in contrast to Rousseau's regrets that he had not undertaken walking tours, Wordsworth was a leading exponent of such as well as constantly walking far greater distances. Quite apart from his literary qualities he must be regarded as one of the world's most remarkable pedestrians. As De Quincey wrote (when Wordsworth still had several years to live and some thousands of miles to go): 'I calculate, upon good data, that with these identical legs Wordsworth must have traversed a distance of 175,000 to 180,000 English miles – a mode of exertion which, to him, stood in the stead of alcohol and all other stimulants whatsoever to the animal spirits; to which, indeed, he was indebted for a life of unclouded happiness, and we for much of what is most excellent in his writings.' Like Rousseau he became an addict when young; and though in both cases those long adolescent walks may have been the physical expression of frustrated sexuality and introverted minds, for Wordsworth the occasion for them arose not from a need to get away from restricted and unattractive surroundings but from an outright and childish love of and admiration for the scenes of nature. Even before the age of nine he was wont to wander among the cliffs and hollows of the hills around Hawkshead, where he lived following the death of his mother. And soon he was taking walks along the roads or doing the 5-mile circuit around Esthwaite Water. But it was when he returned to the Lake District on his first long vacation from Cambridge that his cultivation of walking expanded. His first act was to walk across the moorland to Windermere ferry on his way back home: and during the summer days he wandered over the fells and recesses of Furness and Grizedale, sometimes accompanied by a little dog who warned him of the approach of people, which could be useful when he was working out his poetry by means of reciting it aloud. As he later wrote:

> Those walks, well worthy to be priz'd and loved,
> Regretted! that word, too, was on my tongue,
> But they were richly laden with all good,
> And cannot be remembered but with thanks
> And gratitude, and perfect joy of heart,
> Those walks did now, like a returning spring,
> Come back to me again.

He was also fond of walking in twilight and darkness. His first major poem was 'An Evening Walk' which describes pastoral scenes around the lakes. He walked back home after local dances (which he hadn't enjoyed much), once by moonlight and once at sunrise. And once, as he walked at night along the silent and deserted road, he was surprised by the mysterious figure of the Discharged Soldier – tall, gaunt, destitute, who evoked in Wordsworth first fear, then awe, then fascination and pity. He led this ancient warrior to a cottage for food and rest, but gained the greater benefit for himself; for the Soldier was the first of several Wordsworthian figures encountered on his walks, such as the Tinker, the Beggarman and, most curiously, the Leech-Gatherer. Still, William Wordsworth had so far walked only in a desultory way, sauntering and contemplating, and it was not until his pedestrian tour through France in 1790 that he entered the big league as a walker.

Wordsworth was now twenty and had been at Cambridge for three years. His final year was coming up and he should have spent his long vacation studying. Instead he opted out for an entirely irresponsible jaunt together with a fellow undergraduate of St John's, Robert Jones. Possibly they were inspired by the example of William Frend, a radical and a fellow of Jesus College, Cambridge, who had walked through Europe in the previous year. They were careful not to tell their relatives of their plan, and walked out of London on 11 July, with twenty pounds between them: on the evening of 13 July they landed at Calais. It was probably by design that they picked this particular moment to arrive in France, for the next day was the first anniversary of the storming of the Bastille and was being celebrated throughout the country as a great national festival. Delegates were assembled in Paris for the strange ceremony at the Champ de Mars, and every town and village had its tree of liberty as well as wreaths and garlands and maybe triumphal arches, and public dinners and dancing in the streets. Wordsworth and Jones were ardent admirers of the revolution, as yet innocent of bloodshed or despotism, and participated enthusiastically in the general euphoria. This was helped by the fact that ordinary French people now regarded the English no longer as the hereditary foe but as precursors in the cause of liberty. Consequently these two young men were treated as personal representatives of a friendly nation, a flattering experience which went rather to their heads: though the Gallic greetings were probably tinged with a certain amount of humour, for the two visitors confirmed the French conviction of English outlandishness and eccentricity. They each carried a bundle of personal effects and at times adopted the sensible but somewhat ludicrous method of carrying their bundles on their heads. As they were dressed identically, and each carried an identical oak stick, they must have looked like Tweedledum and Tweedledee, except that one was taller and thinner and the other shorter and fatter.

Nevertheless, despite these distractions they made good progress, pacing along at military speed and averaging over 20 miles a day and reaching Chalon-sur-Saône after a fortnight of steady walking. For most of the way they walked along the highways under avenues of rustling elms and past enormous fields of corn, but for three days they took to paths 'by secret villages and lonely farms' to shorten the route. At Chalon they sailed down the Saône to Lyons, fraternising furiously with a bunch of Delegates now returning from Paris. From Lyons they resumed their walk, now towards Geneva and the glittering Alps. They diverted to visit the Grande Chartreuse, shortly to be desecrated and destroyed, but at the time appearing to them as a bastion of religious bigotism. Then it was into the main Alpine valleys, stopping at Chamonix to see the glaciers, and so up the Valais to the Simplon pass. At the pass they lost the main track and came to a spot where they were surprised to be told by a peasant that they had already crossed the watershed, and Wordsworth later used this incident to develop the theme that imagination depends on hope and expectation and vanishes with accomplishment and completion. Although he respected the Pennine Alps as objects of grandeur and wonders of nature, he didn't really like them. He found them cold and impersonal and felt much happier along the shores of Lake Como. In those days the western side of this lake had no road along it, so for three days Wordsworth and Jones walked along a series of rocky paths that led through woods of oak and chestnut on the steep slopes above the lake on whose surface their greens and golds were reflected, while sailing boats stole lazily by. In between the woods were vineyards and cornfields and cheerful villages with attractive dark-eyed girls who sang as they went about their work. They observed this Elysian scene at all hours of the day, and even at night, perched on a rock and waiting for the dawn. From here it was through the Grisons to Lucerne and Zurich, and then by Lake Constance to Berne and Basle, sidetracking to see the falls of the Rhine at Schaffhausen and the valley of Lauterbrunnen. From Basle they sailed down the Rhine to Cologne and then walked back to Calais, returning to England on about 10 October.

This mighty walking tour had a profound effect on Wordsworth. Not only was his inward and retentive mind now imbued with images of the natural scene which could be drawn upon throughout his life, but by the very undertaking of it he had given up his opportunities of obtaining a fellowship and had lost the impetus to acquire a good professional post. Increasingly he saw himself as a wanderer and a poet. The following summer he spent nearly four months staying with Robert Jones and his family at Plas-yn-Llyn, during which they went on a three-week pedestrian tour of North Wales. They climbed from Beddgelert to the summit of Snowdon at night and enjoyed the unforgettable experience of emerging from the lower-lying fog into a crystal-clear moonlit scene, with mountain peaks appearing as islands upon a misty sea. After this visit to Wales he went to France for a year and then followed another pedestrian tour, this time alone. Beginning on Salisbury Plain 'along the bare white roads lengthening in solitude their dreary line', he walked to Bath and Bristol and then up the Wye valley past Tintern Abbey, and so into central Wales. In 1795 he and his sister Dorothy went to live in a house at Racedown in Dorset. Two years later a young man called on them, his arrival memorable in that he didn't come by the road but cut a corner through a field, leaping over a gate. This was Samuel Taylor Coleridge, who had just walked 40 miles to visit them, and here we must consider the man who, together with William and Dorothy, made up 'three persons and one soul', or perhaps rather, so far as their walking exploits are concerned, six legs and one soul.

Coleridge was eighteen months younger than Wordsworth and had

also been at Cambridge, was also a radical, and had likewise lost both
his parents when young. As a pedestrian his main qualification had
been a tour of Wales in 1794 in company with another undergraduate
of Jesus College, Joseph Hucks. Their purpose was mainly to discover
grass-roots opinion about the political issues of the day. Coleridge was
in effect a revolutionary. He had Utopian ideas about an ideal
communistic society presided over by twelve Pantisocrats, of whom
he would be one. After he and Hucks had walked the 90 miles from
Cambridge to Oxford, he mulled over these ideas with Robert South-
ey so deeply that three weeks passed before the two Cantabrians
pursued their way westwards on 5 July. The weather was extra-
ordinarily hot and the roads appallingly dusty, the Pantisocrats being
choked by the Aristocrats:

> The Dust flies smothering, as on clatt'ring Wheels
> Loath'd Aristocracy careers along.
> The distant track quick vibrates to the Eye,
> And white and dazzling undulates with heat.

The great heat did at least break down social barriers in one respect,
for at Gloucester they observed a group of men bathing naked in the
Severn and bandying words with a girl in a boat. As for Coleridge's
revolutionary concepts, he mostly kept them to himself though once
or twice expounded them to some astonished locals. Their route led
through Hereford into central Wales, to Montgomery and Bala;
thence by Llangollen to Wrexham and so along the north coast to
Conway. The mountain scenery duly impressed him. 'From Llangun-
nog we walked over the mountains to Bala – most sublimely terrible! It
was scorchingly hot. I applied my mouth ever and anon to the side of
the rocks and sucked in draughts of water cold as ice and clear as infant
diamonds in their embryo dew.' Hucks, more concerned with creature comforts, writes of the maid who, noticing that he had thrown
aside the sheets which he supposed were damp, said 'Lord, Sir, it be
impossible, for they have been slept in four or five times this week.'

At Conway they were joined for a while by two other Cambridge
men. With their sticks, knapsacks, trousers and generally wild
appearance, these early pedestrians were often thought to be French
revolutionaries. They walked towards Anglesey, climbed to the summit of Penmaenmawr, and then began their journey south via Caernarvon, Beddgelert, Aberystwyth, Llandovery, Abergavenny and

Chepstow, to Bristol. They had walked over 600 miles, and though the cause of revolution had not much progressed both had immeasurably broadened their experience and Coleridge had had plenty of time for 'melancholizing by myself, or else indulging those day-dreams of Fancy, that make realities more gloomy'. But of course it wasn't all gloom and melancholy, and we have a glimpse of the brilliant high-spirited Coleridge who could keep all sorts of people spellbound for hours in the announcement he required the town crier of Abergele to make, relating to his lost stick which, as a result, was immediately found:

> Missing from the Bee Inn, Abergele, a curious walking-stick. On one side it displays the head of an eagle, the eyes of which represent rising suns, and the ears Turkish crescent; on the other side is a portrait of the owner in woodwork. Beneath the head of the eagle is a Welsh wig, and around the neck of the stick is a Queen Elizabeth's ruff in tin. All down it waves the line of beauty in very ugly carving. If any gentleman (or lady) has fallen in love with the above-described stick, and secretly carried off the same, he (or she) is hereby earnestly admonished to conquer the passion the continuance of which must prove fatal to his (or her) honesty. And if the said stick has slipped into such gentleman's (or lady's) hands through inadventure, he (or she) is required to rectify the mistake with all convenient speed. God save the King.

As for Dorothy Wordsworth, she had when in her teens come to walking through William:

> We used to walk every morning about two hours; and every evening we went into the garden, at four or half past four, and used to pace backwards and forwards till six. Unless you have accustomed yourself to this kind of walking, you will have no idea that it can be pleasant . . . Nothing but rain or snow prevented our taking this walk. Often I have gone out, when the keenest north wind has been whistling amongst the trees over our heads, and have paced that walk in the garden, which will always be dear to me – for the remembrance of those very long conversations I have had upon it supported by my brother's arm.

Thanks to William also, she soon escaped from the garden and in 1794, when they were staying with friends near Keswick, the two of them walked in one day from Kendal to Grasmere and thence to Keswick, a total of 33 miles. This exploit incurred the disapproval of some members of her family, in particular her great-aunt Mrs Crackanthorpe who wrote to reprove her for 'rambling about the country on foot'. To her Dorothy replied, 'I cannot pass unnoticed that part of your letter in which you speak of my "rambling about the country on foot". So far from considering this as a matter of conde-mnation, I rather thought it would have given my friends pleasure to hear that I had the courage to make use of the strength with which nature has endowed me, when it not only procured me infinitely more pleasure than I should have received from sitting in a post-chaise, but was also the means of saving me at least thirty shillings.' It was probably as a result of this exchange that Wordsworth wrote his poem 'To a Young Lady who had been reproached for taking long walks in the country', though alas the consolation the poem envisages for the tomboy, that when she becomes a contented wife and mother she will look back with pleasure at her healthy youth, was a mirage, for Dorothy was never to marry.

The trio who hit it off so well at Racedown became inseparable two years later when the brother and sister rented a house at Alfoxden close by their friend's cottage at Nether Stowey near the coast of Somerset. His wife Sara generally stayed at home while they walked together daily, often for hours on end. Coleridge did most of the talking but they equally shared the walking; and their walking styles are of interest. Wordsworth had a rolling, lounging gait, but neverthe-less walked straight and rhythmically; Coleridge's gait reflected his unstable nature in constant adjustments of pace and shiftings from one side of the path to the other in complete disregard for his companions' line of march: to this one must add the unflattering description of him by Carlyle – 'a fat, flabby, incurvated personage, at once short, rotund, and relaxed . . . He never straightens his knee joints. He stoops with his fat, ill-shapen shoulders, and in walking does not tread, but shovel and slide.' For her part Dorothy adopted a rather masculine gait together with a slight stoop of the body. And it was in the course of walking that the two men composed their poems. The passionate Coleridge preferred to compose over uneven ground or breaking through the straggling branches of a copse; whereas the orderly Wordsworth found inspiration best when walking up and down a straight gravel path or (in Hazlitt's words) 'in some spot where the continuity of his verse met with no collateral interruption'.

Meanwhile the intelligent and perceptive Dorothy was guiding their minds and often pointing out aspects of the natural scene from which poetic images could be drawn. A typical entry in her journal reads: 'February 13th 1798 Walked with Coleridge through the wood. A mild pleasant morning, the near prospect clear. The ridges of the hills fringed with wood, showing the sea through them like the white sky, and still beyond the dim horizon of the distant hills, hanging as it were in one undetermined line between sea and sky.'

In early November 1797 they all set out on an extended walk westwards along the coast for some 30 miles. After spending the night at Lynmouth they visited the Valley of the Rocks and headed back. It may have been on this occasion, or else shortly before, that Coleridge was seized with dysentery when resting at a farmhouse near Porlock, about half-way between Lynmouth and Stowey. He took two grains of opium and eventually fell asleep while reading a passage from *Purchas his Pilgrimage* which begins: 'In Xamdu did Cublai Can build a stately Palace . . .'; and, when he woke, he wrote out the first fifty-four lines of his poem 'Kubla Khan', including the words which so well describe his own walking style, 'meandering with a mazy motion'. Shortly after, during the same month, they walked as far as Watchet and on the way developed the theme which resulted in 'The Ancient Mariner'. Although the poem has the roll and swell of the ocean for its setting it contains six lines which have since haunted many solitary walkers in remote places:

> Like one that on a lonesome road
> Doth walk in fear and dread,
> And having once turn'd round, walks on,
> And turns no more his head;
> Because he knows a frightful fiend
> Doth close behind him tread.

In the following year Coleridge retraced his steps along the coast accompanied by two young men who were thirsty for the heady brew of his extraordinary eloquence. One of these was William Hazlitt. In January Coleridge had visited Shrewsbury as minister-elect of the Unitarian Church there, a position which would offer him financial security. Among those who heard him preach was William Hazlitt, who had walked 10 miles from Wen, where his father was the Unitarian minister. Two days later Coleridge came to stay with them.

Next morning he received a letter from Thomas Wedgwood offering him enough support to keep him going as a poet, and decided to decline the clerical post there and then, just as he was in the act of tying his shoe-laces. Young William then accompanied him on foot for the first 6 miles and received an invitation to visit him at Stowey in the spring. Hazlitt walked the whole way from Wen to Nether Stowey, 'with unworn heart and untired feet'. The other young man was John Chester who, although a great admirer of Coleridge, did not really have the intelligence to understand him. He was short and bow-legged, 'had a drag in his walk like a drover', and 'kept a sort of trot by the side of Coleridge, like a running footman by a state coach, that he might not lose a syllable or sound that fell from Coleridge's lips'. Thus it was that the three of them walked over 35 miles to Lynton. 'We walked for miles and miles on dark brown heaths overlooking the Channel, with the Welsh hills beyond, and at times descended into little sheltered valleys close by the seaside, with the smugglers' faces scowling at us, and then had to ascend conical hills with a path winding up through a coppice to a barren crown.' They arrived at Lynton at midnight and next day, after a good breakfast of tea, toast, eggs, and honey from the beehives in the garden, they duly visited the nearby Valley of the Rocks and then loitered around the 'ribbed sea-sands'. On the third day they returned to Nether Stowey. A few days after that Hazlitt set off back home and Coleridge accompanied him as far as Bristol, covering the 33 miles from Bridgwater on the second day.

But all this pedestrian activity by Wordsworth and Coleridge in Somerset was only a prelude to the ranging walks that they took in the Lake District, where they were both living by 1800. The first of these was in November 1799. The two poets plus William's brother John set forth into the area on foot and on the fourth day they came to Rydal and Grasmere, where they stayed for a few days. The rough November weather in no way lowered their spirits: by Grisedale Tarn (where John left them to return to his seafaring) Coleridge found that 'light and darkness coexisted in contiguous masses, and the earth and sky were but *one*! Nature lived for us in all her grandest accidents.' For the following ten days they walked all over the place with the object of seeing as many of the lakes as possible – Wastwater, Buttermere, Loweswater, Bassenthwaite, Derwentwater, Ennerdale Water and Ullswater. What was significant was that in order to make this transit they left the beaten track at several points and crossed the hills by rough passes such as Sty Head, Black Sail Pass, or across Floutern Tarn and Matterdale Common. Mist, frost, snowy peaks, black rocks, they were in among them all.

Nor was this the end of Wordsworth's walking in Cumbria that winter, for he was back next month with Dorothy to move into Dove Cottage by Grasmere. Approaching from Yorkshire they decided to walk along the road across the Pennines. Starting one afternoon at Wensleydale they got 12 miles to Askrigg, arriving after dark and with ice on the road. Next day the ground was thinly covered with snow, enough to make the road soft but not slippery: a strong east wind blew flurries of snow into their backs. After 1½ miles they took a lift in a cart for 2 miles to the inn at Hardraw, suitably named. Here they inspected a frozen waterfall, and then it was over the pass and with the good tail-wind they did 10 miles in two and a quarter hours, 'a marvellous feat of which D will long tell'. After resting for a quarter of an hour at Garsdale, they covered the remaining 7 miles to Sedbergh in an hour and thirty-five minutes. Next morning it was 11 miles to Kendal in three hours, and so on by post-chaise to Grasmere. This winter walk was complemented next May when William and John Wordsworth walked from Grasmere east into the Yorkshire Dales on their way to visit the Hutchinson family near Scarborough (William was to marry Mary Hutchinson in 1802).

A beneficial by-product of their journey was that Dorothy began her Grasmere Journal so as to combat her loneliness. The daily entries reveal in full clarity the way in which walking provided the principal release for the pent-up physical energies of the Wordsworths, over and above their gardening and household chores. Some of the walks had a purpose, the 6-mile return trip to Ambleside being frequently done for posting letters or buying provisions. But for the rest it was walking for its own sake, whether the 5-mile circuit around the two little lakes or the 4-mile return to the head of Easedale or shorter strolls to Mary Point in Bainriggs Wood or White Moss Tarn and the Upper Rydal path, or merely in the garden of Dove Cottage: morning, noon and night. Just after Christmas 1801 they made a tour with Mary, first walking the 13 miles along the road to Keswick to stay with Coleridge at Greta Hall: on the way William exhibited appropriate signs of poetic vagueness in leaving his copy of Spenser on a bank (Mary turned back to retrieve it) and his gloves at an inn where they ate. Next day they walked 16 miles to stay a month with Thomas Clarkson at Eusemere, cutting across Matterdale Common by the Old

Coach Road. It hailed. 'The wind drove and eddied about and about, and the hills looked large and swelling through the storm. We thought of Coleridge. O! the bonny nooks and windings and curlings of the beck, down at the bottom of the steep green mossy banks.' William and Dorothy made their return to Grasmere late in January, on horseback to Grisedale and then on foot for 8 miles over the pass by Grisedale Tarn. At the top they lost the path in the mist but thanks to William's sense of direction they came down the right way.

The Great Earth Mother, the goddess Nature, who exercised such a calming influence over William and Dorothy Wordsworth failed to cast the same soothing spell over the tortured mind of Coleridge. In vain he had upped sticks and followed them to the Lake District: in vain he paced the hills. His febrile brain now sought to penetrate the mysteries of metaphysics instead of devising lyrical poetry. His health was becoming seriously imparied by the onset of opium addiction. He was perpetually in debt. And his marriage was becoming intolerable, especially since he had become emotionally attached to Sara Hutchinson and ever more neglected his own Sara (always referred to by him as Mrs Coleridge). All the same, walking was still important to him and on 1 August 1802 he set off on a ten-day foot excursion ostensibly to visit a library at St Bees but really to get away and be alone. In letters to his 'dearest Sara' he gives a graphic description of most of it, starting with the departure: 'On Sunday Augt. 1st – half after 12, I had a shirt, cravat, 2 pair of stockings, a little paper and half a dozen pens, a German book (Voss's poems) and a little tea and sugar, with my night cap, packed up in my natty green oil-skin, neatly squared, and put into my *net* knapsack, and the knap-sack on my back, and the besom stick in my hand, which for want of a better, and in spite of Mrs C. and Mary, who both raised their voices against it, especially as I left the besom scattered on the kitchen floor, off I sallied . . .' The first day got him to Long Moore Farm by Ennerdale Water, crossing to that lake from Buttermere on the same pathless line he had taken when there with Wordsworth, 'soft mossy ground, with many a hop, skip and jump, and many an occasion for observing the truth of the old saying: where rushes grow, a man may go'. After a couple of days around Egremont and St Bees he walked back into the hills to Wastdale. His letters abound in startling analogies. A waterfall 'glimmered through the trees, that hang before it like bushy hair over a madman's eyes': a scree-slope is like 'a pointed decanter in shape, or an outspread fan, or a long-waisted old maid with a fine prim apron'.

Then he ascended Scafell, at 3210 feet the highest point in the Lake District, and from the summit continued his letter: 'O! what a look down just under my feet! the frightfullest cove that ever might be seen, huge perpendicular precipices . . .' Scrambling down a steep stream bed he got to Eskdale, and so on via Coniston and Grasmere having covered around 90 miles in all.

The rejuvenating effect of a walking tour is inevitably reduced and even warped when soft options are taken to make use of wheels and only walk when one feels like it. Such was the plan of the 'three persons and one soul' when they set off on their tour of Scotland in August 1803 in an Irish jaunting-car. This was a two-wheeled carriage in which two passengers could sit behind the driver, facing backwards; it was roughly sprung and hoodless and pulled by a placid horse. The idea was Wordsworth's (he always adopted it on later tours) and was perfectly sensible, and the horse and carriage performed excellently. But it was a contributory factor to the end of the intimate relationship between the three. Coleridge had begun to perceive that his god Wordsworth had feet of clay: purporting to be the most unworldly and unselfish of men, Wordsworth was at heart conceited and ungenerous and was constantly mollycoddled by his sister. Sitting on the carriage cushions in the rain Coleridge also brooded on his own supposed illness, his 'atonic gout', his sickness, his nightmares. Sometimes riding, sometimes walking (usually up hills and to lead the horse), they progressed to Carlisle and across the lowlands to Glasgow and thence into the Highlands up Loch Lomond-side. At Tarbert they decided to leave the horse and cart for a few days and make a purely pedestrian venture into the Trossachs. They crossed Loch Lomond by the ferry to Inversnaid, William dropping their bundle of provisions into the water and so spoiling their sugar, coffee and cake. From here it was up Glen Arklet, where Highlanders were busy making hay while the sun shone, to Loch Katrine. After some debate they decided to walk around the head of the loch to a house on the opposite shore, where they were well received and put up for the night. Next day was cold, rainy and windy. Coleridge walked the 6 miles to the foot of the loch, the Wordsworths going some of the way in a ferry-boat, William swiftly appropriating the ferryman's plaid and wrapping it around himself for warmth. But the gloom of the day was forgotten when they fetched up at the ferryman's thatched and peat-blackened longhouse, where they spent the night, fortified by drams of whisky and diverted by the colourful character of the ferryman: 'We caroused our cups of coffee, laughing like children at the strange atmosphere in which we were: the smoke came in gusts, and spread along the walls and above our heads in the chimney, where the hens were roosting like light clouds in the sky.' Also sheltering there for the night was an Edinburgh drawing master on his way on foot to John o'Groats.

Heavy rain next morning induced them to return to Tarbert as quickly as possible: waiting for the ferry at Inversnaid for some hours they were enchanted by a girl who was later immortalised by William in a rather sickly poem. Still the August rain persisted and at Tarbert Coleridge decided to cut short his tour and make his way to Edinburgh as best he could (his case sent ahead by carrier), while the Words-worths continued with the jaunting-car. This they did all around Argyll and through the Grampians and all the way back to Grasmere. At one point they diverted to revisit the famous ferryman's hut, evidently for them the spiritual centre of the Highlands, and once again took the Inversnaid ferry. In the boat were a man and woman with their child and Dorothy demonstrated her sense of social concern when she reflected on 'the difference in our condition to that poor woman, who, with her husband, had been driven from her home by want of work, and was now going a long journey to seek it elsewhere: every step was painful toil, for she had either her child to bear or a heavy burthen. *I* walked as she did, but pleasure was my object, and if toil came along with it, even *that* was pleasure – pleasure, at least, it would be in remembrance.'

Meanwhile an extraordinary change had come over Coleridge. After they parted he walked 10 miles up Loch Lomond to Glen Falloch, spending the night at Inverarnan. Here he resolved to go north and not to Edinburgh, 'having found myself so happy alone – such blessing is there in perfect liberty', and so headed for two days through Strathfillan and Glen Orchy and across the lonely moor of Rannoch. After an uncomfortable night in the remote Kingshouse Hotel where he was kept awake by drunks, he went on down Glen Coe to the Ballachulish ferry and on towards Fort William. He staggered into the town having walked nearly 30 miles in the day and with intense pain in his thighs, inflammation in his left leg, and torture in a bad toe. What is more his shoes were in very bad repair, having been partly burnt when he dried them by the fire of the Loch Katrine ferryman, and he had walked some of the way barefoot. At Fort William, although his single pair of stockings was washed and darned, he could get no new shoes. By the time he got to Fort Augustus next day – 36 miles on, some of it along the hilly parallel roads above Loch Lochy – 'the shoes were all to pieces and three of my toes were skinless and I had a very promising hole in my heel'. Here he was put in the lock-up as a spy, but when released was able to get new shoes and march next day through the Great Glen to Inverness. Then it was south for five days more to Perth, by which time he had marched for over 250 miles, doing 33 miles on the final day. Such was Coleridge's last great walk. Despite unpleasant withdrawal symptoms he had refrained from drugs during it. Henceforth the addiction became too intensive for anything as purposeful and energetic as pedestrianism.

Although the Wordsworths had abandoned walking tours in favour of carriage tours with some walking thrown in, they continued to walk extensively as part of their daily routine at Grasmere and later at Rydal Mount. For William this continued till 1840, but Dorothy in 1828 became an invalid and partly lost her reason: a feature of her illness was that she deluded herself into believing that she was incapable of walking at all, and was wheeled about in a chair. To the Lake District came disciples who were keen to walk and write as part of the same Romantic experience. One such was Thomas De Quincey, who had discovered for himself the pleasures of walking at the early age of sixteen when, although head boy and generally recognised as a brilliant pupil, he ran away from Manchester Grammar School on the sensible grounds that they had nothing more to teach him. Or rather, he walked away; for having tiptoed down the staircase past the headmaster's bedroom he set off on foot to his relatives at Chester, doing the 40 miles in two days and becoming a confirmed pedestrian in the process. 'Life on this model was but too delightful; and to myself especially, that am never thoroughly in health unless when having pedestrian exercise to the extent of fifteen miles at the most, and eight to ten miles at the least.' After some aimless weeks at Chester he set off into Wales via Llangollen to Bangor. Here he would have stayed some time but for some imagined slight which induced him to leave as abruptly as he had from school. He rambled away to Caernarvon and from there it was through Dolgelly to Harlech and into Powys. Travelling on an allowance of a guinea a week he had to be careful about expenses and, though the inns were plentiful and in no way hostile to pedestrians, he eked out his money by staying sometimes in cottages for sixpence, where milk, bread and goat's flesh were offered, though no tea, coffee or sugar. He also for some time experimented with camping, and carried 'a canvas tent manufactured by myself, and not larger than an ordinary umbrella: but to pitch this securely I found difficult; and on windy nights it became a troublesome companion': on fine nights he used it as a pillow. From this interesting initiative De Quincey has been called the 'father of backpackers'. By the time he got to Oswestry he decided to run away from home also and head for the big city. But to walk there would, he felt, be impossible because of the way the English landlords despised pedestrians and, like Karl Moritz, young De Quincey was extremely susceptible to slights and insults. So when he got to Shrewsbury he boldly walked into the main hotel and demanded a room as being a passenger booked for the night mail-coach. Obsequious lackeys lit his way with candelabra for, as he wrote, 'the scandal of pedestrianism is in one respect more hopefully situated than that of scrofula or leprosy; it is not in any case written on your face.'

All this was in 1802: by 1809 De Quincey was actually living in Dove Cottage, leased from the Wordsworths. He was particularly fond of walking in the silence and solitude of the mysterious night, watching the way in which the natural scene took on a different tempo and snatching glimpses of the diurnal routines of the villagers as they sat around their fires or prepared for sleep. Had not the Master himself written:

> A favourite pleasure hath it been with me,
> From time of earliest youth, to walk alone
> Along the public Way, when, for the night
> Deserted, in its silence it assumes
> A character of deeper quietness
> Than pathless solitudes.

The locals thought him mad, a diminutive figure flitting by, his arms held rigidly beside him, and indeed madness was not so far away as he started to drink more readily from the decanter of laudanum that stood at his elbow while he read avidly. His walks were not always alone, for there were by now other Wordsworthians taking to the paths and slopes of the Lake District, with *Lyrical Ballads* in their knapsacks, though not all of them were true Romantics like De Quincey. An admiration of nature was central to his imaginative and intuitive mind, not so much through the meticulous attention to detail that Dorothy Wordsworth practised as by a more comprehensive appreciation of the scenery. As for his walking, it developed in a most curious way; for when he became completely addicted to opium he found that the only method of combating the torpor and melancholia it induced was to take exercise. For several years he paced the streets around his house in Edinburgh, but his nervousness at meeting people soon became so pathological that he had to retreat to his garden where he walked around a circuit of 44 yards four hundred times every day.

When John Keats set out with his friend Charles Brown for a pedestrian tour of Scotland in June 1818 he was quite clear about his reasons for going: 'I should not have consented to myself these four months tramping in the Highlands but that I thought it would give me more experience, rub off more prejudice, use me to more hardship, identify finer scenes, load me with grander mountains, and strengthen more my reach in poetry, than would stopping at home among books, even though I should read Homer.' This suggests a slightly different approach to that of Wordsworth since it ignores the pleasure of walking as such, indeed implies that it is an ordeal to be gone through so as to broaden the mind and gain poetic inspiration. But in fact when Keats wrote this in a letter he had been walking for nearly a month and was not feeling well; and besides in the same letter he dashed off some lines which, although not great poetry, at least rectify the omission:

> There is a joy in every spot, made known by times of old,
> New to the feet, although the tale a hundred times be told:
> There is a deeper joy than all, more solemn in the heart,
> More parching to the tongue than all, of more divine a smart,
> When weary feet forget themselves upon a pleasant turf,
> Upon hot sand, or flinty road, or Sea shore iron scurf . . .

Starting their walk at Lancaster they first headed into the Lake District: of one thing we may be sure, that from start to finish they walked out of step, for Keats was several inches shorter than Brown. Keats was suitably impressed by the first proper hills he had ever seen; they 'weighed very solemnly' upon him, and the sight of Windermere made him forget 'the divisions of life; age, youth, poverty and riches'. Around the hallowed shores of Rydal Water and Grasmere they took a short day: 'We stopped; we strolled; we stopped again. At every third step, something new, some change came upon us.' After a night in a flea-ridden house by Thirlmere they proceeded to Keswick and took a circuit around Derwentwater, and next day attempted to climb

Skiddaw but retreated when the mist came down. As with other pedestrian tourers they were not specially keen to reach the tops of hills. As Brown put it: 'I was not much gratified by this sort of bird's-eye view. If you would be delighted with a garden, it is surely better to walk in it, than to stare down upon it from a garret window. It must be acknowledged there is some thing grand in looking down on a country as if it were a map; but the strangeness of the sight, more than any thing else, is its attraction.' By the time they got to Carlisle and the border they had covered 114 miles in six days, 'merely a little tired in the legs, and a little blistered', and Keats found the scenery so interesting that 14 miles seemed to be less than the 4 miles from Hampstead to London.

At Dumfries they found a horse-fair that day and large numbers of men and women were on the road, the women nearly all barefoot and carrying their shoes and stockings to wear when they got to town. Keats 'expatiated on the beauty of the human foot, that had grown without natural restraint, and on the beautiful effect of colour when a young lassie's foot was on the green grass'; though Brown opined that 'to see the same foot stumping through the dust of the road, or, what is worse, dabbling in the puddles of a town is the reverse of beautiful'. Keats had his only coat repaired overnight – the knapsack had worn it at the seams – and they took to the road again. They equipped themselves with plaids, those practical all-purpose garments; Brown's coat and trousers were also tartan and, with his white hat (Keats wore a fur cap), gave him a somewhat theatrical appearance and increased speculation on who they might be: besides the usual suspicion that they were spies or excisemen they were taken for linen-drapers, jewellers, razor-sellers and, because Brown wore a pair, spectacle-vendors. In this way they walked westwards to Stranraer and sailed over to Ireland, landing at Donaghadee. But after walking the 22 miles to Belfast they were so depressed by 'the nakedness, the rags, the dirt and misery of the poor common Irish' that they returned to Scotland forthwith. Then it was up the coast to Ayr, stopping to visit Burns' Cottage, and thence to Glasgow, regularly walking around 20 miles a day.

By 16 July they were at Tarbert on Loch Lomond-side, scene of the parting of Coleridge and the Wordsworths fifteen years ealier and now definitely on the tourist circuit with pleasure boats plying the loch. From here they walked 24 miles to Inverary, of which 13 were before breakfast: this was due to a misconception that the Rest and Be

Thankful between Glen Croe and Glen Kinglass was an inn, when in fact it was – and is – merely a stone at the top of a pass with 'Rest and Be Thankful' written on it, commemorating the construction of the road by General Wade's soldiers in 1753. Breakfast was at Cairndow and after it Keats bathed in Loch Fyne, bitten continually by midges. By the time they reached Inverary Brown's feet were in bad shape, blistered by a new pair of shoes, but they made it in four days to Oban, weakened somewhat by the limited diet, now confined to eggs and oatcakes. From Oban they spent a few days on Mull, walking across it to visit the islands of Iona and Staffa. Accompanied by a guide, and walking barefoot over boggy ground, they spent their first night on Mull in a shepherd's hut in Glen More: 'The family speak not a word but Gaelic and we have not yet seen their faces for the smoke.' Brown believed that his family came from Mull and sought out people of the same name, with much mutual incomprehension. After seeing the ruins on Iona and Fingal's Cave on Staffa they crossed back through Mull by a shorter route. The weather had been raw and Keats had ominously got a sore throat (a prelude to the consumption that was to kill him three years later) and so they rested several days at Oban, where the poet read from the three slim volumes of Dante that he carried in his knapsack.

Then began the final section of their tour, three days' walking to Fort William and another four to Inverness. Brown describes the usual routine:

> . . . prosing over the map, calculating distances, packing up knapsacks, and paying bills. There's so much for yourself, my dear. 'Thank'ye, sir.' How many miles to the next town? 'Seventeen lucky miles, sir.' That must be at least twenty; come along, Keats; here's your stick; why, we forgot the map! – now for it; seventeen lucky miles! I must have another hole taken up in the strap of my knapsack. Oh! the misery of coming to the meeting of three roads without a finger post! There's an old woman coming, God bless her! she'll tell us all about it. Eh! she can't speak English! Repeat the name of the town over in all ways, but the true spelling way, and possibly she may understand. No, we have not got the brogue. Then toss up heads or tails for right or left, and fortune send us the right road! Here's a soaking shower coming! ecod! it rolls between the mountains as if it would drown us. At last we come wet and weary to the long wished for inn. What have you for

dinner? 'Truly nothing.' No eggs? 'We have two.' Any loaf bread? 'No, sir, but we've nice oat-cakes.' Any bacon? any fried fish? 'No, no, no, sir!' But you've plenty of whiskey? 'Oh yes, sir, plenty of whiskey.' This is melancholy.

They also took a day at Fort William to climb Ben Nevis. Keats was fascinated by the cloud formations, the rock corries, and the loose stones which covered the summit which they traversed 'sometimes on two, sometimes on three, sometimes on four legs – sometimes two and a stick, sometimes three and a stick, then four again, then two, then a jump, so that we kept on ringing changes on foot, hand, stick, jump boggle, stumble, foot, hand, foot, (very gingerly) stick again, and then again a game at all fours': all this perhaps more difficult than it might have been, due to regular nips of whisky. By Inverness his throat was so bad that he sailed back from Cromarty to London, having walked some 560 miles since Lancaster. In the short time remaining to him Keats made little use of the experiences of this walk or the images of the Highlands as strands in his poetry but he continued to get inspiration when walking, and one of his greatest poems, the 'Ode to Autumn', was written one evening in Winchester when he had returned from a walk along the valley of the Itchen.

These writers and poets of the Romantic movement are distinguished from ordinary pedestrian tourers of the same period because they endowed walking with an extra dimension. For those who could or would appreciate what they were saying, walking was the best means of comprehending for oneself the cult of nature. All other means, whether merely reading, or observing nature from the security of a garden or the comfort of a coach or the superiority of a horse, were inadequate substitutes. Effort, attention and sensory experience were all desirable ingredients, and walking provided them all. Admittedly the Romantic poets mostly came into the habit because they couldn't afford to keep horses: but having made a virtue of necessity they converted it into an integral part of their philosophy. In them poetry was linked to walking as never before or since and most of them were practitioners, Byron being the leading exception, his wealth and pride precluding him from such a menial pursuit. When young, James Hogg had served as a shepherd in Ettrick; and Walter Scott regularly went for long walks with fellow law students of Edinburgh, boasting in later years of having done 20-30 miles a day, in spite of his lame right leg. Shelley also walked throughout his brief life: at Oxford, where he used to strike daringly across the fields, in Wales, where from his uncle's house he walked in order to admire the scenery and observe the peasantry, and at Marlow, from where he occasionally walked the 32 miles to London. (Though it can hardly be classified as an example of the genre described in this chapter, there is also the extraordinary episode when for five days in 1814 he walked south from Paris with two girls in tow, his wife Mary and her stepsister. Keen to push on to Switzerland and further from her angry father they elected to walk on the grounds that they were short of cash: though when they reached Troyes five days later they evidently had enough money to hire a special coach for themselves. More likely, they did it for a lark; but the laughs must have been few towards the end when, having trudged across the war-stricken plain where foreign foot-travellers were neither expected nor welcome, and having had to make do with straw for a bed and sour milk and stale bread for supper, Shelley sprained his ankle. So it was he that rode on the mule that also bore their baggage while the two girls, still wearing their long black dresses, walked.)

To conclude the theme let us return to the continent of Europe and observe two famous Romantic writers – Heine and Balzac – at the moment when they first discovered the liberation of walking nearly a century after Rousseau had stepped forth from Geneva. When Heinrich Heine marched out of the university town of Göttingen one fine day in June 1824, a fresh morning breeze was blowing, and it seemed to him that it also served to blow away the dusty cobwebs of Justinian and other Roman law-makers which had been woven into his brain by pedantic professors. He was heading for the nearby Harz hills and that evening, after 25 miles, he reached their foot at Osterode. From a strictly pedestrian point of view his greatest effort was that after some days in the Harz he walked 150 miles to Berlin, but it was in the hills that he experienced the Romantic ideals as expounded by his English predecessors. At times he walked along the roads, encountering various other foot-travellers including a rather weedy tailor's apprentice who walked with him for a while but then became exhausted: 'He still made a brave pretence of marching, and blustered about girding his loins, but he soon gave in and complained that he had blistered his feet, and that the world was far too wide. At last he sank down at the foot of a tree, rocked his poor little head, as a lamb in distress waggles its tail, and exclaimed with a melancholy smile, "Knocked up again like an old screw, only fit for the knacker."' At other times he took to the hillside, walking up through woods to the rocky summit of the Brocken and next day down the eastern slopes with a group of students, as they 'crossed the boggy places at a run, stepping over tree-stems that served as bridges; clambered down precipitous hollows by help of projecting pines'. Sauntering rather than marching, with frequent stops to admire the view, he proceeded in this way from valley to valley, clad in a shabby brown overcoat and with a knapsack on his back. Ever recurrent are his joyous recognitions of the natural scene – the 'thread of silvery water trickling beneath the stones', the 'whispering of leaves like myriad maiden voices', the 'notes of the birds like snatches of love songs'. And although unlike several of the Romantic walkers he found no difficulty in his relationship with women (sharing pleasure with another 'lover of kisses' in a dark doorway in Goslar, or presenting flowers to an elegant beauty at the Brockenhaus), yet he was so full of love that it overflowed into the scenery and in particular into the three little rivers – Ilse, Bode and Salke – which, when he had conquered them with his feet, he converted into seductive women with his pen, inspiring so many to get out into the countryside on foot.

Heine's experience is complemented by that of the fifteen-year-old Honoré de Balzac who, at about the same time, walked 15 miles southwards from Tours across the heathlands to where he came in sight of the great emerald swathe of the valley of the Indre: at which point he sat down to rest beneath a walnut tree. 'For the first time in my life I was able to stop under a tree or to walk either slowly or quickly without being pestered by anyone. For a miserable boy, crushed by the various forms of authority, large and small, which weigh down upon all young people, this first taste of freedom, physically experienced through the leg muscles, brought an indescribable alleviation to my soul.' That the passionate figures of Heine and Balzac should have felt the same as the fastidious Rousseau indicates the pervasiveness of the Romantic attitude as expressed through walking.

Athletes

COMPETITIVE walking was unknown in the ancient world: all the foot-races were run, none walked. And when it was necessary to deliver urgent messages on foot, the fastest method was by running, maybe in relays. The runners of Israel brought David the news of Absalom's death; or rather, the first runner, Ahimaaz, muffed the message, and it was left to the second, Cushni, to speak the words that brought the tears to a father's eyes. The runners of Greece are immortalised by the exploit of Pheidippides, who delivered the good news of Marathon to the Athenians. Not until the eighteenth century was there any form of race-walking or endurance-walking; but once these had become established they rapidly caught on in popular appeal. It all started back in the days of Charles II. The Merry

Monarch and his courtiers were constantly placing heavy stakes at horse-races. Casting about for other contests it was natural they should fix on their running footmen: Pepys mentions such a race in his diary entry for 30 July 1663, 'between Lee, the Duke of Richmond's footman, and a tyler, a famous runner'. Occasional wagers of this sort took place for several decades and the sport began to be known as pedestrianism, which meant both running and walking, as appropriate to the length and type of contest. What got pedestrianism really moving was a number of truly long-distance exploits which were done very largely by walking, not running, and undertaken by a number of gentlemen amateurs. Of these, the one who gave the greatest initial impetus to the sport was Foster Powell in his walk from London to York and back in 1773.

Foster Powell was a clerk at the Inner Temple. He was five foot eight inches high, thin but with stout legs, and of a rather sallow complexion. As with many great walkers, it was not till his youth was past that his exploits began. In 1764, when he was thirty, he did 50 miles along the Bath road in under seven hours, running the first 10 miles in one hour. Sometime after this he went to Switzerland and in the course of his journey walked 200 miles beyond Paris. These achievements of speed and distance encouraged him to undertake that he would walk the 400 miles from London to York and back within six days, for a bet of a hundred guineas. On Monday, 29 November 1773, wearing his ordinary clothes of breeches and tail-coat, he left London in the small hours and late at night was at Stamford, 88 miles away. After a short rest he walked 72 miles on Tuesday, as far as Doncaster. Then on Wednesday he covered the remaining 37 miles to York by 2 p.m., speeding into a jog towards the end. Having delivered a letter he repaired to the Golden Anchor for some light refreshment (he was always particular about his diet and ate very little during his exploits, keeping going on snacks of tea and toast, and also beer), and then lay down for one and a half hours. At 5.30 he set out on the return journey and reached Ferrybridge that night, 22 miles off. On Thursday he covered 65 miles to Grantham, and on Friday 54 miles to Eaton. He reached his starting-point in London at 6.30 p.m. on Saturday, after the final 56 miles: as he approached the city thousands came to cheer him in. Ruminating on this crowded hour of glorious life the quiet and retiring Powell emerged from the shadows of the Inner Temple again in 1786 for a number of other stunning performances: indeed, since he was by now fifty-two years old, it is probable that he had retired from his clerkship. In that year he undertook the classic walking challenge, to walk 100 miles within twenty-four hours, which he did along the Bath road (50 miles out and 50 miles back) in twenty-three and a half hours. The next year he improved on this with 109 miles in twenty-three hours and fifty minutes, from Canterbury to London and back. 1788 was a peak year, for in June he repeated his walk to York, this time doing the return journey in five days and nineteen hours; and in July he walked 100 miles in twenty-two hours. Testing his powers of endurance he walked to York twice again: and amazingly, unlike most ageing athletes who gradually deteriorate, Foster Powell improved on his times.

By now a constant series of pedestrian contests were taking place, their timings duly noted in the *Sporting Magazine* with dubious accuracy, and attracting increasing interest among the sporting fraternity who placed wagers on the contestants just as they did on the horses. Although the lesser distances up to say 30 or 50 miles involved running or a mixture of walking and running called 'go as you please', the really long distances were walked throughout, nearly all on the turnpike roads where the milestones provided useful markers. The contests were completely unstandardised, just individual challenges, some against time (for instance, the number of miles in twenty-four hours), some against distance (how long to walk 400 miles), some at set rates (say, to walk 2 miles in each hour for a hundred hours), some solo performances, some against a competitor. The contestants were generally amateurs, that is to say, they were in theory doing it for the sport and not the money: a high proportion of these were army officers, men such as Captain Agar, Captain Acres, Lieutenant Fairman or Lieutenant Groats. But there were also professionals (easy to spot, because not prefixed with a Mr), as well as 'gentlemen of fortune', who could certainly do with an extra bob or two. The style of these walkers was eagerly noted. Lieutenant Fairman walked in such a way that 'his arms are compressed, and pinioned close to his sides, and their weight is supported by a loop pendent from each shoulder, into which he places his thumbs'. Abraham Wood, of Mildrew in Lancashire, 'is a remarkably fine, tall, well-made man, and is not only a swift runner, but is also possessed of good *wind* and great *bottom*'. But the king of the long-distance pedestrians was Captain Robert Barclay Allardice, usually known as Captain Barclay.

From his youth Robert Barclay had excelled in physical strength, inspired by legendary tales of the Barclays of yore, one of whom had wielded a sword no one else could lift. At twenty he could lift half a ton. When commissioned into the 23rd Regiment of Foot, he lifted the eighteen stone paymaster from the ground and on to the mess table, by means of clutching his legs. But walking was his real love. Already at fifteen he had walked 6 miles in an hour 'fair toe and heel'. At nineteen he walked 70 miles in fourteen hours, and at twenty-one, 64 miles in twelve hours. He was now set for the big league and in 1801 a group of supporters bet him the enormous sum of two thousand guineas to walk 90 miles in twenty-one and a half hours. Unfortunately, after doing 67 miles in thirteen hours, he incautiously took some brandy and was violently sick and had to withdraw. Confident that he could do it perfectly well, Captain Barclay arranged for a replay in November, and went into serious training beforehand. The prize was now five thousand guineas, and the course was fixed on a straight section of the road between York and Hull of exactly one mile in length. Gas lamps were placed along the road, and turning posts at each end, which added some three paces to each mile; and a rest-house was ten yards off course. The start was at midnight: six stop-watches were placed in a sealed box. Barclay was dressed in a flannel shirt, flannel trousers and night-cap, lamb's-wool stockings, and thick-soled leather shoes. Hour after hour he kept unchangingly to a rate of 2 miles every twenty-five minutes. By afternoon a large crowd had assembled and many were making their own bets on whether he would make it: odds in his favour began at 2:1, and after 60 miles had increased to 7:1. He finished fresh and strong at twenty hours, twenty-two minutes, which was one hour, eight minutes within the allotted time, and was carried away shoulder high amid loud cheers.

Six years later the Captain was in the lists again, this time at Newmarket in a race against Abraham Wood as to which could cover the greater distance within twenty-four hours. The winner was to get two hundred guineas. Wood scrapped after 40 miles, and some of the backers refused to pay Barclay on the grounds of suspected collusion. But this slur was soon forgotten; the Captain was clearly the champ and so it was natural that he should be offered a truly amazing challenge: he was bet one thousand guineas to walk 1000 miles in one thousand hours, and to cover 1 mile in each and every hour, a test which others had attempted and failed. This is as much a test of sleeping as of walking, for over the forty-two days in question it is necessary to use the rest periods to maximum effect: Captain Barclay in fact altered the time within each hour in which he took his mile's walk, so that sometimes he had rests of nearly an hour at a time. He was also meticulous in his diet which, in that meat-eating age, was highly carnivorous. For breakfast he had roast chicken and a pint of strong ale, followed by two cups of tea with bread and butter. For lunch it was beefsteak or mutton chops. For dinner, roast beef or mutton chops, with two or three glasses of wine. For late supper, cold chicken. It does not seem that he went into any special training, but he was at the height of his powers. For instance, in the previous year, he rose one day at five and walked in all 30 miles through the day over the moors of Aberdeenshire in pursuit of grouse then, after an early dinner, 60 miles through the night back to his house at Ury. Next afternoon he walked 16 miles to Lawrencekirk to attend a ball, and after some vigorous dancing walked back and was home by seven in the morning.

The scene was a special course on Newmarket Heath; the date, 1 June 1809; and he was off. Round and round he walked, all through June and into July. He walked in a sort of lounging gait, without appearing to exert himself, and leant his body forwards and bent his knee slightly on impact; his steps were short in relation to his height. The daily log tells us the precise timings of each mile, the state of the weather, and his physical condition. During the initial weeks he did his mile in around fifteen minutes, but towards the end this had slowed to around twenty minutes. At times he suffered severe muscular pains; on the thirty-fourth day the pain in his legs was so excessive that he 'could not move without crying out'. Eventually his ordeal came towards its end, the crowds began to assemble, and at 3.37 p.m. on 12 July he concluded his final mile in twenty-two minutes and was once again a popular hero. None the worse for this exploit, except for a loss of weight of 32 lbs, Captain Barclay reported for duty with his regiment five days later and was soon embarking for Walcheren with the British military expedition. Later, he retired to his estate and lived to the age of seventy-five. He was often quoted as an authority on training, but his methods would not appeal to athletes today. He was a strong supporter of the induced sweat: the pedestrian should drink a lot of liquid, then run 4 miles in thick flannels, then lie on a bed under six or eight blankets, then strip and rub off. It was with training methods better than these that his great record was easily beaten by others later. In 1851 Richard Manks walked 1000 miles in one thousand successive half-hours, and in 1877 William Gale walked 1500 miles in one thousand successive hours.

By now the development of athletics had forced a distinction between walking and running in competitive events, except for some 'go as you please' races. Race-walking was to be strictly 'heel and toe', that is to say, a gait in which one foot touches the ground before the other leaves it. For some time it was thought that this definition was enough, but it overlooked the fact that one can achieve a faster speed over shorter distances by adopting a sort of non-leaping run with the knees bent, really a type of jogging. As anyone will know, when someone is moving in this way it is extremely difficult to tell whether or not the back foot has left the ground before the front foot makes contact. Thus it was that a second criterion came to be introduced into race-walking, namely, that during each step the foot must be straightened, making a firm differentiation from any form of running. Speed is obtained by a very long stride and rapid pace. Full use is made of the mobility of the hips by swivelling them in such a way that they draw the leg forward and reduce the rise and fall of the body with each stride. This action is counterbalanced by using the arms to absorb the rotation, swinging them across the chest with elbows out. And the fullest use is made of the hip-wobble by placing the feet as it were on either side of a straight line, and pointing the toes straight ahead. In this way the stride can be extended and by doing three paces to the second speeds of up to 10 m.p.h. can be attained as one skims over the ground with the sensation of floating.

Unfortunately it has to be said that this race-walking style is as ungainly as it is unnatural. It is something which the human frame simply was not designed to do. For, whilst ordinary walking is the most natural thing in the world, when speed is required the whole body is ready to break into an elegant run. To remain at the walk when at great speed is to restrict the natural potential and inclination, as with horses trained for trotting races, producing a distinctly ludicrous effect reminiscent of the jerky movements in early movies. The practitioners have to exercise an iron control to prevent themselves from running. No wonder that race-walking has been elbowed out from the central position it briefly held in the last century, or that of truly long-distance events it is the running marathon that now captures the public imagination. After all, the main attribute of walking as opposed to running is endurance rather than speed: the story of race-walking is thus, to my mind, a specialised subject which is part of the history of competitive sport rather than that of walking in general.

At the outer edge of the recognised and established track and road race-walking events, however, there have been a number of unusual and localised contests of endurance which at times have attracted great public attention, and which are more in the tradition of Powell and Barclay. One such were the 'go as you please' contests of the 1880s, first instituted in London in 1878. The idea here was for the contestants to go around a circuit for six days aiming for maximum distance: they could run or jog if they wanted, though in practice they mostly walked. As in the early days of pedestrianism, the event was financed by heavy public betting. As with Captain Barclay's Newmarket walk, the management and discipline of eating and sleeping were almost as important as the walking, and the contestants staggered at intervals into their tents to be tended by their assistants. The champion of these events was George Littlewood, an Englishman who in 1882 at the Madison Square Garden in New York covered 623¾ miles over the allotted period despite an accident in the course of it when the alcohol in which he was bathing his feet caught fire.

Another group of fringe events were the inter-city walks, such as the Vienna-Berlin walk, the Manchester-London walk and the long-standing London-Brighton walk. Mostly these were abandoned as traffic made them impracticable: one exception is the Paris-Strasbourg (now Colmar) walk, revived in 1970. This walk, of slightly varying length through the years, is at present 518 km (322 miles). The record is held by Robert Pietquin who in 1980, exclusive of four hours' statutory rest periods, covered the ground in sixty hours, one minute and ten seconds. Then there are the twenty-four-hour events. The best performance here is that of Jesse Casteneda who in 1976 covered 142 miles 448 yards. In Britain anyone doing 100 miles in twenty-four hours qualifies for membership of a select group called the Centurions.

From time to time men have tested themselves to destruction by seeing how far they can walk non-stop. Richard Crawshaw threw his gauntlet into the ring in 1974 by covering 255.84 miles before he stopped, taking seventy-six hours, twenty-one minutes. Aged fifty-six, a former colonel and a Member of Parliament, he was sponsored for the benefit of the NSPCC. For the first 155 miles he was accompanied in his race-track circuits by a previous British record holder, but after that he walked alone. In the end it was not so much exhaustion of the leg muscles that forced him to stop as a stomach chill brought on by his decision to walk through the third night thinly clad so as to ward off sleep. When he got home he took a tranquilliser and went into a deep slumber while his wife massaged his legs. After two bouts of eight hours' sleep he was back in the pink of health. The right honourable and gallant Colonel (who has appropriately since been President of the Long Distance Walkers Association) saw his record broken by Warrant Officer Norman Fox of the Royal Horse Artillery who in 1982 walked 401.44 miles in one hundred and forty-three hours, twenty-nine minutes, when aged thirty-five. One wonders to what extent the slower speed helped to achieve the longer distance. Certainly these two men were probably at the respective ends of the age-bracket for this particular test, for anyone over sixty must surely lack strength, anyone under thirty mental discipline. But for sheer pedestrian plodding no one can touch the achievement of Dimitru Dan, a Rumanian who entered a contest on a track in France starting on 1 April 1910, to cover 100,000 km. On 24 March 1916 he called a halt after he had covered 96,000 km (60,000 miles), averaging 27.5 miles a day. Towards the end he was the only contestant, which is not surprising in view of the outbreak of world war and general conscription. It is macabre to think of the carnage on the battle front while this solitary Rumanian footed futilely around the empty track.

To be an athlete does not necessarily mean to participate in a competitive event, and it is not a far step from Richard Crawshaw or Dimitru Dan to the so-called marathon road walkers. The British end-to-ender is the road walk between Land's End and John o'Groats. The fastest time for the 851 miles is held by the same Norman Fox, who in 1983 did it in twelve days, twenty-one hours (some 65 miles daily average); and for women, by Ann Sayer, who took thirteen days, eighteen hours in 1980 (61 miles daily average). This tall Amazon is a metronomic walker, with the ticker set permanently somewhere between allegro and presto to give an unalterable 4 miles to the hour for the entire day without ever stopping for rest. The US equivalent to the Land's End to John o'Groats walk is the 2876 miles between the City Halls of Los Angeles and New York, and this was walked in 1972 by John Lees who took fifty-three days (54 miles daily average). These achievements evoke the memory of the man who has been called the father of the marathon walkers, Edward Payon Weston. He got his first taste for the sport when at the age of twenty he walked from Boston to Washington to be present at Lincoln's inauguration, doing the 450 miles in ten days. When he was twenty-eight he walked 1326 miles from Portland, Maine, to Chicago in twenty-six days (51 miles daily average); and, even more remarkably, did it again forty years later when he was sixty-eight, beating his record by twenty-nine hours. Two years later he still retained enough strength to walk from New York to San Francisco at a daily average of 37 miles. But perhaps his most amazing feat was earlier, in 1879, when he wagered a hundred pounds to Sir John Astley's five hundred pounds that he would road-walk 2000 miles in a thousand hours in England. Because Sundays were to be observed as a day of rest, this meant eight hundred and fifty-six hours. He completed the distance in twenty-two and a half hours over the top (55.5 miles daily average), and so had to forfeit his hundred pounds to the rapacious baronet.

All these feats were done with back-up teams and without carrying anything. There were some really cranky ones such as G. H. Johnson who in 1926 walked 577 miles from Chicago towards New York without eating anything, or Plannie L. Wingo who in 1931–2 walked backwards on a route from Santa Monica, California, to Istanbul – that is, excluding the Atlantic and other sea passages. But there is also a wilder and more individualistic type of marathon walking undertaken by solo backpackers out to cover even greater distances. The problem is that their endeavours are so dependent on their own ground rules. Should they carry their full equipment on their backs?; camp out always, or sometimes accept accommodation?; walk consecutively, or take occasional lifts?; walk only on roads, or partly on paths and tracks?; walk every day, or take rest days?; walk absolutely alone, or with some sort of back-up?; be completely out of touch, or ring home every night? Only by knowing all these things can we properly assess them; and the trouble is that often, in their own or press accounts, vital facts are obscured. Verification is impossible (though sometimes false claims can be exposed through irreconcilable references). Sean Maguire in 1978 walked the 7327 miles from Yukon to Florida in three hundred and seven days (24 miles daily average). Then there has been George Meegan, who spent six years nine months in walking 19,019 miles (I like that final 19, it shows real exactitude) from Tierra del Fuego at the tip of South America to Prudhoe Bay in Northern Alaska. If his daily average mileage was short it may be partly because he was accompanied by a Japanese girl, and after marrying her at Mendoza, Argentina, he sired two children in the course of his journey. And despite several so-called 'round the world' walkers, whose achievements are less remarkable than the term implies because their route is so split by sea, George Meegan has a good claim to have completed the longest continuous walk ever. In the first half he emulated Sebastian Snow, who a decade before had made an epic walk of 8700 miles up South America in a year and a half, thus averaging about 16 miles daily. His account of it in *The Rucksack Man* is most revealing and merits close inspection for its insight into the trials and tribulations of marathon walkers.

On 5 February 1973 Sebastian Snow set out from Ushuaia in Tierra del Fuego, the southernmost city of South America and the world. He wore Italian leather boots, pure wool knee stockings, tweed knicker-bockers, a hand-knitted sweater, and a heavy double ventile anorak. On his head was a cap and on his back a 60 lb pack containing the usual tent and sleeping-bag, spare boots, underclothes and shirts, books, medicines, maps, compass, torch, mug; and also, unusually, several pairs of contact lenses. In a body belt he carried his passport and large amounts of travellers' cheques. His self-imposed rules were that he would walk alone, carry all he needed, and walk every yard of the way never accepting a lift; though he could make use of transport for the purposes of lodging or other local 'side' trips. He did not lack for influential contacts and enjoyed periodic interludes of rest and re-freshment in elegant houses which must have seemed all the more luxurious in contrast to the rigours of the march. The goodwill of his hosts must at times have been strained by his steadfast refusal to indulge in a bath (he believed it was bad for the pores), though a forthright hostess obliged him to take one after eight months' abstinence.

The successive ordeals of Sebastian Snow in his great walk have all the quality of ancient legends where capricious gods impose fearsome tests upon their victims. In such legends the usual number of tests is either three or seven – both magic numbers – and I think I can detect the Seven Ordeals of Sebastian Snow. The first was Wind. In the flat pampas of Patagonia he encountered terrible winds that made even those of Tierra del Fuego seem mild, for autumn was now advancing. There were 125 m.p.h. gusts which changed direction and threw him to the ground on four occasions; and a headwind that was so strong that it took him two hours to erect his tent, which then blew down twice on him in the dark. On the Plateau of Death, a roadless wilderness now largely under snow, he duly encountered mist, hail, snow, fast-flowing torrents, and the inevitable fierce winds. These winds were additionally hazardous for him because he insisted on wearing contact lenses, not spectacles, when walking. So when dust or pebbles got thrown into his face the lenses became agony to wear and often could not be extracted. Next came Drought: for though it was easy going along dirt roads across a dry plain at around 20 miles a day, there was a complete lack of water. Fortunately Sebastian was always strict about water consumption and avoided drinking during the march; so his litre of the 'precious liquid' saw him through three days without impediment.

Across the flat expanses as he progressed northwards, Sebastian was increasingly plagued by his third test, Traffic. He walked on the verge of the asphalt which stretched endlessly ahead, the monotony broken only by the corpses of dogs or the glitter of shattered windscreens, facing the oncoming vehicles. Even this had its hazards when trucks threw up clouds of dust in their wake which blinded him, or when one overtook another from behind him. The consequent everlasting dance with death almost went to his head and at times he walked straight at oncoming trucks, daring them to swerve before he did. Close behind Traffic came Heat. In the Peruvian desert north of Lima he was not far from hell. The temperature was usually over 30°C in the sun and the water in his bottle was near to boiling point, but through sheer obstinacy the Abominable Snowman kept his double ventile jacket on and still wore his tweed breeches, 'so that the net result was a daily nine hours sauna bath'. It was acts of defiance such as these that kept him going, as did many routine disciplines such as marching by the watch and stopping for five minutes in the hour. The gods meanwhile had bowled some other mean tricks at him, which may generally be called Distractions. Perhaps in revenge for the fact that after six months he became newsworthy and was recognised along the way as *El Mochillero* (The Rucksack Man), they arranged for the aluminium frame to break, and some days later a new backpack to split. More alluring distractions followed in the shape of Anna and her Aunt Emma, who lured him to Macchu Picchu; though the Ascot-educated girl who begged him to take a lift with her, and the girls at the roadside brothel, were all sternly rejected. But more serious was the intervention of Chris Bonnington, who came out to meet him in Ecuador by arrangement, courtesy of the *Observer*. The ensuing ten days provided a most instructive example of the differences between walkers and climbers, for here were two leading practitioners of their respective skills walking together, the climber seeking to influence the walker. Bonnington was all for taking short cuts: 'he leapt from tussock to tussock up the hillside at a tremendous pace' and then stood waiting for Snow to catch up; or he plunged off the road on to railway tracks or paths. But the hare just couldn't keep up with the tortoise and on several occasions ended the day on wheels (at least, according to the tortoise's account). I think that Officialdom must be rated as the sixth test. In Bolivia the security police ranged from the studiously attentive to the ruthlessly tough. Ham-footed detectives tried all their arts to establish whether he was a drug smuggler. The army arrested him for photographing their men. In Peru he had to pass through at least ten police control points in 100 miles.

It is an interesting feature of Sebastian Snow's walk that as the months went by his pedestrian achievements became ever more remarkable while his physical and mental strengths were being subjected to ever greater cumulative strains, for 'the loneliness became so depressing that if I had fifteen minutes of pleasure out of any twenty-four hours, I felt surprised'. Fantasy helped him: at times he saw himself as Tom Thumb in his Seven League boots, or as Charlie Chaplin with his jaunty waddle. At other times self-pity dominated, and he saw himself as an old blinkered cart-horse heading for the knacker's yard, plodding on and on and with brain emptied of all thought. The constant brushes with death from the monstrous vehicles brought bouts of sudden but impotent fury. But curiously these moods served him well, for they strengthened his determination to continue. Another mental trick was to refer to himself as 'we', as if some ghostly companion was with him: over and over he would repeat to himself, in time with his steps, 'We shall arrive, when we shall arrive.' In this way he at times averaged 25 miles at 8000 feet altitude, and his most memorable day was 62 miles in eighteen hours into Quito, the last part of it in pelting rain and utter darkness, blinded by oncoming lights dazzling his lenseless eyes. By the time he reached Medellin in Colombia it was calculated that he had taken 11,745,000 paces.

But now came the final ordeal – Jungle; for Sebastian was set on reaching Panama City, still with half a mind to continue into North America. For this exploit he bought a complete refit, including tropical clothes, hammock, two machetes and a twelve-bore shotgun. Joined by a Canadian student (Wade Davies), he set off into the jungle, for the Pan-American highway was not yet built. Each step was slow motion in the gluey quagmire. Sebastian suffered from an ingrown toenail and injured his hand on a spiky palm. Five days of fording rivers, slithering through mud and pushing through creepers got them to the Panamanian border. Here he slipped and sprained his left ankle, which swelled alarmingly. 'From now on until I reached Panama City three weeks later every bloody step I took became an individual act of will.' Despite the forebodings of missionaries, the shock of a police search and the dangers of bandits, they staggered on, Sebastian now spraining his right ankle also, and Wade ill with dysentery. When he arrived at Panama City Sebastian Snow was some five stone underweight; both ankles were sprained, swollen and discoloured; his feet were covered with blood and sores; his body was spotted with insect bites, ticks and leeches; his skin was rotting through lack of vitamins. Yet only insistent advice from friends dissuaded him from continuing north. So this fanatical walker decided to call it a day. With typical understatement he concludes his account of it by saying – just as if he had been on a 20-mile saunter over Dartmoor – 'It had been a good walk.' Amazingly, he had been exempted from military service with the British Army on the grounds that, following a rugger accident when aged sixteen, his left leg was about half an inch shorter than his right; so he had walked the whole way with a fractional limp!

Although he is not exclusively a road walker, this is also the place to mention John Merrill, perhaps the greatest British long-distance hiker of today, because he certainly considers himself as a competitive walker and is undoubtedly an athlete. His books tell us how he undertakes his journeys and sets his self-made laws. For him the walk must be continuous and if possible without any rest days. Indeed, once he has started his walk each day he doesn't even stop for rest or food till the end of it. He carries no water and tries to consume none when on the march, during which his only sustenance is chocolate, of which he eats two or three bars a day in the early stages, rising to eight bars a day after the first few weeks. His backpack, containing all his needs except food purchased en route, weighs some 50 lbs. He wears traditional walking boots of 4½ lb the pair; two pairs of pure woollen socks, the inner of short loop stitch, the outer long ragg, which he changes every two or three days; a cotton shirt; Rohan breeches, or else shorts; a balaclava helmet when cold. He steadfastly refuses all offers of a lift, and he always walks alone. Other principles enshrined in 'Merrill's Law' include some spartan restrictions such as 'limit your conversations with people you meet', 'do not let illness get you down', and 'turn a blind eye to blisters', as well as two mental guidances – 'have faith', and 'develop the three D's: drive, dedication and determination'. Another precept is 'use your evenings to recover', and in this Merrill strictly means what he says, for at the end of the day's walk he immediately lies down and rests his legs throughout the remainder of the evening and night. The evening meal is generally a bowl of soup, a hot main course, followed by a tin of fruit, a mug of tea, and half a packet of biscuits. Finally, 'when it is time to go to sleep I lay the boots flat, heads together, forming my pillow. I generally fall asleep instantly.'

By sticking to drills such as these John Merrill has succeeded in becoming Britain's most redoubtable long-distance walker. In all, he has already done twelve walks each of over 1000 miles. When on a major walk, and where the going is easy, he averages at least 25 miles a day at around 3 miles an hour. It is clear that only a man of iron determination could sustain such inexorable achievements over so long a period. The physical wear and tear itself is severe enough, and he has suffered from ailments such as the fatigue fracture of a toe. But equally important is the question of temperament, and here John Merrill's remarkable equanimity undoubtedly comes into play as a major factor, helped also by a sympathetic and understanding wife who respects the solitary aspects of his character. Certainly it is evident that the leading marathon walkers can only achieve their targets by adopting self-disciplines just as severe as those of any other leading athletes. The main difference is that for all track or road races – walking or running – the preparatory training is of primary import-ance, whereas for walking very long distances it is the physical and mental disciplines during the performance which count for most.

John Merrill has a serious disposition, a characteristic shared by another great marathon walker, Hamish Brown. Hamish first came to prominence by climbing hundreds of the highest Scottish peaks in the course of a single expedition which he made entirely on foot, never using a vehicle. This involved a total of 1639 miles and a cumulative ascent of 449,000 feet. With this under his belt he next set out to walk from John o'Groats in the general direction of Land's End, but keeping so far as possible to the highest ground and over the tops of the hills. His route (which also involved a side walk across southern Ireland) this time totalled 2500 miles, which he covered (in 1979) over a period of one hundred and seventy-five days. Of these one hundred and forty-six were walking days, giving a daily average of about 17 miles. His self-ordained rules permitted him to make side-rides, so as to stay in occasional hotels, though he mostly camped. Also, though his backpack weighed 24–30 lb, he arranged for supply parcels to be waiting at a series of post offices. These parcels contained books, magazines and newspapers, for Hamish Brown did not feel that the walk need cut him off from ordinary pleasures (he even carried a transistor in the later stages); they also contained a very important item of food – Storm's dog biscuits. For he wasn't altogether alone, but had his dog, Storm, trotting at his heel: and throughout his book (*Hamish's Groats End Walk*) he refers to the whole affair in terms of 'we' and not 'I'. Mention should also be made of another really tough marathon walker, Chris Townsend, who after walking from John o'Groats to Land's End completed the Pacific Crest Trail in 1982.

But marathon walking doesn't have to be confined to soloists, and an example of a walking event that gave as much pleasure to people as a modern marathon mass run was Billy Butlin's challenge walk from John o'Groats to Land's End in 1960. Anyone could enter and the first prize was a thousand pounds each for men and women. They could stop where they liked or where they could, but there were checkpoints and roving motor monitors. The nicest things about it were the ways in which many competitors helped each other, especially in the severe winter conditions in which they started down the main roads of Ross and Sutherland, and that they were given hospitality by the local inhabitants. Some were incredibly ill-prepared and ill-shod. In the true spirit of Foster Powell, a twenty-one-year-old stockbroker wore a city suit with bowler hat throughout, changing into top hat and tails for the finish; ludicrous, of course, except that the bowler is actually an eminently practical form of headgear in rough weather. Of the 715 who started only a minority trickled in to the finish. The two winners were, for the men, J. Musgrave aged thirty-eight, in eighteen days, and for the women, W. Lewis aged eighteen, in twenty days.

This splendid Billy Butlin event also serves to remind us of the constant succession of single-minded people who trudge up and down the route without trying to break the record. One such was Barbara Moore, born Anya Cherkasova, who occupies a special place in the story of marathon walking because her achievements were in support of her advocacy for a vegetarian diet: one wonders what Robert Barclay would have made of it. This redoubtable woman had endured imprisonment in the Russian revolution but emerged from it to become the USSR's first woman aviator and a motoring and motorcycling champion. Her conversion from these violent mechanised pursuits to the gentle motion of walking came after a period of study and meditation in India, followed by residence in England. She hit the headlines first in a walk from Edinburgh to London during which she wore sacking tied around her blistered feet, in the manner of the Russian peasants of her youth; and in the following year, 1960, came her John o'Groats to Land's End walk which she made in twenty-two days, entirely on a diet of honey and fruit and vegetable juices. (She also made marathon walks across Australia and the USA, during which she was knocked down by a car but insisted on keeping going.) Most recently we have had Ian Botham, the cricket hero, and three friends striding down the route in great publicity in aid of Leukemia Research, taking thirty-five days. And in between times there has been Ben Haywood, who did it, in one direction or the other, no fewer than six times when over the age of sixty and often sleeping rough by the roadside. As Ben put it, with admirable simplicity, 'Walking was agony, but it had to be endured if I was to beat the challenge.' It is good to learn that the civic dignitaries turned out and gave him a hero's welcome when he finally stomped into home base at Bromwich.

Strollers

HIDDEN between the hedgerows or wending across the meadows, hugging the stream-banks or running in a straight line through the cornfields, the ancient village paths of rural England, which now seem like delicate gossamer webs, were once the vital arteries of local life and unlike the roads were entirely for pedestrians. Along them people walked daily to work, whether from outlying cottages into the village or from the village into the fields. They walked to the shops or the post office, and the children walked unwillingly to school. For many these daily chores involved a good two miles each way and for the unlucky ones even more: unlucky, because the additional walk was on top of the manual labour of the day, as 'the ploughman homeward plods his weary way'. Yet there was an obverse side to that half-hour trudge. It provided a blessed moment of privacy in a life crammed communally into crowded rooms, and an intimate touch with the natural scene in all its annual variety. On market days the paths were full of people going to town carrying baskets of fruit or vegetables or poultry to sell in return for tea or sugar or haberdashery. The paths themselves were sources of marginal benefit, for herbs, mushrooms, blackberries and nuts could all be picked along them.

It was not merely as the route to work that paths played an important part in rural life: they were also the scenes of assignation and love. The convention was that unattached young men and women could 'walk out' together, and on Sunday afternoons and summer evenings the paths were lovers' lanes. Walking out of the village due decorum was preserved as the young couple started sedately side by side; once past the houses they were holding hands; between the hedgerows there were kisses; and in the long grass there was every-thing else. Stiles provided great opportunities for physical contact, as also did stepping-stones and foot-bridges. At any stage, except perhaps the last, the girl had the opportunity to reject, and maybe was soon walking out with someone else: for this was the only way to get to know a boy as they mostly didn't have parties at home, except for their immediate families. It would have been a bold couple, however, who walked out thus on a Sunday morning, for that was the time when everyone in their Sunday best walked to church or chapel in the direction of the tolling bell and long and solemn service.

Elihu Burritt wrote of the English footpaths: 'They run through all the prose, poetry, and romance of the rural life of England, permeat-ing the history of green hedges, thatched cottages, morning songs of the lark, moonlight walks, meetings at the stile, harvest homes of long ago, and many a romantic narrative of human experience widely read in both hemispheres.' But, since the lower the social status the greater part that walking played in social life, it is most fitting that walking of this sort should be described by John Clare, the Northamptonshire peasant. In 'Stray Walks' he writes:

> 'Tis sunday and the little paths that wind
> Through closen green by hedges and wood sides
> And like a brook corn crowded slope divides
> Of pleasant fields – their frequent passers find
> From early morn to mellow close of day
> On different errands climbing many stiles

Oer hung with awthorn tempting haste to stay
And coolsome moments of the road away
When hot and high the uncheckt summer smiles
Some journeying to the little hamlet hid
In dark surrounding trees to see the friends
While some sweet leisures aimless road pursue
Wherever fancys musing pleasure wends
To woods or lakes or church thats never out of view.

At the time when rural depopulation followed from industrialisation and agricultural decline the attractions of the rural byways drew discerning members of the gentry on to them: or, to be more exact, the genteel who inhabited the smaller residences rather than the farmers or the squirearchy or the very grand in their parks and gardens, some of which were designed so as to offer extensive walks. Such a one was Mary Mitford whose book *Our Village* was first published in 1824 and charmingly describes her discovery of her locality, the village of Three Mile Cross, near Reading. Mary Mitford was one of a then all too common breed of spinsters who sacrificed their lives in looking after their elderly parents. But she was also a highly intelligent woman who had already published several works and was on friendly terms with literary figures such as Elizabeth Barrett. Lack of money drove Mary and her parents from their house in Reading to a cottage in Three Mile Cross, but this jolt into the country made her name. In *Our Village* she describes how after walking across the common she comes on to 'the meadows, and out of the world. Robinson Crusoe, in his lonely island, had scarcely a more complete or a more beautiful solitude.' From here 'I shall meet no one now; for I have fairly left the road, and am crossing the lea by one of those wandering paths, amidst the gorse, and the heath, and the low broom, which the sheep and lambs have made – a path turfy, thymy, and sweet.' And when she walks in the winter, with the countryside in frost, the mile-long avenue of oaks is 'like the roofs and columns of a cathedral, every tree and branch encrusted with bright and delicate congelation of hoar-frost white and pure as snow, delicate and defined as ivory'. When a coach passes her she notices 'how much happier the walkers look than the riders – especially the frost-bitten gentleman, and the shivering lady with the invisible face, sole passengers of that commodious machine!'

From the days of Mary Mitford and other pioneers of the practice the country walk became a recognised and established way of taking exercise among the upper and middle classes who lived in the country, and their guests. Not everyone was keen of course. Max Beerbohm in an essay describes feelingly the perils of going to stay in the country and being obliged to go for a walk. Feeble excuses such as having some letters to write were usually ineffective so, Beerbohm advises, 'you might as well go quietly'. His reason for disliking a walk is that in his experience inspiration in thought or conversation comes more readily on the hearth-rug than on the farm-track. On the former one can enjoy the cut and thrust of witty talk, on the latter one is reduced to dull repetitiveness. From this he concludes that though walking may be good for the soul it is bad for the brain, which eventually decides to go to sleep until it is all over. But Beerbohm was such an ethereal man that we need not take his strictures too seriously, delightful writer though he was. No more serious is the categoric statement by Mrs Millamant in Congreve's *The Way of the World*. When the country boor Sir Wilfull Witwood suggests a walk with the obvious intent of proposing that she should become Lady Witwood, she delivers the terrible retort, 'I nauseate walking; 'tis a country diversion. I loathe the country and everything that relates to it.'

Mrs Millamant's outburst would carry more weight were it not that shortly after in the play we find her making full use of the possibilities of a walk in St James's Park for ensnaring the lover of her choice with honeyed insults and disdainful affectation. Since Congreve wrote in the seventeenth century, Mrs Millamant's is an early instance of urban promenading, a form of social walking which was then at its most fashionable, with Charles II himself around on the prowl for a pretty face. The promenade was as conducive to romance as was the village footpath, though in a different sort of way. There was no privacy, but there were introductions and assignations and flirtations, all conducted under the guise of simply taking a stroll. But urban walking also took more energetic forms, and it is Congreve's contemporary Jonathan Swift who must be our first example of a really determined exponent.

Swift was possibly the best-known figure in the London society of his day, a brilliant conversationalist and Tory political activist. His *Letters to Stella* contain several references to his habit of walking in London whenever he could, such as 'a good walk, and dined with Ford' or 'I walked today into the city for my health'. He found walking so efficacious that it was one reason why he moved out of town to live in Chelsea, so as to 'put myself under the necessity of walking to and from London every day'. Usually he walked in daylight hours but sometimes after supper, which was dangerous because of footpads and for which Stella admonished him. When in attendance on the Court at Windsor he wrote to her: 'I led Mr Lewis a walk up the avenue, which is two miles long: we walkt in all about five miles: but I was so tired with his slow walking, that I left him there, and walkt two miles towards London, hoping to meet the lord treasurer, and return with him; but it grew darkish, and I was forced to walk back, so I walked nine miles in all'. Inspired by these achievements Swift actually thought of walking all the way to Chester together with his servant on his way to Dublin, where he had secured the position of Dean of St Patrick's Cathedral, and calculated that it would take him a fortnight to do it. But in the event he rode it all, confining his further walking to the streets of Dublin and the surrounding parks, where he is said to have walked at an 'electric pace', fanatical for his daily exercise.

Perhaps it would have been better for the health of Samuel Johnson if he too had walked for exercise in London, as an antidote to his obesity and melancholy. But although he boasted of having in his youth often walked the 32 miles from Lichfield to Birmingham and back to dissipate his early hypochondria, his walking was all too soon circumscribed to his immediate social needs. Like other large fat men, he appeared to glide when walking: as Boswell writes, 'When he walked the streets, what with the constant roll of his head, and the concomitant motion of his body, he appeared to make his way by that motion independent of his feet.' When they undertook their celebrated tour of the Hebrides in 1773 Dr Johnson rode virtually all the way, and the only reference we have to his actual walking is when he arrived in Edinburgh and Boswell led him home through the narrow streets of Auld Reeky: 'A zealous Scotsman would have wished Mr Johnson to be without one of his five senses upon this occasion. As we marched slowly along, he grumbled in my ear, "I smell you in the dark!"' He supported himself with a large oak stick which also served as a measure, for one nail was driven into it at the length of a foot and another at that of a yard. On the barren and treeless island of Mull he lost it and would not be comforted by Boswell's optimism that it might yet be found but growled, 'Consider, sir, the value of such a piece of timber here!' In his famous dictionary his prime definition of Walking reads: 'To move by leisurely steps, so that one foot is set down before the other is taken up.' The word 'leisurely' seems gratuitous, and possibly reflects his personal attitude to the motion in question. (Mention of the great lexicographer may remind us also that walking was often used as background exercise when reading, especially in gardens and other secluded places, something that cannot be done with running, despite the intriguing first line of Keble's hymn, 'There is a book who runs may read'.)

In the following century we find other famous writers who walked in the style of Swift. Charles Dickens at one time was driven by insomnia to go for night walks. He describes how, after the 'flickering sparks' of revelry had died away, he was quite alone as he walked through the 'interminable tangle' of London streets, encountering only occasional policemen or shifty characters lurking in doorways. He would walk across Waterloo Bridge then downstream through Southwark to recross the Thames into the City, contemplating buildings such as the Sadlers Wells Theatre, the Newdigate debtors' prison, or the Billingsgate fish market. We may be sure that he went at a great pace, for he was a doughty walker who often did 30 miles, as for instance from his house at Gads Hill into London. At about the same time another literary giant with an excess of physical energy was regularly pounding the pavement, putting in his 6 miles before breakfast. John Ruskin practised what he preached when he wrote: 'Of simple exercises, learn to walk and run at the utmost speed consistent with health: do this always going at the quickest pace you can in the streets, and by steadily, though minutely, increasing your pace over a trial piece of ground, every day.' He also had theories about the relationship of walking to music, as well as to poetry. His contention was that the normal pace was two to the second, which corresponded to a reasonable tempo for minims: likewise it was the equivalent to a spondee, the classical poetic measure of two equal syllables.

Dickens and Ruskin were only two of a legion of fast pacers through the foggy gaslit streets of Victorian London. They resembled the joggers of today except that they walked and didn't run: despite Ruskin's reference to it, running was then a more specialised activity and quite impracticable in the clothing which was then obligatory; and besides, many of them were not so pushed for time. One winter evening in the 1840s young John Horsley was walking briskly back from the studios of the Royal Academy at Somerset House, where he was an art student, to his family home in what is now Kensington Church Street, a 4-mile stint that he did twice each day. As he strode past Apsley House down Knightsbridge he began to pass another man who was also walking fast. This figure immediately responded to his unspoken challenge and they paced ahead at a great lick along the newly laid pavement at the outside of Hyde Park and Kensington Gardens. Horsley was a strong walker and had indulged in such 'silent races' before, but this was the toughest and he was determined not to be beaten. As they approached Kensington neck and neck, their lungs bellowing loudly, he became convinced he would have to give up, when the stranger, who hadn't said a word before, suddenly blurted 'Damn it! you can have your own way', and staggered to a stop. John Horsley had just enough energy to struggle on around the corner of Kensington Church Street where he collapsed in a doorway puffing and panting and helpless, hoping his antagonist would not see by how narrow a margin he had won. When, as a senior portrait painter and Royal Academician, he came to write his memoirs, this was one of the achievements of which he was most proud.

Although the efficacy of walking was recognised as long ago as in classical Roman times, and the symptom of sweating was known to be a good thing, it was only with the modern understanding of physiology that the practice of walking for reasons of health really took off in urban societies. Nowadays we know exactly why walking is good for us. It stimulates the muscles which assist the heart in circulating the blood, thus increasing the heart's efficiency and decreasing such dangerous things as cholesterol levels, clot formations, blood sugar, and hormone production. Also, through the exercise of the lungs, it improves the oxygenising capacity which, among other things, activates the brain cells. Besides this, it triggers off responses from the nervous system, so releasing tensions and providing an outlet for pent-up emotions. And it slows down the ageing process of bone-demineralisation, particularly in the legs and feet. All these attributes are more than ever important today when most urban people are overstimulated and underactive and grossly neglect their legs, those massive limbs which constitute over a third of normal body weight. Walking is thus the simplest and easiest way of keeping fit; and a brisk pace of around 4 miles an hour consumes about four times as much energy as a slow stroll, and about half as much as a moderate jog or run. But it is enough to know these things in a general sort of way: for when people become obsessed with quantification of their calorific expenditures and target heart rates, the whole procedure starts to take the form of a cult. The wisest are those who seize every opportunity to walk in the course of their ordinary daily rounds (in effect, like John Horsley) rather than in special exercise sessions (like John Ruskin), difficult as this may be in a world of cars. For casual walking, whether urban or rural, provides more than mere exercise when it becomes part of the social scene.

To see how walking integrated into social life in the past one can do no better than turn to English fiction, which is speckled with references to walks, ordinary and extraordinary. Any selection must include Dickens, though it has to be said that for such a strong and committed pedestrian his walking scenes are surprisingly undescriptive; this is perhaps because for him the countryside was of no interest in itself but only as a background to the colourful townsfolk whom he occasionally launched into it. For instance, when Nicholas Nickleby stormed out of Dotheboys Hall in Yorkshire we are told that he intended to walk all the way to London together with the unfortunate Smike, mainly because he started off with only about four shillings. In the following chapter we see them both in London 'disfigured with every mark of fatiguing travel' and 'both perfectly worn out by their unwonted and protracted exertion': of the journey itself we are told nothing. Neither is anything known of what lay behind the bland statement by Traddles to David Copperfield that when he had gone to court Sophy in Devon, 'I walked there, and I walked back, and I had the most delightful time.' Likewise, of Oliver Twist's 20-odd-mile walk to rob a house in Chertsey, of David Copperfield's 23-mile walk from Blackheath to Chatham, and of the Pickwick Club's 25-mile walk at Dingly Dell, we are given no details. The flight of Little Nell and her grandfather at least occasions one brief pedestrian image, as 'she bounded on before, pointing her tiny footsteps in the moss, which rose elastic from so light a pressure and gave it back as mirrors throw off breath'; and it is nice to think of Mr Tupman in his retirement walking constantly on Richmond Terrace 'with a youthful and jaunty air, which has rendered him the admiration of the numerous elderly ladies of single condition, who reside in the vicinity'. But only in *Martin Chuzzlewit* is there any interesting walking scene. Martin and Tom Pinch have decided to dine in nearby Salisbury. As they cannot borrow Mr Pecksniff's gig they decide to walk and soon discover the benefits, for it is so much better than a gig for circulating the blood and sharpening the wits: though it is cold, in a gig it would be far colder. They don't mind the snow flurries as they see the wind sweeping over the grassy downs. 'A rare, strong, hearty, healthy walk – four statute miles an hour – preferable to that rumbling, tumbling, jolting, shaking, scraping, creaking, villainous old gig'.

Notable walking incidents occur in the pages of Trollope, Charlotte Brontë, Meredith and D. H. Lawrence, illustrative of quite different sorts of experience. In Trollope's *Can You Forgive Her?* Kate Vavasour has two memorable walks on the Cumberland fells overlooking Vavasour Hall. On the first occasion she and her cousin Alice go for a four-hour walk on a clear cold day up to 'the big stone on Swindale Fell' where Alice reads her an ill-judged letter of proposal she has received from Kate's brother, George. They get back late for lunch, braving the wrath of the crusty grandfather. On the second occasion Kate is led up to the same place by George immediately after they have heard their grandfather's will read, in which George had been disinherited in favour of her. George is furious and vents his wrath on his sister by hurling her from him with great violence, so that she falls heavily on to the stony ground and breaks her arm. While she staggers back in agony to the Hall, George – 'the wild beast' – marches on across the fells in heavy rain to Bampton. He knows that he faces social ostracism from his family and friends but 'he was still, at this moment, a member of parliament; and as the rain drenched him through and through, he endeavoured to get consolation from the remembrance of that fact in his favour'.

Kate Vavasour may have been bruised by her brother but her mental state was not nearly so disturbed as was Jane Eyre's when she crept out of Thornfield Hall before dawn so as to escape from the unwelcome advances of her employer, Mr Rochester. Charlotte Brontë is more passionate than Trollope and Jane's flight is less of a walk than a wander as she staggers around what are evidently parts of Hallam Moors and Stanage Edge in Derbyshire. 'I was weeping wildly as I walked along my solitary way: fast, fast I went like one delirious.' She stumbles across fields to a road and after a lift in a coach is deposited in the middle of nowhere, from where she has just enough energy to strike up the hill and sleep in the heather. Next day she goes on for some hours along the road, a pathetic figure in her long dress, straw bonnet and shawl, till, after being coldly refused food or shelter at several houses, she finally walks at night across a marsh towards a light where kindly help awaits her.

Meredith's novel *The Egoist* abounds in walking scenes. In the gardens, parterre and park of Patterne Hall and its surrounding estate the drama unfolds around the uncertainties of Clara Middleton in her engagement to its maddeningly egotistic owner, Sir Willoughby Patterne. She seeks for sounding-boards to her doubts in a series of walks with others. First, with Vernon Whitford, a cousin of Sir Willoughby who acts in the capacity of secretary to his estate and tutor to his heir-presumptive, young Crossjay. Vernon Whitford is apt to disappear from time to time to go for long walks of up to nine and a half hours at a time to train for his summer visit to the Alps and also to work off his temper. In her shorter walk with him and Crossjay 'he led at a swing of the legs that accelerated young Crossjay's to the double, but she with her short swift equal steps glided along easily on a line by his shoulder'. This impresses him so favourably that he pays her a rare compliment: 'It's not the first time I have thought you would be at home in the Alps. You would walk and climb as well as you dance.' And, what is more, after some talk about her fanciful Alpine ascents to come, she gets him to give his view that in principle it is better to break off an engagement than marry the wrong person. Clara's second walk is with Laetitia Dale, a lovely girl of rather lower social rank who lives with her father in a small house at the edge of the park. They have to be content with only a short walk because Sir Willoughby has insisted that if they take a longer route they must be accompanied by a footman. Laetitia is a not entirely disinterested confidante, for she much admires Sir Willoughby, and Clara feels the need for an hour's further walk alone along the road after she has dropped Laetitia at her father's cottage. In so doing she is nearly run over by a fly carrying Colonel de Craye who is being driven from the station and, the fly being upset, de Craye walks back with her and Laetitia to the Hall. Clara's crisis comes to a head next day when she decides to escape by means of some energetic walking. First, before breakfast, she walks with Crossjay to Aspenwell village where she intercepts the postman and takes a letter written to her by a girl friend who has offered to have her to stay in emergency. Breakfast is at 9 a.m. and shortly after 9.45 she slips out of the Hall in driving rain and heads off briskly through the park and past the West Lodge and towards the station, some 3 miles distant, to catch the 11 a.m. train. Her absence is noticed at about 10.15. Now is the moment for Vernon Whitford. He walks as he never walked before, welcoming the rain, for 'rain, the heaviest you can meet, is a lively companion when the resolute pacer scorns discomfort of wet clothes and squeaking boots'. Taking a short cut from the road he springs across the fields and finally, back on the road with a better foothold than on the slippery field-path, he runs. By means of moral blackmail he persuades Clara not to catch the train but return to the Hall, though it is Laetitia and not Clara who in the end is destined to marry Sir Willoughby.

D. H. Lawrence is definitely the writer for lovers' lanes. In *Sons and Lovers* it is Paul and Clara who walk out along the banks of the Trent. 'No one was on the path that went along the green river meadow, along the elm-tree colonnade.' Once into a grove, she jumps from a stile into his arms and he covers her face with kisses. 'She stirred against him as she walked, and his body was like a taut string.' Then it is down beside the river where the flood had swamped the path as they scramble along getting muddy and dishevelled. In *The Rainbow* it is Anton and Ursula, meeting after an absence in a café in Nottingham.

> They came out of the café.
> 'Is there anything you would like to do?' he said.
> 'Is there anything we *can* do?'
> It was a dark, windy day in March.
> 'There is nothing to do,' she said.
> Which was the answer he wanted.
> 'Let us walk then – where shall we walk?' he asked.
> 'Shall we go to the river?' she suggested timidly.
> In a moment they were on the tram, going down to Trent Bridge. She was so glad. The thought of walking in the dark, far-reaching water-meadows, beside the full river, transported her. Dark water flowing in silence through the big restless night made her feel wild.

(But walking as a prelude to love-making is only desirable if you like the man. It was not so for Flora in Stella Gibbons' *Cold Comfort Farm*. 'Flora was now in a dreadful fix. For if she said that she adored walking, Mr Mybug would drag her for miles in the rain while he talked about sex, and if she said that she liked it only in moderation, he would make her sit on wet stiles, while he tried to kiss her.')

In Jane Austen's novels the many walking scenes are where her characters reveal their real selves, where confidences are exchanged or home-truths bluntly stated, in contrast to the stifling formalities and falsehoods of the drawing-rooms. The walks may not be long or exhausting but they are used to extremely good effect, never more so than by Elizabeth Bennet in *Pride and Prejudice*. On hearing that her sister Jane has been taken ill when staying with the grand neighbours at Netherfield, Elizabeth decides immediately to walk the 3 miles there. Her two sisters accompany her from Longbourn along the road as far as Meryton (a frequent walking destination for them) but after that 'Elizabeth continued her walk alone, crossing field after field at a quick pace, jumping over stiles and springing over puddles with impatient activity, and finding herself at last within view of the house, with weary ankles, dirty stockings, and a face glowing with warmth of exercise.' As soon as her back is turned the ladies of the house are assiduous in criticising her. 'She has nothing, in short, to recommend her, but being an excellent walker. I shall never forget her appearance this morning. She really looked almost wild,' pronounces Mrs Hurst. 'To walk three miles, or four miles, or five miles, or whatever it is, above her ankles in dirt, and alone, quite alone! what could she mean by it? It seems to me to show an abominable sort of conceited independence, a most country-town indifference to decorum,' observes Miss Bingley. Later, when staying at Hunsford parsonage in Kent, Elizabeth is seen frequently walking in the park of Rosings, seat of Lady Catherine de Bourg, especially along a nice sheltered path through a grove at the edge of the park. On these walks she encounters the proud Mr Darcy, Lady Catherine's nephew, on at least three occasions. She is entirely prejudiced against him, so when he quite unexpectedly proposes to her in the parsonage drawing-room, he is coldly rejected. Next day, although she alters her walk so as to avoid the park, he comes up and hands her a long letter of explanation for his conduct, which she reads and ponders as she wanders along the lane for two hours more. Elizabeth next meets Mr Darcy in Derbyshire when her uncle and aunt take her with them to visit his stately home as sightseers. He comes across them in the garden, then joins them as they are walking in the park by the lake, and manages to be alone with Elizabeth as they outpace the aunt and uncle on the way back to their carriage. Back at Longbourn there follow various garden scenes including one when Elizabeth refuses to be bullied by Lady Catherine de Bourg into renouncing her interest in Mr Darcy. And soon after, it is on a walk that she and Darcy become engaged. 'They walked on, without knowing in what direction. There was too much to be thought, and felt, and said, for attention to any other objects.' Eventually, 'after walking several miles in a leisurely manner, and too busy to know anything about it, they found at last, on examining their watches, that it was time to be at home.' Next day, as if to cement the new family relationship, Darcy goes with Elizabeth and her sister Kitty on a long walk to Oakham Mount to admire the view.

The action of walking sounds like the recurrent beat of the drum through the tonality of Thomas Hardy's prose. It was by means of walking daily when young that he learnt to love his native Dorset, and he was able to evoke the sensuality of a rural walk in a way which the urban Dickens was quite unable to do. Take, for example, the opening scene in *The Mayor of Casterbridge*. A man is walking along a road: 'His measured, springless walk was the walk of the skilled countryman as distinct from the desultory shamble of the general labourer; while in the turn and plant of each foot there was, further, a dogged and cynical indifference, personal to himself, showing its presence even in the regularly interchanging fustian folds, now in the left leg, now the right, as he paced along.' Or this from *The Return of the Native*: 'Along the road walked an old man. He was white-headed as a mountain, bowed in the shoulders, and faded in general aspect. He wore a glazed hat, an ancient blue coat, and shoes; his brass buttons bearing an anchor upon their face. In his hand was a silver-headed walking-stick, which he used as a veritable third leg, perseveringly dotting the ground with its point at every few inches interval.' In *Far from the Madding Crowd* Hardy describes a man who through an innate sense of modesty walked small, not tall: 'Oak walked unassumingly, and with a faintly perceptible bend, quite distinct from a bowing of the shoulders.' But of all his novels *Tess of the D'Urbervilles* is the most imbued with walking, which provides the setting for most of the scenes and is often explicitly described.

The book opens with her father walking homeward to the village of Marlott: 'The pair of legs that carried him were rickety, and there was a bias in his gait which inclined him somewhat to the left of a straight line.' And soon after we are introduced to her future husband, Angel Clare, as he passes through the village on a walking tour with his two brothers, knapsacks on their backs. Stopping for a few minutes to talk to the girls, he catches up on his brothers by running downhill then 'bending himself to a rapid walk' uphill. The story ends with Angel and 'Liza-Lu leaving Wintocaster after Tess's execution, walking rapidly but with bowed heads, 'which gait of grief the sun's rays smiled on pitilessly'. Tess's own walking covers a wide range. There are the love scenes, when she and Angel are 'walking out' with his arm around her waist. 'Thus, during this October month of wonderful afternoons they roved along the meads by creeping paths which followed the brinks of trickling tributary brooks, hopping across by little wooden bridges to the other side, and back again.' And later, in the flight of love, they walk aimlessly and helplessly away, arm in arm, following obscure paths: 'To walk across country without much regard to roads was not new to Tess, and she showed her old agility in the performance'; 'I feel strong enough to walk any distance,' she says. Then there are the scenes of acute distress. The pregnant Tess is overwhelmed by a sense of guilt and takes to lonely night walks. 'On these lonely hills and dales her quiescent glide was of a piece with the elements she moved in. Her flexuous and stealthy figure became an integral part of the scene.' 'Walking among the sleeping birds in the hedges, watching the skipping rabbits on a moonlit warren, or standing under a pheasant-laden bough, she looked upon herself as a figure of Guilt intruding into the haunts of innocence.'

But her longer walks are the most remarkable, especially those to and from her menial work at Flintcomb-Ash farm. She approaches it by means of a three-day walk, trudging across the county like a wild animal, impervious to the bad weather, disguised beneath her shabbiest field-gown and scarf and with her eyebrows cut so as to deface her beauty. 'Thus Tess walks on: a figure which is part of the landscape; a fieldwoman pure and simple, in winter guise.' The frightful conditions at the upland farm force her to appeal to her parents-in-law at Emminster Vicarage, even though it means walking 15 miles each way on a Sunday in December, starting off at 4 a.m. in the starlight, 'the ground ringing under her feet like an anvil'. 'Still, to start on a brisk walk, and on such an errand as hers, on a dry clear wintry morning, through the rarefied air of these chalky hog's-backs, was not depressing.' It is only as she nears her destination that her courage fails her. She dithers outside the vicarage; and the final straw is when her walking-boots, which she had secreted under a hedge so as to put on her pretty thin shoes, are summarily expropriated and she hasn't the courage to prevent it. Instead she starts her return walk in tears, leaning on gates and pausing by milestones, but shambling on. 'Her journey back was rather a meander than a march. It had no sprightliness, no purpose; only a tendency.' Some time later she leaves the farm when 'Liza-Lu arrives on foot with the news that their mother is ill. Tess does not hesitate. 'She plunged into the chilly equinoctial darkness as the clock struck ten, for her fifteen miles walk under the steely stars.' After mile upon mile, first on the chalky upland then on the clay of the valley, the winding road just visible, and in utter silence, Tess reaches her home and sickly family. In the image of Tess as she walks we can perhaps detect the archetypal figure of a wanderer who, like the Ghost in Hamlet, is 'Doom'd for a certain spell to walk the night'.

Intellectuals

THE daily walk known as a 'constitutional' or earlier a 'stretch' was an established feature of university life at Oxford and Cambridge. Apart from those who merely perambulated around Christ Church meadows or the backs along the Cam there were many who regularly took longer walks up or down the river towpaths or to well-established points such as Cumnor or Grantchester. Some of these were along routes known as 'grinds' which were used for running steeplechases, such as Cambridge's 'Gog Magog grind' and 'Grantchester grind'. *Ambulando cogitans* or *ambulando solvitur* were the Latin tags which recognised that walking was good for cogitation and problem-solving. It could also generate lively discussions. Not always, however, as for instance when young F. E. Smith was asked to take a constitutional with an

Oxford don. This don was notorious for getting particularly bright undergraduates to babble away about their philosophic views, and then demolishing their concepts with ruthless and sarcastic savagery. Smith was resolved not to be ensnared and they began their walk in silence till the don eventually said, 'They tell me you're very clever, Smith. Are you?' 'Yes,' replied Smith; and for the remaining hour of the walk not a word passed between them. Not for nothing did he become Lord Chancellor of England!

Besides these cerebral triumphs or disasters university walkers imbibed the beauty and mystery of the surrounding countryside as expressed for them in Matthew Arnold's poem 'The Scholar Gypsy'. The elusive wanderer is variously seen on the 'green-muffled Cumnor hills', by the 'stripling Thames at Bablock-hithe', by the 'Fyfield elm in May', 'above Godstow Bridge when hay-time's here', 'on the skirts of Bagley wood', and finally battling with a snowstorm 'towards Hinksey and its wintry ridge'. Although he is often loitering around the place, as for instance lying in a boat or sitting on the river bank or watching the passing scene, he is also capable of strong walking – 'with a free onward impulse brushing through, by night, the silver'd branches of the glade'. The Scholar Gypsy also represented a tradition of wandering scholars of earlier generations, familiar figures on the roads from the fact that many undergraduates used to walk between their homes and colleges. A charming story relates to Richard Hooker, a boy at Oxford in the time of Queen Elizabeth. He lived in Exeter, but on his long walk home diverted to Salisbury to call on his patron, Bishop Jewel. Next morning the Bishop announced that he would lend young Richard his horse, but the 'horse' proved to be a special walking staff which the Bishop in his turn had used when young and studying in Germany. It was of great sentimental value to him and the fifteen-year-old boy was to be sure to return it when he passed on his walk back for the Michaelmas term.

As the Victorian era progressed the cult of organised games became so dominant that fewer students walked among the fields for exercise. Soccer, rugger, cricket and, above all, rowing absorbed their energies and indeed took up so much time and effort that several of them spent their whole time at sport. For some, the experience of a long walk still occurred when they joined reading-parties in the summer. In between the hours allotted for reading they might go on long ranging walks through the hills, such as described in the classical hexameters of Clough's 'Bothie of Tober-na-vuolich':

So they bathed, they read, they roamed in glen and forest;
Far amid blackest pines to the waterfall they shadow,
Far up the long, long glen to the loch, and the loch beyond it,
Deep, under huge red cliffs, a secret; and oft by the starlight,
Or the aurora, perchance, racing home for the eight o'clock
    mutton.
So they bathed, and read, and roamed in heathery Highland . . .

But, this apart, for many undergraduates golf now took the place of a country walk. The Master of Magdalene College, Arthur Benson, viewed this development with dismay, as he wrote in *From a College Window*:

> The delights of the countryside grow upon me every month and every year. I love to stroll in the lanes in spring, with white clouds floating in the blue above, and to see the glades carpeted with steel-blue hyacinths. I love to walk on country roads or by woodland paths; on a rain-drenched day of summer, when the sky is full of heavy inky clouds, and the earth smells fresh and sweet; I love to go briskly homeward on a winter evening, when the sunset smoulders low in the west, when the pheasants leap trumpeting in their roosts, and the lights begin to peep in cottage windows. Such joys as these are within the reach of everyone; and to call the country dull because one has not the opportunity of hitting and pursuing a little white ball round and round among the same fields, with elaborately contrived obstacles to test the skill and the temper, seems to me to be grotesque, if it were not also so distressing.

But while they may have neglected the fields the undergraduates did not neglect the roads, and pedestrian prowess was always esteemed by some. The 'big one' was to walk to London: Marble Arch is 55 miles from Carfax, Oxford and 51 miles from King's Parade, Cambridge: and in the opinion of G. M. Trevelyan, 'Every aspiring Cantab or Oxonian ought to walk to the Marble Arch at a pace that will do credit to the college whence he starts at break of day.' Two men in particular did this walk: Hilaire Belloc with a fellow undergraduate at Oxford made it to Marble Arch in a record time of eleven and a half hours; and Leslie Stephen when a Cambridge don walked to London in twelve hours to attend a dinner of the Alpine Club. (One imagines the scene. 'Evening, Stephen. Come up from Cambridge?' 'Walked up, actually.') In their different ways both were to exercise a powerful influence on walking.

In his own estimation, Belloc's life after going down from Oxford had been one of complete failure. Despite his fame as a writer he knew in his heart that oratory was his finest but frustrated skill. His inability to get on with people precluded the parliamentary or legal career for which he was so obviously suited as President of the Oxford Union, or even an Oxford fellowship which he might have got with his First at Balliol. There was an awkwardness about him and an inner conflict which were not to be found in the slightly younger man who in other ways so resembled him, Winston Churchill. Perhaps it was in part this awkwardness that drove him towards long walks. He was of powerful physique, fond of talking and singing as he strode along, and speaking with an unusual accent which derived from being half French. He had, indeed, served as a conscript in the French Army; and, as he put it, he had 'in his gait the narrow seas'. When still at Oxford he walked with others from York to Edinburgh and alone from Oxford to Holyhead; and, besides his record effort to London, frequently walked at a great pace around Oxfordshire. A few years later, despite being completely out of funds and responsible for a wife and baby, he set out on his great walk to Rome.

Although it seemed quite irresponsible at the time, this venture did help to keep the home fires burning because *The Path to Rome* was an instant success and brought him in a tidy sum, which is more than could be said of most of his scores of other books. In some ways his walk to Rome was indeed the pilgrimage it purported to be: he was on foot, alone, without much money, in tatters, uncomfortable, and ostensibly a devout Roman Catholic. But in other ways he was essentially different from the pilgrims in his eye for literary copy, his topographical dissertations, his intellectual approach, and his tortured soul: indeed, at one point he doubts the very existence of the soul, writing that 'every pleasure I know comes from an intimate union between my body and my very human mind'. His ferocious determination to cover the ground at tremendous speed also puts him into quite a different category to the gentlemen 'tramps' who, as we shall see, were starting to wander along the roads at this time. The true greatness of *The Path to Rome* is that besides describing his journey in brilliant style it also expresses the free run of his mind as he walks along – the thoughts, the imaginary conversations, the obsessions, the fantasies. All this is utterly different from the educative, reasonable and relevant wodges that serve to fatten so many travel books. Belloc simply lets himself go. Thus, trudging in the remorseless rain across the monotonous plain of Lombardy, he conjures up the image of the antithesis of himself, a smug bank manager with a secure salary and pension, as if to reassure himself that despite the sore legs and damp clothes he would still rather be a wanderer than a bourgeois. He also devotes the first five pages to a scornful demolition of the saying that it is the first pace that counts: on the contrary, says Belloc, 'it is the five-hundredth that counts'. Ruminating in this way, his outer eyes observe the grandeurs of nature in her larger canvases – the sunrise, the line of Alpine peaks, the chestnut forests, rivers and lakes: but of plants and wildlife, flowers and birds, he notices absolutely nothing.

He covered the 700-odd miles from Toul in Alsace (scene of his military service) to Rome in twenty-seven days, on some days doing over 40 miles along roads. It was an impressive achievement, and far tougher than expected; indeed, he hadn't planned it at all well. His idea was to walk in as straight a line as possible, a constraint which involved crossing several mountain ridges, though for the rest he was on roads. His maps were quite inadequate. He wore a plain cotton suit. He often rejected the softer option of a night at an inn, but pressed on and slept by the roadside. His food was primitive, and hot meals irregular. He walked on despite severe knee pains. He carried virtually no money and twice ran out of it. He arranged no contacts through influential friends. So if he failed to walk some of the way it should not seriously detract from his achievement.

Carrying a satchel containing 'a large piece of bread, half a pound of smoked ham, a sketch-book, two Nationalist papers, and a quart of wine of Brule', Hilaire Belloc strode out of Toul into the dusk, for his general plan was to walk by night. He slept out next morning, woken by the sun shining through the branches of the trees 'like a patient enemy outside a city that one watches through the loopholes of a tower'. After two days he had done 50 miles and had a stiff pain in one knee, which was not helped by taking a series of short cuts involving much more effort than sticking to the road. He walked over the Ballon d'Alsace and across the gap of Belfort into the Jura. At the end of a day which involved crossing two ridges he was utterly exhausted and accepted the assistance of a cart, thereby breaking his vow to walk the whole way: but 'I clung to the waggon in such a manner that it did all my work for me, and yet could not be said to be actually carrying me.' More Jura ridges faced him, but on the last of them he was rewarded with a distant view of the Alps: 'sky beneath them and sky above them, a steadfast legion, they glittered as though with the armour of the immovable armies of Heaven.'

Now entering the second week and with 180 miles done, Belloc was feeling deeply depressed. Not only was his knee pain dull and chronic but he was out of the French-speaking area and had a loathing for all things German. He shuffled on so lethargically that he actually allowed himself to be ordered to hold the bridle of a horse while its owner entered an inn for a drink. But next day, fortified by a good night's sleep, he decided to take his most ambitious short cut by making a bee-line across the massive mountain wall of the Brienzer Grat. After a good lunch in Brienz he tramped on, the sole of one boot now loose at the toe, along the road over the Grimsel pass amid black rock and smooth ice, and so down to the valley of the Rhône at Ulrichen. It was his intention to head straight across the valley and attack the rougher Gries pass, but he was warned that it was still in thick snow. (Incidentally, Richard Wagner had walked over the Gries half a century before, spending a night at a hut near the col and then walking 22 miles down to Domodosola.) Belloc hired a guide, and they set off at three next morning. Plunging through the deep untrodden snow they were caught in a snowstorm and his thin cottons were soon soaked. He had to admit defeat, and retreated to Ulrichen; but didn't stay to lick his wounds and was soon off by the longer route over the Furka and St Gothard. By now he was only 90 miles from Milan, though obsessed by the fractional costs of food and lodging, as he had scarcely any money left. At Como he decided to break his vow uncompromisingly and take the train. He had only 1.8 francs, and the ticket cost him exactly that. 'I had become that rarest and ultimate kind of traveller, the man without any money whatsoever – without passport, without letters, without food or wine.'

'There are no open views in Lombardy, and Lombardy is all the same.' The third week of the walk found Belloc striding across the dull alluvial plain in steady drizzle. Tiring of the monotony he deviated to the town of Lodi Vecchio, doubtless in hope of seeing the place where General Bonaparte had seized the Tricolor and led his men to rush the bridge. But no, that was at Lodi itself, and Lodi Vecchio was merely a sodden village from which he now attempted to regain the main road by a cross-country ramble, pushing through long grass, ditches and oozing ground. He trudged along the Emilian Way for two more days, and all the time it rained. Then came the moment when he veered off so as to pursue his 'direct' route to Rome, which involved crossing three distinct spurs of the Apennines, each divided by wild rivers now swollen by rain, which he had to get over on the back of a guide who knew how to ford them. At Calestino he was arrested as a vagrant, and no wonder: 'A man unknown, unkempt, unshaven, in tatters, covered with weeks of travel and mud, and in a suit that originally cost not ten shillings; having slept in leaves and ferns, and forest places, crosses a river at dusk and enters a town furtively, not by road.' But the magic words 'English' and 'tourist' secured immediate release. The following day was to be his greatest test of endurance of the whole walk, for due to a misconception of the distance he pressed on through the night till he had outwalked his strength, yet 'I still went forward a little, because when I sat down my loneliness oppressed me like a misfortune; and because my feet, going painfully and slowly, yet gave a little balance and rhythm to the movement of my mind.' At dawn he lay down and fell asleep in adoration of the sun. At last he gained the main range of the Apennines. Down into cool dark chestnut woods, the haunts of charcoal burners, to the valley of the Serchio. At Sillano, 'An inn received me; a great kitchen full of men and women talking, a supper preparing, a vast timbered roof going up into darkness.' The air was warm, the summer had come. Winter's rains and ruins were over, and Hilaire Belloc felt youth reviving in his veins: 'Youth came up that valley at evening, borne upon a southern air.' A few days later he was walking up Val d'Elsa between the rounded Tuscan hills when he noticed the railway line: he succumbed to temptation and rode the 'twenty-five miserable miles' to Siena. But he didn't linger and that same evening 'took up the ceaseless road' along the Cassian Way. On it he admits to two more short rides in carts. 'It broke my vow to pieces; there was not a shadow of excuse for this use of wheels; it was done openly and wantonly in the face of the wide sky of pleasure.' And the last two days were covered so quickly that Belloc is under suspicion of not revealing further rides. After a final night on straw he is last seen entering the eternal city in time to celebrate the feast of St Peter and St Paul.

After this Hilaire Belloc was widely known as a Walker, and he went on to make full use of his feet to provide material for his books, though in none of them did he reveal the physical experiences of his walks as he had in *The Path to Rome*. He had a passion for topography and loved to analyse the shape and relationships of hills, rivers and passes. Sometimes he succeeded brilliantly in this, but all too often his descriptions are riddled with inaccuracies, which is not surprising since he seldom checked his facts and dictated his books as if they were speeches. He wandered in the Pyrenees, getting lost in the mountains more than once, but advising his readers tediously of all the planning they should do and the precautions they should take. He stomped around the sites of the battlefields of Waterloo and Blenheim. He walked across the weald of Sussex in four days and alone, though when he wrote of it he split himself up into four characters who hold long disputations with themselves. And he walked in winter from Winchester to Canterbury by way of the North Downs. (In his description of this walk he rightly stressed the significance of the ancient ridgeway path as a drove road of prehistoric times, but his contention that it was also the main route of the medieval pilgrims is misleading. Although certain sections may have been used by them, they mainly kept to the roads which already linked the towns and villages along the lower ground. And besides, very few pilgrims were travelling direct between Winchester and Canterbury; rather, they would have been going to either one or the other.) In all these ventures Belloc liked to walk for a purpose and despised those who walked for exercise. Once past forty he deteriorated physically and no longer had the will or energy for walking. In fact he was soon shuffling, and only in imagination could he think of 'the men that were boys when I was a boy, walking along with me'. His habit of consuming a bottle of wine with every meal didn't help and his legs were fully employed in supporting his massive frame. In retrospect there are few people today who would care to defend any of the opinions of Hilaire Belloc but there are many who admire him for the manner in which he expressed them: and we can also admire him for adding romance to the idea of walking, even though few have followed in his footsteps to Rome. Appropriately, one who has done so is his great-grandson Louis Jebb who, in 1983, reached St Peter's, Rome, like Belloc, for the celebration of the feast of St Peter and St Paul in June. Unlike Belloc, who only started from Alsace, Louis Jebb began in London and covered 1050 miles in thirty-eight days; and he took no lifts in carts, though he did stick more to the roads.

Leslie Stephen presents an interesting contrast to Hilaire Belloc. A tall thin man, his deepset eyes gazing from a face disguised behind a bushy beard, he was capable of silence and solitude as well as conviviality. A true scholar and a humanist, he devoted his later life to editing the *Dictionary of National Biography*; that is, after he felt obliged to give up his position at Cambridge because he had resigned from holy orders. Leslie Stephen first came to walking when studying German at Heidelberg: touring for a few days in the Odenwald he relished the sense of freedom from the 'prison house of respectability' that came from doing away with collars and ties. As a young don at Trinity Hall, Cambridge, he personified the 'muscular Christianity' that was sweeping the schools and colleges, and coached the college boat to the coveted position of head of the river in the bumping races. Already he was a compulsive walker, and even when coaching the boat from the towpath he forebore to ride a horse but chose to walk or run as he bellowed through his megaphone. Besides walking to London he also excelled in shorter distances, such as doing 6¾ miles in an hour, or walking 2 miles against another man who ran 3 miles: the first time he did this he won by 230 yards, but the second time he just lost despite the desperate resort of discarding his shirt. He organised long walks on Sundays after chapel. One favourite destination was Ely, 15 miles away as the crow flies, its great cathedral towering over the flat fenland and visible all the way. Stephen is said to have devised a new cross-country route to Ely every term. He was presented with a walking-stick by the undergraduates for having 'out-walked them all'. From a later description of his walking we learn that 'there was no swaying of shoulders or swinging of arms. The step looked short but those who tried to keep by his side knew that it was long.'

Meanwhile Stephen had discovered the Alps (seeing them first when on a walking tour of Bavaria and the Tyrol in 1855) and climbing in them became his passion for a good twenty years of his life. He was a natural climber – calm, patient, poised and fearless but not rash – and made a number of first ascents. The Alps were his playground and also his cathedral and he held that only those who come to grips with nature can truly worship her. Alpine climbing in the mid-nineteenth century was very different from what it is today and one feature was the long walks of approach to and return from the ice and rocks: his fellow climbers always recognised Stephen's distinctive walking prowess. His guide, Melchior Anderegg, declared that he was the best walker he had ever seen (a compliment which Stephen rather contemptuously dismissed on the grounds that Anderegg 'has only seen a few Germans and a stray English': ordinary working-class people were never supposed to be first-class walkers!). Whymper referred to him as the 'fleetest of foot of the whole Alpine brotherhood'; and he was said to stride from peak to peak 'like a pair of compasses'. On one occasion, after an accident on the Col de Miage, he was deputed to leave the rest of the party and seek help from Chamonix. He had had no sleep up on the rocks the previous night and was dozing as he walked the last few miles, imagining that he saw Cambridge friends approaching him along the road, and carts and horses which flitted into the scenery and then disappeared. Of course, besides these Alpine triumphs he always kept up the habit of long walks at home; but it was not till he was forty-seven and past climbing that he formed the Sunday Tramps, as we shall see. Towards the end of his life he walked in Cornwall and, though by now an ill man, strode from Land's End to his holiday house at St Ives across the granite outcrops of the Penwith peninsula in wild weather.

It is interesting to compare Stephen's attitude towards the Alps with that already propounded by John Ruskin, the Golden Boy of Oxford, who had been even more influential in generating an aesthetic appreciation of them. Ruskin, as we have seen, was a compulsive walker but he drew the line at climbing. When first he visited the Alps he went for some immensely energetic walks with his guide, Joseph Couttet, while his parents lingered in the hotel for their adored son. At the Simplon pass he dashed up a col to see the sunset 'five miles up hill against time (and a walk against time up a regular slope of eight feet in the hundred is the most trying footwork I know), five miles back under the stars'. But when Couttet took him up a real mountain it was not a success: 'On 29th July [1844] I went up the Buet and down to Sixt, where I found myself very stiff and tired, and determined that the Alps were, on the whole, best seen from below.' And this remained his contention, so that when discoursing on the art of landscape-drawing his advice was '. . . take knapsack and stick, walk toward the hills by short day's journeys – ten or twelve miles a day – taking a week from some starting-place sixty or seventy miles away; sleep at the pretty little wayside inns, or the rough village ones; then take the hills as they tempt you.' It was in the spirit of either Ruskin or Stephen – that is to say, either as walkers at the intermediate levels or as climbers on their approach routes – that so many of the professional classes, particularly academics, schoolmasters and clergymen (and their ladies) experienced the pleasures of walking in the Alps.

Belloc, by contrast, never established much of a following for his particular brand of mountain walking, though he had several disciples. One such was J. B. Morton who in the 1930s walked with tremendous energy in and out of the Pyrenean passes all the way from

Mediterranean to Atlantic. Like his master he frequently got lost and had a divine disregard for the weather, a disregard fortified by wine. A typical description reads: 'I stopped in the shelter of an enormous rock, and ate some chocolate and drank some wine, for I had determined to force the pass in one burst.' An hour or so later: 'Having drunk a little more wine I blundered on until I came to a small precipice . . .' After a wet night crouched on the rocks he quaffed even more of the wine, but this time it not surprisingly tasted horrible. This is not to disparage what was one of the greatest of mountain walks and a description (in *Pyrenean*) marvellously perceptive of the scenery and the mountain people, seen immediately before road and rail construction brought to an end their romantic isolation. Apart from all the slithering and scrambling the journey included an heroic forced march of 40 miles down the valley of the Cinca to Ainsa, a joyless slog through drizzle.

As his contribution to walking literature, and in complete contrast to Belloc's tempestuous books on the subject, Stephen has left us his essay *In Praise of Walking*. Walking, he says, is 'primitive and simple; it brings us into contact with mother earth and unsophisticated nature; it requires no elaborate apparatus or extraneous excitement.' It is in itself delightful and needs no other purpose. But over and above this basic pleasure there is another, which can only be fully appreciated by intellectuals. For the true walker is one to whom the 'muscular effort of the legs is subsidiary to the "cerebration" stimulated by the effort' and who can 'generate the intellectual harmony which is the natural accompaniment to the monotonous tramp of the feet'. This harmony does not imply constant 'cerebration', for the walker can also if he wishes put his intellect 'out of play for a season'. He sees the benefit both ways also on the subject of companionship: 'Never, at least, have I found talk flow so freely and pleasantly as in a march through pleasant country. And yet there is also a peculiar charm in the solitary expedition when your interlocutor is yourself.' To be dependent on yourself is best, and is more important than the scenery. In fact, paradoxically, you can be more alone and more able to think effectively when walking in a crowded London street than in a quiet place such as your own study. In looking back over his life he recalls such things as friends, ideas or important events in a generalised way: 'The memories of walks, on the other hand, are localised and dated.'

These thoughts of Leslie Stephen were expressed in a slightly different way some years later in another essay by another academic, George Trevelyan, Master of Trinity, Cambridge. His longest walk, he tells us, was done alone: 54 miles from Muirkirk to Dumfries. He also walked extensively in central Italy when writing his histories of Garibaldi, in particular following the line of retreat of the dwindling band of republicans as they made their way through the Apennines to San Marino. He recalls how he would rise with the dawn and walk till it became too hot, only resuming after the siesta; and on one occasion 'making the steep ascent to Volterra, for the first time, under the circlings of the stars; the smell of unseen almond blossom in the air; the lights of Italy far below us; ancient Tuscany just above us, where we were to sup and sleep, guarded by the giant walls'. His *Essay on Walking* opens with the brief but splendid sentence: 'I have two doctors, my left leg and my right.' Having established the medicinal use of walking he goes on to distinguish between road walking and cross-country walking and comes down firmly for the latter. Road walkers are the 'Puritans of the religion', and 'the secret beauties of nature are unveiled only to the cross-country walkers'. He even goes so far as to maintain that scrambling is an integral part of walking. And he is all for inducing a sense of adventure such as by night walks or losing one's way – 'a half-conscious process, which in a sense can no more be done of deliberate purpose than falling in love'. But Trevelyan devotes his strongest passages to emphasising that the efficacy of walking is only found if one exhausts oneself. Particularly if a man has a crisis in his life; 'Let him walk until his flesh curse his spirit for driving it on, and his spirit spend its rage on his flesh in forcing it still pitilessly to sway the legs.' As regards the chronic question of companionship, his solution is that it is not to be despised on a single day's walk such as a Sunday ramble, but for really hard walking or walking tours one should go alone. There follow lyrical passages of the sensual pleasures of walking tours in various places – Tuscany, Devon, Wales and Northumberland – including the softer moments when watching the sunset at the end of a long day, or taking a day off from walking during the tour, and lying in the long grass.

Fearless, gallant and intensely patriotic are the clean-cut figures of Richard Hannay and Archie Roylance who stride across the heathery hills in tweed suits in pursuit of the baddies in the pages of *The Thirty-nine Steps* or *John Macnab*. But neither is as interesting as their originator, the wiry little Scotsman John Buchan. A self-made man who became one of the pillars of the establishment as Governor-

General of Canada, he is particularly associated with Oxford, studying at Brasenose and later living a few miles away at Elsfield Manor. Otmoor and Wychwood were where he often walked, but his heart was in the hills of the Borders. In *Scholar Gypsies* he describes how once when young he persuaded a shepherd, Sandy Scott, to walk up Tweedsdale with him and give him an insight into local country lore. Young Buchan soon found it hard going. 'Onward we trudged, one stolidly, the other with many occasional haltings and turnings-aside. I had not yet learned the secret of that swinging walk with firmly grasped stick and body slightly bent forward, which enables shepherds to tramp their thirty miles with ease over the roughest country. On the contrary, I limped and dragged, now walking with great strides, and now loitering at a snail's pace behind.' After a night spent in a barn, 'the morning came blue and cloudless, and we, who had been tired and dispirited on the previous night, rose in a hopeful frame of mind and regarded the world with serene equanimity'. But in the course of the second day Buchan felt he had had enough, settled up with Sandy, and retreated to a friend's house nearby. 'We bade each other good-day, and I turned aside, while my former comrade, with his stick flourished in the air, and reproach in his retreating footsteps, went stolidly on his way. Then I learned something of the feelings of Orpah when she chose to return alone to Moab.' Later, Buchan made up for this rather feeble exit by walking 63 miles one day in Galloway.

In *Scholar Gypsies* John Buchan also contributed his own essay to the subject of walking. In his words: 'As a man's mind is richly advantaged, so also is his body. He loses the sickly humours, the lassitude, the dulness, which oppress all sedentary folk. His sinews grow firm and his nerves strong. Tramping many miles over heather and inhaling the wholesome air of the uplands, or basking in the sunlight among the meadows, make his frame hardy and active and his skin brown and clear as a moorland trout-stream.' The essence of all this is the 'blessedness of mere movement, free and careless motion in all weathers and in all places'. As for thoughts, 'rhymes run in his memory, confused lines of great poets'. Buchan also stresses the benefit which association with beautiful natural sights brings to the intellectual senses, and he makes the interesting point that today's educated mountain wanderer can appreciate the wonders of nature in a way denied alike to the sickly townsman and to the animistic pagans of the past. 'Most people witness fine natural sights as exiles, feeling with a living regret that such are foreign and beyond their narrow world. But to the man who is much abroad these come with pain or pleasure, according to their nature; but not as scornful, uncontrollable giants who mock his impotent wonder, but rather as forms of the great mistress whom he seeks to know.'

Many are the examples of other leading Oxbridge figures who walked far and furiously. William Gladstone walked regularly in the country; for instance, doing the 13 miles from Montrose to his home at Fasque in two hours, forty-seven minutes. At the age of fifty-three, when Chancellor of the Exchequer and in attendance on Queen Victoria at Balmoral, he wrote in his diary: 'Walked 24¾ miles. Found it rather too much for my stiffening limbs. My day of long stretches is, I think, gone by.' One doubts if he received any sympathy from the Queen at dinner that evening. Another Liberal heavyweight, Richard Haldane (later to become Lord Chancellor), was proud of his walking prowess and when a young barrister had walked from Brighton to London overnight. The 50 miles were not excessive for one who as a boy with his brother had set off from his Perthshire home to walk up Ben Lawers in a day. Ben Lawers was over 30 miles off and by the time they got back late at night they reckoned they had walked 72 miles. Later we find William Temple, Archbishop of Canterbury, who boasted that he could walk 6 miles in an hour and 50 miles in a day without difficulty. The prowess of Edward Bowen, a Harrow schoolmaster, is attested by Trevelyan: he was a fanatical road walker who made a point of never doing less than 25 miles. I also like the story of the historian R. H. Tawney who, on being asked by a postgraduate research student for advice on how to better his researches into local parish records, drily replied, 'Get thicker soles for your shoes.'

If, in describing the walking of the university men, especially Oxonians and Cantabrians, I have drawn as examples so many eminent people, it is not merely because of the mileages they walked but because they wrote so well about walking. What Benson, Belloc, Stephen, Trevelyan and Buchan said is still true today and still reads well: and we can still walk in the manner and spirit that they did. Where our resources will be really put to test is in keeping up to the level of conversation and 'cerebration'. It can be seen that both solitude and companionship were important to the intellectuals in their full experience of walking. To argue that only the one or the other is the better way is fruitless. Even William Hazlitt, the walking companion of Coleridge, was ambivalent on the subject. Though he was not a university man, his essay *On Going a Journey*, written in

1822, was one which these later walkers had all read and which set the pattern for their own essays. He starts off by asserting that walking and talking don't go together, just as in his day the old English custom was not to eat and drink at the same time but to have water with dinner and only afterwards to settle down to the port. 'I cannot see the wit of walking and talking at the same time,' he says; and, 'I am never less alone than when alone.' There follows his classic passage: 'Give me the clear blue sky over my head, and the green turf beneath my feet, a winding road before me, and a three hours' march to dinner – and then to thinking! It is hard if I cannot start some game on these lone heaths. I laugh, I run, I leap, I sing for joy.' But then Hazlitt qualifies his stance. He has in all honesty to admit that Coleridge had held him spellbound on walks: 'He could go on in the most delightful explanatory way over hill and dale a summer's day, and convert a landscape into a didactic poem or a Pindaric ode.' Also, when travelling abroad, a companion is most desirable. Thus, in considering Hazlitt and the subsequent essayists we can see that the aesthetic pleasure of walking comes from a series of experiences, some alone, some shared: but the sharing is best with a single congenial companion, never a group. Anyway, the old English custom of separating the eating from the drinking was really rather barbaric, and a meal without wine has been said to be like a day without sunshine. So also walking and talking can indeed complement each other; and as the best meals are those with the perfect companion, so are the best walks.

Discoverers

THERE are some who have come to appreciate walking not because it was their prime purpose to take the exercise but because by walking they were able to discover what they were looking for or explore places they wanted to get to. One such group has been the geologists who sooner or later penetrated into every unknown gully or unexplored cliff, tapping away at the rocks. In Britain a notable example was Hugh Miller, who wandered all over Caithness in search of the Old Red Sandstone in a formidable attempt to fight a rearguard action against Darwinism. More interesting from a walking point of view were those who first went to the Alps and whose scientific preoccupations led them up to the pinnacles and glaciers and so to the peaks and the new-found sport of mountain climbing. For instance James

Forbes, the Professor of Natural Philosophy at the University of Edinburgh, first entered the High Alps in 1841 when he took a five-hour tramp from the Grimsel Hospice to an encampment on the Unteraar Glacier. Though to become one of the leading Alpinists, he always maintained that the walks over the lower slopes and the passes provided an essential part of the appreciation of the whole, and describes a typical approach walk: the rise before dawn, the walk through the valley still in shadow with knapsack on back and trusty alpenstock in hand, through the forests of pine and larch, up to the pass and pastures new.

John Tyndall, who was deeply involved in glacier theory, first approached the Alps on foot in 1849 as a student at Marburg, admittedly for the sake of the walk rather than for science. 'In those days it was a pleasure to me to saunter along roads enjoying such snatches of scenery as were thus attainable. I knew not the distant mountains; the attraction which they afterwards exercised upon me had not yet begun to act.' The word 'saunter' was in his time used for something much more energetic than a stroll, and he certainly cannot have been strolling in that he covered the initial 150 miles to Heidelberg in three days. When he entered the deep valleys he rejected mules and conveyances, and 'trusting to my legs and stick, repudiating guides, eating bread and milk, and sleeping where possible in the country villages where nobody could detect my accent, I got through amazingly cheap': which was important, since Tyndall, like several other of the Victorian Alpine giants, was of poor and humble origin. Also in the 1840s, the scientist Michael Faraday walked 44 miles from Leukerbad over the Gemmi pass to Thun in ten and a half hours and two hours' rest, in spite of illness. And his contemporary, the pioneer geologist Thomas Bonney, was still keeping fit at seventy by a regular 7 miles a day.

Artists, too, have walked in pursuit of their calling, particularly landscape artists. Some, like Turner and Constable, made foot excursions to points at which they could sketch out a scene which would then be transferred to a larger canvas back in the studio. Others, especially water-colourists, perfected their scenes on the spot. But it has to be said that artists have seldom given prominence in their paintings to the action of walking. There are plenty of figures on roads in classical art, of course, but they usually portray the humble peasantry who give the appearance of shuffling along in a desultory way rather than striding out with purposeful intent. Nor does modern representational art help us much in a visual interpretation of the wider ramifications of walking. We are left with some nineteenth-century artists, such as Hans Thoma, who captured the impression of the energetic hill walker amid scenes of natural beauty: but perhaps the most arresting pose is that in the self-portrait of Gustave Courbet in *The Meeting*. In this picture, painted in 1854, Courbet sought to portray the proud inner superiority of himself, the bohemian and radical artist, as against the bourgeois values of his patron, Alfred Bruyas. He chose to depict himself on the road outside Montpellier in the guise of a walker, and the inspiration for the style and grouping of the figures was from a print of the Wandering Jew, a sort of eternal walker. Thus, in the striking and independent pose with head held high, staff and hat in either hand, pack (in this case, with artist's materials) on back, and gaiters over shoes, we observe a representation of many of the virtues inherent in walking through the ages: and it is good to see, on this occasion at least, that the wealthy non-walker is greeting the humbler walker with a proper deference. The picture also demonstrates most effectively how it is that meetings are more satisfactory when on foot than when on wheels or horseback, and how walking brings different sorts of people together on equal terms.

Not gazing at the glaciers through telescopes or with an artist's eye but scrutinising the plants through magnifying glasses, the naturalists were also afoot. Richard Jefferies, a mystic who experienced a cosmic consciousness through a spiritual love of nature, as a boy used to walk up Liddington Hill in Wiltshire: 'The labour of walking three miles to it, all the while gradually ascending, seemed to clear my blood of the heaviness accumulated at home. On a warm summer day the slow continued rise required continual effort, which carried away the sense of oppression.' For years he regularly took an identical walk every day so as to observe the ever-changing cycle of the year. Another great naturalist, W. H. Hudson, walked extensively over areas such as the chalk downs of Sussex or the New Forest of Hampshire, though he was a rotten walker. Not only was he of weak physique and usually underfed, but he clearly took no care to acquire a rhythm in his pace. At the start of the day he would rush ahead, force through hedges, climb hills, and explore woods and thickets. At the end of the day he was so exhausted that he was unable even to keep up with the snail's pace of his diminutive but dominating wife. Sometimes they adopted the expedient of alternately walking and bicycling (one cycling ahead and leaving the bike while the other walked and then caught up) to cover more of the country, putting up for the night with villagers, 'often footsore, and in need of their ministrations': though on a Midsummer's Eve he walked for two hours through the night to see the dawn at Stonehenge. Hudson's private life was gloomy, but his written descriptions of nature are enchanting and in reading them we visualise the tall gaunt figure as it advances across the grassy down, frequently stopping to make notes and sometimes lying down to examine or contemplate, for instance, the thistledown detaching from its stalk and floating away into the valley of the Ouse.

Hudson became famous in his own time, but this was not so of his disciple Edward Thomas who was killed in the First World War. Thomas was also a naturalist, though his finest form of expression was through the medium of poetry; unlike his mentor he was a keen walker. He was tall and slim and walked with a long slow stride, evidently incompatible with the gait of D. H. Lawrence who, after a walk with Thomas, muttered darkly, 'I must teach you to walk like a tramp.' He wore long baggy flannel trousers, a jersey and a Burberry, but was bareheaded and impervious to wet weather. In describing a walk which had ended at Winchester or Salisbury (he could not remember which) he wrote exultantly how everything had been annihilated save 'the wind, the rain, the streaming road, and the vigorous limbs and glowing brain . . . We and the storm were one and we were triumphant; and in mid-triumph we came down to the lighted streets.'

In the summer of 1910 Edward Thomas set out to walk along the Icknield Way, the prehistoric track that follows the low ridge of the Chilterns from East Anglia to the Thames and on along the Berkshire Downs. He was clearly influenced by Belloc's recent book on the North Downs Way and reasoned that if Belloc could write a popular book on the basis of one week's walk and a one-inch-to-the-mile map, so could he. But here the similarity ends for Thomas was concerned with a constant observation and specification of little things such as flowers, bushes, crops, ditches, hedges and trees, and did not attempt the prosy evocation of the topographical entity at which Belloc excelled. More important for us, he was almost painfully frank about his physical walking experience as well as his motives. He agonised over the justification of walking for literary copy ('it has not been decided whether this is a worthy object') and as to whether one should have a purpose for a walk – both of which certainly applied to him – and then concluded rather lamely: 'We walk for a thousand reasons, because we are tired of sitting, because we cannot rest, to get away from towns or to get into them, or because we cannot ride; and for permanent use the last is perhaps the best, as it is the oldest.' He began his walk at Thetford and for the first couple of days it was along the flat fens and brecklands of East Anglia. The new enemy of walkers, the motor car, was much in evidence, tyrannically dominating the road at a time when there were no speed limits. Although on some roads the new smooth surfaces were being laid, on others it was still earth and gravel and the dust raised by the cars was most unpleasant. He was so disheartened by this that on the second day, after leaving Newmarket, he would have hitched a lift in a cart if one had been passing him; in fact, 'in Cambridgeshire I recommend elephant, camel, horse, mule, donkey, motor car, waggon, or cart, anything except a covered cab or a pair of hobnailed shoes'. As the day wore on and he stumped along 'on a shoeful of blisters', 'essays on walking and walking tours began to wear very thin'. But at the same time his attention was constantly diverted to the larks and blackbirds, the bryony and the dog-rose, the elder bushes and the lime trees, that he understood so well; so that in retrospect he could write of the last few miles of his second 20-mile day: 'I am glad now that I walked them. It seems to me now that my purely physical discomfort intensified the taste of the evening's beauty, as it certainly made sweeter the perfection of enjoyment which I imagine possible at such an hour and in such a place.'

But that was in retrospect. By the end of the third day he was suffering badly, limping and leaning heavily on a stick which had a knob, not a handle, causing agonies to his arm and shoulder. He therefore decided to take a lift next day in a cart on the rather unconvincing grounds that he had 'about 40 miles to cover before the end of daylight', which surely cannot have been his original intention. Still, by a combination of riding and walking he did get to the Thames at Streatley. Now began a few days of march and counter-march: Edward Thomas was concerned with the inter-relationship between the ridgeway and the parallel underhill lane at the foot of the escarpment, so in this central section of the Icknield Way he walked on both. He had by now assumedly got through the worst of his blisters, though we catch a hint of continuing trouble in the sentence: 'Some country people say that silver-weed is good for the feet, a belief which might well have no better foundation than the fact that it grows commonly close to the road which is cruel to the feet.' His daily mileages were not great except on the final day when he trudged nearly

20 miles to Swindon. Actually, he had intended to find a bed in the village of Chisledon, but no one would take him in. He attributed this rejection to his nondescript appearance. In his Burberry and baggy trousers and with a two-days' beard, he was unclassifiable. He was clearly not a country gent, nor a tradesman, townsman or tramp; nor even a foreigner 'with a foot of hair, broad-brimmed hat, and corduroy or soft tweeds, a cloak and an ostentatious pipe'; nor 'the hairy and hygienic man in sandals'. So it was 'four unexpected miles to Swindon in the volcanic heat of evening, which produced several pains and a constant struggle between impatient mind and dull, tired body'.

But none of these walks by English naturalists can compare with those of a group of American naturalists who in the nineteenth century welded walking to science in a manner similar to that in which the English Romantics had earlier welded it to poetry. In the New World there was little equivalent to the walking tours or country walking that were already an established aspect of the English social scene. So it was left to indigent naturalists rather than comfortable clergymen, lawyers or academics to be the first to experience and describe the joys of walking. Besides, they needed to examine larger areas than did their English contemporaries. It is part of the greatness of Gilbert White that his observations mostly took place within a mile or so of Selborne in Hampshire, but he had no walking experience in the true sense of the term. If he had lived in New Hampshire he would surely have felt the need to travel further. In America the three who in different ways were walking pioneers were Henry Thoreau, John Burroughs and John Muir.

From his home in Concord, Massachusetts, or from his self-built hut on the shores of Walden Pond a mile and a half outside the town (where he lived in solitary self-sufficiency for over two years), Henry Thoreau was wont to take long walks. These led him into the heart of the countryside, whether cultivated land or forest or swamp. In his journal he would record the observations that he made on these walks – the effect of sun, rain, frost and water; the habits of muskrats, frogs, toads and turtles; the migrations, songs and nestings of birds. The country was empty enough for him to be able to walk for 20 miles or more without passing a house. In his prime he sometimes walked at least 30 miles each day for a week. He tried to avoid roads, and there was little impediment to his wandering into the bush because the greater part of the land was not as yet privately owned. He had a bias towards wandering towards the south and west of Concord because that was the direction of the Appalachians and the wild, and away from civilisation. Often he walked and wandered at night. On these walks he was usually alone, though he made a number of expeditions in the company of others. These included a pedestrian tour over the Hoosacs and the Catskills, and climbs to the summits of such mountains as Mount Washington, Wachusett, Saddleback, Katahdin and Monadnock. When he came to write specifically about walking he saw it in the first instance as an almost mystical experience and compared the Walker to a Pilgrim or a Knight-Errant – the Wanderer of folk-consciousness. He implies that one is either born with this wandering instinct or one is not, for 'it requires a direct dispensation from heaven to be a walker'. This quasi-religious association with walking is strengthened by his supposition (without evidence) that the word 'saunter' derives from the pilgrims who walked to the '*sainte terre*'. From this he goes on to say that walking is an adjunct to the appreciation of nature, and so is not mere exercise. By it one shakes off urban thoughts and worries and for himself he finds it essential to walk for at least four hours daily 'sauntering through the woods and over the hills and fields, absolutely free from all worldly engagements'. He despises the townsfolk who so neglect their lower limbs: indeed, he despises urban and industrial life in totality. To support the paradox that 'the swiftest traveller is he that goes afoot', Thoreau cites as instance that if he took the railroad to Fitchburg it would cost him ninety cents. As this is at least a day's wages, he would first have to spend a day earning it. Whereas if he walked the 30 miles there he could go now, for it would cost him nothing. Such naïve innocence of economics is what has since earned him so many admirers, though one can understand the irritation that some of the residents of Concord felt towards him. One of the first to appreciate Thoreau, incidentally, was Nathanial Hawthorne, himself an habitual walker in his bachelor days at Salem.

Twenty years junior to Thoreau, and indebted to him for his own appreciation of nature, John Burroughs was superior in terms of accuracy of observation and, by means of publishing a book or two a year, became a populariser of the scientific method in the study of birds and flowers, even though he was not strictly speaking a scientist himself. Until middle age he worked unhappily in the US Treasury Currency Department in Washington, but then moved to New York State and lived in a remote house in the Catskills called Slabsides. But his approach to walking was utterly different to that of Thoreau, reflecting an energetic and optimistic nature, as summed up in the title of his essay on walking, *The Exhilaration of the Road*. Indeed, he was the American prophet of road walking as Thoreau was of cross-country walking, and he dilates on its pleasures in a triumphant but slightly unreal way. He seems to have been on a real high as he wrote:

> The pedestrian is always cheerful, alert, refreshed, with his heart in his hand and his hand free to all. He looks down upon nobody; he is on the common level. His pores are all open, his circulation is active, his digestion good. His heart is not cold, nor his faculties asleep. He is the only real traveller; he alone tastes the 'gay, fresh sentiment of the road'. He is not isolated, but one with things, with the farms and industries on either hand. The vital, universal currents play through him. He knows the ground is alive: he feels the pulses of the wind, and reads the mute language of all things. His sympathies are all aroused; his senses are continually reporting messages to his mind. Wind, frost, heat, cold, are something to him. He is not merely a spectator of the panorama of nature, but a participator in it.

When he goes on to describe the ideal companion for the walk he becomes almost manic. Maybe this is the mood in which many have begun their journeys, but it is very far from that in which they have ended them. For a companion he would by preference choose someone who had served in the army, a healthy and experienced man, past his first youth (not a woman and certainly not gay in the present sense). 'He catches your step and away you go, a gay, adventurous, half predatory couple.' And then: 'What adventures we should have by the way, what hard pulls, what prospects from hills, what spectacles we would behold of night and day, what passages with dogs, what glances, what peeps into windows, what characters we should fall in with, and how seasoned and hardy we should arrive at our destination . . .' The conversation is vigorous and manly. 'By the camp-fire at night or swinging along the streams by day, song, anecdote, adventure, come to the surface.' But then Burroughs reflects and suggests that, after all, the ideal companion may be of an inferior species. Perhaps it is better to take a dog rather than a neighbour. 'The dog enters thoroughly into the spirit of the enterprise; he is not indifferent or preoccupied; he is constantly sniffing

121

adventure, laps at every spring, looks upon every field and wood as a new world to be explored, is ever on some fresh trail . . .' Such is John Burroughs' happy vision, where men are men, big-hearted and big-footed; for, in a throwaway line that must lose him several admirers and put him under grave suspicion of sexism, he also vouchsafed that 'a little foot never yet supported a great character'.

For all their writing, Thoreau and Burroughs must yield to John Muir when it comes to walking achievement. As Abraham Lincoln was to the political world, so was John Muir to the natural world: a stern, dedicated, self-taught, 'log-cabined', middle-western prophet. Just as we owe the Union to Lincoln, to Muir we owe the national parks: as Lincoln was not afraid to be in the firing line, Muir led from the front in his discoveries of the wonders of the Yosemite and his pedestrian penetration into the wilderness. Rejecting all opportunities of conventional advancement, he chose the life of a lonely wanderer; and shaking off the Presbyterian theology of his father, he embraced Darwinian humanism. When still a boy he had walked with two others westwards from Wisconsin towards the Mississippi on a gigantic geological study. This was a prelude to his final break with conventionality, which he made, dramatically and irrevocably, in his 'Thousand Mile Walk to the Gulf' four years later. The name given to his walk is misleading: it was around 800 miles and done in two sections with a sea passage in between.) His purpose was botanising and his destination South America, and on 1 September 1867 he left his home in Wisconsin by train for Jeffersonville on the Kentucky border where his great walk was to begin.

He carried a backpack which contained a plant-press as well as a comb, brush, towel, soap, change of underclothing, and three books: Burns' poems, Milton's *Paradise Lost*, and the New Testament. He aimed to advance 'by the wildest, leafiest, and least trodden way I could find'. But the greater part must have been by earth road or track, and by the end of the first week he had covered some 175 miles – 'my feet were sore, but oh! I am paid for all my toil a thousand times over.' By winding river bottoms, through groves of Kentucky oaks, past rows of twisted vines, he had by then reached the Cumberland river and the Tennessee border. The next few days involved crossing the wild and inhospitable Cumberland Mountains, where good luck steered him between a series of potential disasters. A man on horseback offered to carry his bag, rode ahead, searched it for ready money, but finding only the items already mentioned, handed it back to him intact. In a desolate area of plateau he faced hostility at the only house because he had no change for a five dollar bill and was not working profitably, but was given food and bed. Next day the track petered out and as he pushed along a path he came face to face with a band of guerrillas who had been on the run ever since the Civil War. There were ten of them, all mounted and riding abreast. He decided to brave it out. 'I advanced rapidly with long strides as though I intended to walk through the midst of them': which indeed he did, the only spoken word being his cheerful 'howdy'. Once through them he didn't dare to turn his head, and the dumb-witted grey-headed outlaws left him unhindered because they imagined, from the plants which protruded from the plant-press, that he was a herb doctor. That night he obtained a much-needed meal of string-beans, buttermilk and corn bread at the house of a Negro, after which he slept in the open.

A few days later he reached the border of North Carolina and stopped for three nights with an educated man who led him down to the local gold mines and up to the ridge of the hills: 'such an ocean of wooded, waving, swelling mountain beauty and grandeur is not to be described.' Overwhelmed by the scene, he expressed his admiration in almost biblical terms: 'Oh, these forest gardens of our Father! What perfection, what divinity, in their architecture! What simplicity and mysterious complexity in detail!' By now the scenery was changing as he walked down the southern slopes of the Alleghanies in dark pine woods and descended towards the plain. At one point he lost his way and found himself by a river, which he forded. He considered the possibility of acquiring a boat and floating downstream, but 'I finally concluded that such a pleasure sail would be less profitable than a walk, and so sauntered on southward as soon as I was dry.' After Athens, Georgia, he entered a land of magnificent tall grasses with forests of Southern Pines and Taxodiums, broken by cypress swamps and sandy tracts, where many of the plants were unfamiliar to him. Despite receiving hospitality from a number of strangers who were clearly impressed by him, he was by now out of money and had to do without his evening meal more than once. His daily stages became appreciably shorter after one final forced march in which he did 40 miles to Atlanta. At last he reached Savannah to find that the expected banker's draft from his brother had not arrived. He had to wait for several days, half starved and sleeping in a graveyard at Bonaventure 3 miles off, staggering daily to the bank in Savannah and feeling giddy. 'The ground ahead seemed to be rising up in front of me, and the little streams in the ditches on the sides of the road seemed to be flowing uphill.' The thrill of being alone with nature had worn off and he felt indescribably lonely.

The second part of John Muir's walk began after he had gone by boat down the coast from Savannah to Fernandina, Florida, where he set off to cross the peninsula to the Gulf. At first he found that the area was so waterlogged and dense that he could not advance through the bush, so he proceeded along a railway line; but later in the day he managed to get into some trackless woods and slept on the ground. From here it was across country for four more days, the scenery varying from dry ground covered with tall grasses or pine barrens, to cotton plantations and occasional alligator-infested marshes which had to be carefully negotiated. But the human danger was greater, and he encountered barbarous white loggers and predatory Negroes who would certainly have attacked him had they known he was not armed. He slept out most nights and went breakfastless for want of bread, but still walked briskly. After stopping for three nights with the hospitable Captain Simmons, he reached the sea in one final day's walk. But here fate caught up with him, for he went down, not surprisingly, with malarial fever and contracted typhoid. Because of this he abandoned his plans for South America and went west – fortunately for us, as it transpired.

While Muir was walking extensively in the Sierra Nevada and the Rockies and writing impellingly on the need to preserve the wilderness, the pleasures of walking in a greater mountain chain, the Himalayas, were being discovered by a young Englishman, Francis Younghusband. Younghusband's purpose in mountain wandering was very different. He was an ignoramus in natural science and his motives were political and military – the Great Game of influence and intelligence between the British and the Russians in the deep recesses of Central Asia. But he was more than just an energetic and intelligent cavalry officer, for he was able to cross the barriers of race and class and establish warm relationships with the hill tribes, and there was a strong element of mysticism in him. From the point of view of pure walking his first expedition is of the greatest interest, for it was neither so high as to involve climbing nor so far beyond the mountains as to reach into Tibet and the Gobi (where he also went) where horses were used. It was in 1884 that the twenty-one-year-old strode out of

Pathankot on the edge of the plain and up to Dharmsala. With his retriever at his heel he walked briskly and at the end of the day waited for his servant and a couple of baggage mules to catch up. It was all so tremendously exhilarating – the clear air, hot in the sun or cool in the forests of deodar or rhododendron; the panorama of distant snowy peaks; the vast slopes from which emanated streams of tumbling pure water; the extraordinary types encountered, from lamas to traders. Sometimes he walked a normal stage of 12 miles, sometimes a double stage. When he reached the pass above Kulu Valley after several days, he ran down into it. He then dispensed with the mules so as to be able to travel more quickly, with just two coolies who carried his 80 lb of baggage between them. On the Rotang Pass he first experienced mountain sickness as he trudged through the snow, but on his way south, in the valley of the Sutlej, he learnt how to combat exhaustion in walking uphill by forcing his mind into a blank. 'I would think neither of the heat, nor of where I had to get to, nor of future schemes. I would not even look up to where I had to go. I would simply look on the ground and watch my feet going tramp, tramp, mechanically upwards.' In complete contrast to this delightful walk, Younghusband cites the horrors of a regimental route march (the cavalry on this occasion went on foot) which he found a very nasty experience, made worse when the monsoon broke over their heads.

The wide-ranging pedestrian journeys of Muir and Younghusband were on the verge of what might be called exploration. But although explorers have travelled immense distances on foot and in conditions of appalling hardship, they contribute little to our understanding of the art of walking. In the first place, whenever they could avoid walking, they did so. And since they usually had animals with them, they rode for most of the way, normally on horses but otherwise on anything else available – mules, donkeys, camels, cows, oxen, or even elephants. When water was encountered, they would soon be in a boat. Only in Africa do we find sustained bouts of pure walking in the story of exploration, and these mainly in East and Central Africa, where the tsetse fly often precluded horses. Even there explorers were sometimes carried in litters or even on the shoulders of men. Most of David Livingstone's travels were on the back of oxen or donkeys. Most of Stanley's ranging expeditions were on water. Of his 'walk from the Cape to Cairo', Ewat Grogan was actually on his feet for under half the distance. Secondly, even when explorers did walk they went of necessity extremely slowly and at the speed of the most heavily weighted man or beast. Often they were held up by natural obstacles or hostile tribes. As they covered just a few miles a day, it was seldom the walking itself that tired them even when they were diseased or undernourished. (I suppose it could be argued that Scott's Antarctic team achieved a remarkable pedestrian feat, but as they were on skis and hauling sledges they were only walking in a loose sense of the term: to my mind one of the most pathetic aspects of their final martyrdom was that it took them hours to get their boots on in the morning, so frost-bitten were their feet and fingers and so deadened their brains.) Thirdly, walking was no part of the story they wanted to tell, just as it had been of no central concern to the medieval pilgrims. Thus it is hardly mentioned, which is a pity; though fortunately it is not exaggerated either. For obviously in the realm of exploration there have been great opportunities for imaginative accounts, for which there was a ready market, but which were beautifully debunked in Belloc's *The Modern Traveller*. Two instances of this type do, however, dilate on the theme of walking, one an early masterpiece and the other much more recent.

Nine years before Captain Shaw undertook his pedestrian tour through Europe in true military style, another British captain had walked even more extensively on the Continent. But his title was naval, not military, and his sights were set far beyond the restrictive confines of Europe. Captain John Dundas Cochrane RN, on half pay after the Napoleonic Wars, had persuaded the Board of Admiralty to grant him two years of absence in order to explore the landmass of Siberia. His *Narrative of a Pedestrian Journey*, published in 1824, was the result. Of his total story we can swallow as much as we like, and at the time many swallowed it whole. Although largely without dates or daily accounts he told of getting all the way across the steppes as far as Tomsk. Then, as autumn came on, up north to Yakutsk; from there to Nijni Kolymsk; and then in early spring down to Okhotsk on the Pacific coast. After a year in the Kamchatka peninsula, it was back across Russia with a child bride, the fifteen-year-old daughter of a 'Kamchatkan chief'. In the course of his journey he accomplished such feats as covering immense distances into the Arctic Circle in atrocious conditions ($-27°C$), with unbelievable rapidity (averaging 20 miles a day despite snowdrifts and hills), and superhuman courage (capsized on a raft on a freezing river in pitch darkness). Though in appearance a tramp, he was apparently received with honour by the Governor-General of Siberia and the merchants and sea-captains of the east. But for us the main fascination is that he claimed to have walked nearly all the way.

Of his walk as far as St Petersburg we need not be too sceptical. His route was from Dieppe and via Paris, Metz, Frankfurt and Berlin: on more than one occasion he topped 40 miles. Only when out of France did he encounter hostility and in the Rhineland twice had to sleep rough. Things got worse when he entered Prussia: at the border he was immediately arrested but boldly escaped in the middle of the night and continued to Wittenberg. In East Prussia he took a short cut off the road and inevitably got lost in icy swampy ground. His trousers were torn, he lost his cap, but resourcefully retained his shoes by binding them to his legs. By now hobbling with a sprained ankle he suffered from his worn shoes 'which the variations of weather made alternately like sponge and horn'. So he weakened and took a diligence into Danzig at the rate of 2 miles an hour over the pitted roads, and then a boat towards Memel, which became ice-bound. Once in Russia he twice took rides for part of the way to the capital.

It was after St Petersburg that things got rather larger than life. Hardly had he begun his walk towards Moscow than he noticed the Palace of Tsarsko Selo aflame in the night sky: he hurried to the scene, of course, and was later received at breakfast by a Prince Galitsin. Next day, back on the main road, he was seized by ruffians who robbed him of everything – 'my trowsers, shirts, stockings and English shooting-shoes (the last I regretted most of all, as they were a present from Sir D. Bailey) – as also my spectacles, watch, compass, thermometer, and small pocket-sextant, with one hundred and sixty roubles, about seven pounds'. But despite this, once he had been released from his bonds, he 'trotted on with a merry heart' although barefoot and with a sort of kilt around his midriff, and when he got to Novgorod the Governor kindly provided him with a complete refit. Approaching Moscow, he made the last 96 miles in thirty-two hours. The Pedestrian Traveller now headed east to Nijni Novgorod and after continuing by boat down the Volga to Kazan and by carriage to Perm, he was back on his feet again. Once he was across the Urals and into Asia, Cochrane's walks became inextricably mixed with his rides and probably both with his imagination. He saw himself grinding regularly at 30 miles or more a day, diverting so as to see most of the provinces of Asiatic Russia, shouldering his knapsack again when refused a horse in Yakutsk, and walking through the snow so as to keep warm. Later, on the return journey, with his young wife in tow, he took to his feet again on roads which were so rough that to ride in any vehicle was sheer agony. Back in London he could certainly prove the reality of Mrs Cochrane, but the true details of what happened to him in the far north-east will never be known.

At least Cochrane has given us a spirited account of his journey: not even this was so in the case of a strange figure known as 'Walking Stewart' who haunted the streets of London in the same period. Dressed in a faded military coat, breeches and travel-stained boots, he claimed to have travelled extensively on foot in India, Persia, Arabia, Turkey and Europe. But whenever anyone asked him about it he deflected the conversation towards philosophical speculations, on which he talked brilliantly and wrote several tracts. Perhaps his amnesia was due to brain damage since apparently the crown of his head was indented nearly an inch in depth by a blow from 'some warlike instrument'.

The tale told by Slavomir Rawicz in *The Long Walk* is calculated to draw our sympathy and admiration. Seven prisoners escape from the Siberian Gulag Achipelago in 1941 and walk to India: four die on the way, three make it. The author (or rather, his ghost writer) describes in harrowing terms their 3000-mile flight, every inch of it walked. And yet, our credulity is strained. Five are Poles, one a Cossack, and one an American called Smith: but since he neglected ever to mention his first name, he is only 'Mister Smith'. The six males of party have been travelling for about a month when they come across an incongruous figure hiding head-first in a bush. Who is it but an attractive Polish girl, also on the run? From start to finish all are scrupulously polite to each other ('Gentlemen, shall we proceed?') and, of course, protective and gallant towards the girl. Once outside the borders of the Soviet Union they have several encounters with local people and without exception all are courteous and helpful, with much mutual bowing and dumb-crambo and pointings in the direction of Lhasa. They are given gifts of food and in return are able to assist a farmer with his threshing and a shepherd with his cooking.

But it is the pedestrian achievement which astonishes. No sooner are they through the barbed wire in early May than they jog along for several hours. For the first week or so they walk in darkness at the rate of some 30 miles a day. After two months they have covered 1200 miles, or 20 miles a day, over the hills and forests of Siberia and away from all human habitation, and they keep this up as far as the Gobi desert, where naturally their pace slackens. Throughout they have managed on very intermittent food, and now it is the water which runs out. After several days in the desert they come to an oasis where there is water but no food. On they go with only as much of the precious liquid as can be held in their single receptacle, a mug. Naturally this runs out on the first day and soon two of the party succumb. Twelve days after the oasis the remaining five are still shuffling on without water and 'we walked only about six miles on that day'. Next day they come to some mud from which at least a little moisture can be extracted. And their first food for about a fortnight is obtained by killing snakes and cooking them on a stone heated by a fire of dried cattle dung – a handy fuel which one of them has providentially carried all the way from the oasis. By October they are out of the Gobi and not so far from Shangri La, so it is up to 20 miles a day again; this despite sometimes going for four or five days without food and having to climb over rocks so steep that they need improvised ropes. Even then Zaro the Cossack still has enough surplus energy to get down on his haunches and kick out his legs in a Cossack dance to amuse the village children. At length they come to the Himalayas in the depth of winter but, scorning the use of recognised passes, head right across the top. Two more die, one falling into a crevasse, but three get over. Coming down the snow slopes they see two large animals. Back in Siberia near the start of their walk they had noticed a black bear standing on his hind legs twanging the splinter of a fallen trunk in some interesting musical experimentation, but these are far more remarkable. They are around eight feet tall, one slightly taller than the other: their hair is russet-coloured and they have squarish heads and dangling arms. Yes, of course, they are the Abominable Snowman and Snowwoman out for a walk!: and this is perhaps the moment to part company with the survivors of The Long Walk and turn to better accredited foot-travellers.

Tramps

AFOOT and lighthearted I take to the open road,
Healthy, free, the world before me,
The long brown path before me leading wherever I choose.
Henceforth I ask not good-fortune, I myself am good-fortune,
Henceforth I whimper no more, postpone no more, need nothing,
Done with indoor complaints, libraries, querulous criticisms,
Strong and content I travel the open road.

Walt Whitman's 'A Song of the Open Road', which begins with these
lines, makes use of the image of a journey on foot to portray his
message that one should shake off intellectual and social constraints
and start the great quest. Both in philosophic and physical terms it

expresses admirably the attitude of the latter-day wanderers who saw themselves as tramps and walked away from convention and into adventure.

Of course, the word 'tramp' is a loose one, covering many different types. Dickens attempted to describe the principal sorts of tramps in an essay entitled *The Uncommercial Traveller*. He saw the lazy tramp, sleeping by the roadside with his woman beside him; the slinking tramp, who begs; the well-spoken tramp, who pretends to be a gentleman out of luck and who buttonholes you by the cunning trick of walking specially slowly till you pass him at your faster pace, then suddenly increasing his speed to yours while he pours out his hard-luck story. Then there are the men who walk the roads, assumedly in search of work:

> The young fellows who trudge along barefoot, five or six together, their boots slung over their shoulders, their shabby bundles under their arms, their sticks newly cut from some roadside wood, are not eminently prepossessing, but are much less objectionable. There is a tramp-fellowship among them. They pick one another up at resting stations, and go in companies. They also go at a fast swing – though they generally limp too – and there is inevitably one of the company who has much ado to keep up with the rest.

(A touching thought, this, poignantly developed by Browning in 'The Pied Piper of Hamelin'). Finally, there are the working tramps, the tinkers, chair-menders, knife-grinders and bricklayers who walk the dusty roads in summer to make a penny profit here and there. It was not till after Dickens' time that a popular mystique arose around the workless tramps. They came to be known as the 'Gentlemen of the Road'. They left discreet signs for each other: for instance, a cross with a ring around it meant a religious family; a plain cross, a household which either would not or could not give alms; and a dot with a ring around it, danger of arrest. They brewed tea by the roadside, took off their boots, and studied their feet. They were altogether outside the normal structure of society, a sort of caste of untouchables. As such they became a source of fascination; as did the gypsies who, though not entirely foot-bound like the tramps, were also social outcasts. In Masefield's lines:

> Dunno about Life – it's jest a tramp alone
>   From wakin' time to doss;
> Dunno about Death – it's jest a quiet stone
>   All over grey with moss.
> An' why I live, an' why the old world spins,
>   Are things I never knowed;
> My mark's the gypsy fires, the lighted inns,
>   An' jest the dusty road.

One of the first to adulate the tramp's life was Harry Roberts, whose *Tramp's Handbook* was published at the beginning of this century. His aim is to instruct those in the civilised world how to live simply and minimise their needs. For those who are by nature self-contained though with a sense of humour, the gypsy life offers 'quiet dignity, glorious calm, refined simplicity and the companionship of divine things'. Although the gypsy makes good use of horses, he knows that the best way to travel is to walk. 'Beyond the ever-moving horizon are golden cities and great adventures, and the very limitations of our pace give to all the world, its cornfields and its hills and its woodland, a vastness and a grandeur of which they who grind their way rapidly on wheels know nothing.' He also needs to know all about camping and scavenging and roadside cookery (rabbits, hedgehogs, snails, frogs and even insects feature large here), and he should look the part by avoiding a knapsack and using his pockets.

Roberts was followed by W. H. Davies who, depending on how you look at him, was a tramp with a taste for poetry or a poet with a taste for tramping. In *The Autobiography of a Super-tramp* he relishes the discomfiture of the bourgeoisie at his presence and appearance. He was so adept at knocking on doors and inducing sympathy that he tried his luck in America with some success, though he was sometimes jailed for vagrancy. In peregrinations such as these he often walked for only short distances, though he boasted of doing 3 miles an hour for as long as nine hours, and this despite one foot being wooden from the ankle. W. H. Davies had a romantic streak and maintained that an admiration of nature was essential for the good walker:

> The difference between a good walker and a bad one is that one walks with his heart, and the other with his feet. As long as the heart is eager and willing, the strain on the body is not very important: and it is only at night, when his long journey is done,

that a man's muscles feel swollen and stiff. This means that no man should go forth as a wanderer unless he is a true lover of Nature; for it is the everchanging scenery that keeps his head light until the end of his day's walk.

Davies in his turn was followed by Eric Blair (George Orwell), who for a few days walked with the homeless down-and-outs who were forced to keep on the move every day between the doss-houses in South London and Kent: on one day it was 'a sixteen-mile walk over the asphalt, blistering to the heels, and we were acutely hungry'.

All this was a far cry from the preoccupations of the pedestrian tourers with their cravats and sheets. These may have been flouting convention by walking, but once safely in the hotel dining-room they gave the appearance of any other middle-class travellers. Their aim was always to avoid camping or being mistaken for vagrants (though, rather confusingly, some of them at around the turn of the century referred to their walks as 'tramps', for example Bart Kennedy's *A Tramp in Spain*, while other travellers who mainly used coaches or trains also used the word to describe their journeys, as in Mark Twain's *A Tramp Abroad*). Their days were coming to an end. Quite apart from the growth of motor transport, which made road walking so unpleasant especially near towns, the spirit of the age was changing. There were still gentlemen who wanted to wander around on foot, but they also wanted to rough it more. In part this was a protest against the rigid class distinctions of the late nineteenth century and a wish to meet poor people on equal terms: in part a desire to get closer to nature as in normal life people moved further from it, and to test personal self-sufficiency. Indeed, in the story of one man we can trace the transition from one style of walking to the other, a man whose influence on walkers has been far greater than his rather brief and limited walking experiences – Robert Louis Stevenson.

Stevenson when in his twenties made several short pedestrian tours of the old style. He has given us descriptions of two short solo walks in Britain. One was in the Chilterns, a two-day autumn event from High Wycombe to Wendover, stopping the night at Great Missenden. Most of the way was along country lanes, but he also struck across country. In the silent beechwoods 'the wood listened as I went, and held its breath to the number of my footfalls'. But in the fields there was 'a great coming and going of school-children upon by-paths, and, in every second field, lusty horses and stout country-folk a-ploughing'. RLS reflected that he, the quick foot-traveller, obtained a much better impression of the countryside, as it appeared at that particular moment, than did they. In one encounter on this walk we may detect a prophetic warning. As he strode along a green lane he saw a donkey whose halter had got twisted around its neck. He climbed over a fence to unravel it, but as he walked away the donkey brayed at him in what he felt to be a sort of jeer: he laughed back at the donkey. Another similar short walk was in Ayrshire, in the Carricks and along the coast by Dunure. It was winter, 'everything was grey and white in a cold and dolourous sort of shepherd's plaid', and as he walked the snow crunched underfoot.

We next see RLS in France walking with a friend, Walter Simpson. Their intention was to explore the valley of the Loing but their tour came to an abrupt end at Châtillon-sur-Loire. When Stevenson strode into the town he was alone: evidently he and Simpson didn't believe in walking side by side all the time, or else he had far outstripped his friend. Dressed in a smoking-cap, dark flannel shirt, tweed coat, cheap linen trousers and leather gaiters, knapsack on back, he was arrested as a suspicious character and brought before the Commissary. The Commissary was angry at being awoken from his siesta and looked with distaste at the young Scotsman who was ushered into his bedroom. He ordered him to empty his knapsack which proved to contain 'a change of shirts, of shoes, of socks, and of linen trousers, a small dressing case, a piece of soap in one of the shoes, two volumes of the Collection Jannet lettered *Poésies de Charles d'Orléans*, a map, and a version book containing divers notes'. All this was far beyond the comprehension of a country copper, and so it was to the lock-up that RLS was confined till the slower-moving Simpson arrived and provided identification. But he was only released on condition that they left immediately by train for Paris.

At about this time Stevenson wrote an essay on the subject of walking tours. He first defines various types of walker, by what interests them as they walk (for instance, observing nature from the point of view of a scientist or of a writer, or not observing it at all and merely talking or singing), or the speed at which they walk (there is the 'overwalker' and the 'temperate walker', and the latter is to be commended). RLS advocates walking on even ground, though by this he doesn't necessarily mean on roads so much as on smooth cart tracks or paths. 'Uneven walking is not so agreeable to the body, and it distracts and irritates the mind. Whereas, when once you have fallen into an equable stride, it requires no conscious thought from you to keep it up, and yet it prevents you from thinking earnestly of anything else.' More than the other essayists on walking, who were all slightly ambivalent on the subject, he is categoric that one must walk alone. 'Now, to be properly enjoyed, a walking tour should be gone upon alone. If you go in company or even in pairs, it is no longer a walking tour in anything but name; it is something else and more in the nature of a picnic.' This scathing dismissal of companionship would carry more weight if Stevenson had ever walked alone – or even been alone – for long periods. More authoritative is his description of the sense of well-being at the end of a long hot purging walk. 'Your muscles are so agreeably slack, you feel so clean and so strong and so idle, that whether you move or sit still, whatever you do is done with pride and a kingly sort of pleasure.'

The reasons why Stevenson graduated from pedestrian tourism to something akin to tramping have been analysed by Richard Holmes in *Footsteps*. He went tramping, Holmes says, as 'a kind of initiation ceremony: a grappling with physical hardships, loneliness, religious doubts, the influence of his parents, and the overwhelming question of whether he should take the enormous risk of throwing his life with Fanny's . . .' He also went for literary copy, and the result was *Travels with a Donkey in the Cevennes*. From a purely walking point of view his journey can hardly be considered a success, and the blame for this must go to Modestine. The problem lay in his concern that he must be prepared to camp out. But to camp out comfortably a century ago meant carrying some very heavy and uncomfortable equipment. He might have hired a man with a mule, but RLS wanted solitude also. He thought of a horse, decided it was too much trouble, so plumped for a donkey. This she-ass, which he dubbed Modestine, plagued his progress and in large measure spoilt his walk: but the interplay of wills and the endless misadventures provided him with a perfect theme which has secured immortality for his short book about his short journey. For walkers his story presents a caution: never saddle yourself with a donkey; especially a female donkey on heat, as Stevenson's was for the first week.

From the moment when he set out at 9 a.m. on Sunday 22 September 1878 from the small Auvergnat hill-town of Le Monastier-sur-Gazeille, Modestine set a pace that was agony for any walker. 'It was something as much slower than a walk as a walk is slower than a run; it kept me hanging on each foot for an incredible length of time; in five minutes it exhausted the spirit and set up a fever in all the muscles of the leg.' And there was no way of avoiding it, for if he left her side Modestine would come to a halt and start to browse. After a short while a passing peasant showed RLS how to use a switch on the donkey, accompanying the switching with shouts of 'Proot'. This speeded things up a bit but any relief it brought to his legs was paid for by the effort to his arms. Loaded on to Modestine was his specially designed sleeping-bag, made for him at Le Puy. It was nearly six foot square, of green waterproof cart-cloth lined with blue fleece. It also served as a sack in which to carry an empty knapsack, a rug, two changes of warm clothing, a fur cap and a leather pad containing a flask, jack-knife, lantern, candles, spirit-lamp, pan and revolver. Also several cakes of chocolate and tins of sausages. On top of the sack Modestine carried a greatcoat and a basket with provisions – a leg of mutton, a bottle of Beaujolais, an empty bottle for milk, an egg-beater, and both black and white bread. Passing through the village of Ussel this load turned turtle. Before the amused and mocking villagers RLS had to rectify matters and, after another mishap, decided that the only solution was to throw away the mutton, egg-whipper, white bread and empty bottle, and carry the basket of provisions and coat on his own back, leaving Modestine with the loaded sleeping-bag. But to no avail, for a little later the load once more bit the dust. It was dark by the time he reached Le Bouchet St Nicholas and put up at the inn after 13 troublesome miles.

The landlord of this very basic inn next morning provided him with a goad, which had an electrical effect on Modestine: and a further improvement took place at Langogne, where RLS decided to have his knapsack repaired so as to discard the basket, which was agony to carry. But this was succeeded by a couple of bad days, up on the moorlands in a labyrinth of tracks in driving rain, getting lost and camping uncomfortably, and having to abandon his planned route because of Modestine's weakness. All the same his gloomy feelings engendered one of the classic statements about travel, particularly on foot: 'For my part, I travel not to go anywhere, but to go. I travel for travel's sake. The great affair is to move; to come down off this feather-bed of civilisation, and find the globe granite under-foot and strewn with cutting flints.' The only redeeming feature came at the inn at Luc where in a clean and roomy kitchen he enjoyed a dinner of trout, stewed hare, cheese and a Vivarais wine. The

daily distances were getting shorter and shorter when he arrived at
the Trappist monastery of Notre Dame des Neiges and twenty-
four hours of religious reflection and ambivalent thoughts about
catholicism.

From here his route led over Mont Goulet: the sun shone and the
wind had dropped. He was enchanted by the wayside sounds – the
bleating and tinkling of the sheep gathered in the street at Lestampe,
the music of a horn and a flute, men singing, cocks crowing. He
arrived at La Bleymard at dinner time and in late afternoon continued
up the slopes of Mont Lozère to the upper edge of the tree line, where
his 'night among the pines' inspired four lyrical pages on the pleasures
of sleeping out under the stars. He awoke before dawn, lit his lantern,
and brewed some water and chocolate. Preceded by a gust of wind 'as
long as a heavy sigh', the sun rose and the light 'spread at a gallop
along the hillside, scattering shadows and sparkles'. Now he was on
his way over the mountain, guided across the turf by a line of upright
stones. At the Col de Finiels he entered into a new world. A strong
wind blew into his face from the south as he surveyed the ranges of the
Cevennes, receding towards the Mediterranean. Down into the steep
valley of the Rieumalet he went, and to complete his enjoyment
'Modestine herself was in high spirits, and broke of her own accord,
for the first time in my experience, into a jolting trot'. At Pont de
Montvert he reached the Tarn. This was a place of evil memory, scene
of the flashpoint of the insurrection of the Camisards in July 1702
when the psalm-singing crowd led by Pierre Seguier plunged their
knives into the body of their persecutor, the Archpriest du Chayla. He
walked on down the new road towards Florac surrounded by gold-
tinted Spanish chestnuts. By now Modestine was 'in laggard humour';
RLS cast about for a place to camp, and found a small flat piece of
ground above the road. His night was not so peaceful as on Mont
Lozère due to ants, bats, mosquitoes and rats, and in the morning he
was embarrassed to be discovered there by the peasants: but he
enjoyed a good wash in the Tarn – 'To wash in one of God's rivers in
the open air seems to me a sort of cheerful solemnity or semi-pagan act
of worship.'

From Florac he ascended the valley of the Mimente. The scenery
was still beautiful, but RLS was in a black mood, and in his journal
attributes this to having to 'plod at a wearisome slow pace behind
Modestine'. Not that there was now any trouble with the saddle or
pack, for he had learnt how to balance them with stones: it was rather

that he had become bored with the whole procedure and anyway had to carry much of the load in his knapsack. The theme of former religious strife continued to dominate his encounters, whether with a game-hunter on the road or a gendarme and a merchant over dinner. Another camp was succeeded by a long walk, and at the crest of a hill, where the track petered out into several, an aged shepherd, 'hobbling on a pair of sticks, and wearing a black cap of liberty as if in honour of his nearness to the grave', directed him on his way. The last hour or so was along a road in moonlight. RLS took a couple of swigs from a bottle of Volnay. 'It was but a couple of mouthfuls; yet I became thenceforth unconscious of my limbs, and my blood flowed with luxury. Even Modestine was inspired by this purified nocturnal sunshine, and bestirred her little hoofs as to a livelier measure.' Dust rose from his feet and flowed away. 'Our two shadows – mine deformed with the knapsack, hers comically bestridden with the pack – now lay before us clearly outlined on the road, and now, as we turned a corner, went off into the ghostly distance, and sailed along the mountain like clouds.' He reached St Germain-de-Calberte just in time to be accepted at the inn. This was yet another place for the contemplation of old unhappy far-off things and battles long ago, historically a Catholic outpost in a Protestant country, but now a placid place with all passion spent. It was past three when he set out for his final stage of 15 miles to St Jean du Gard; (incidentally, he walked a total of 125 miles over the twelve days). He got there in just over six hours, so Modestine must have kept up a pace of nearly 3 miles an hour, picking up for lost time.

For the benefit of his readers Stevenson in *Travels with a Donkey* affects a sentimental attachment to Modestine, even implying that he burst into tears at their parting. But, as he travelled in the post-chaise from St Jean to Allais, we may be sure that an uppermost thought in his mind was that in future he would never again go for a walk with a donkey. Nor, in fact, did he go for any more adventurous walking expeditions: for these, we have to turn to his novels such as *Kidnapped*, with the flight of James Balfour and Alan Breck, their perilous escape over the heathery hills of Appin and the peat-bogs of Rannoch Moor, and their refuge in the eyrie above Glen Coe while the redcoats searched for them in the glen below. And we think of their author himself not as a pedestrian tourer but as a camper and a tramp, of the sort conjured up by his lines in 'Vagabond':

Wealth I seek not, hope nor love,
Nor a friend to know me;
All I seek, the heaven above
And the road below me.

Stevenson was not the first British walking-camper in France: in this
he was pipped to the post by a mere boy, Edward Knight. Young
Knight had been withdrawn from Westminster School on a quite
erroneous diagnosis of consumption. His father, who had served in
India, now resided at Honfleur, where his small income went further
than in England. The son, who, unusually for those times, was left
very much to his own devices and allowed to wander around the place,
developed a passion for walking on extended journeys, putting the
strength of sterling to extremely good use. 'I used to save all my pocket
money to spend on my walking tours. I reckoned that for two sous I
could travel more than a mile, and that thus I could walk more than
two hundred and fifty miles for every pound that I saved.' This he
achieved essentially by sleeping out, bivouacking 'in the woods, or
under the ferns and heather on the moor, not so much for economics
sake but because I loved to sleep with only the sky and the stars above
me'. He carried an Indian sepoy's ox-hide knapsack in which he
generally had in one pouch a loaf of bread, a sausage and some Gruyère
cheese; and in the other, a bottle of red wine. And very little else, for
not only did he have no tent but he even dispensed with a blanket,
contenting himself with a thin mackintosh. Not surprisingly he
sometimes found it too cold to sleep at night, in which case he altered
his schedule by walking at night and sleeping by day. But either way
he would usually treat himself to a hotel dinner, sometimes washed
down with a 'bottle of extra special burgundy, price sixpence'. His
great advantage was that he spoke French fluently, indeed was so
much taken for a Frenchman that he was approached by the sinister
'men-merchants' – people who sought out youths who for a fee would
take the place of the sons of the wealthy, who had been drafted into the
army by lottery. But generally he was met with Gallic kindness and
warmth and walked, over a number of years, for thousands of miles in
Brittany, the Jura, and the valleys of the Loire, Rhône and Garonne.
Just before going up to Cambridge he tramped through Algeria,
getting as far as Lagouat in company with French soldiers. E. F.
Knight went on to become a formidable proponent of outdoor life as
admired in the pages of *Boys' Own*. He glamorised the Empire and

wrote dispatches from the front during engagements with the Naga, the Matabele and the Boers. He was a strong advocate of sailing as a sport. But from the walking point of view he never sustained the lengths he had achieved long before in France during the days of the Third Empire.

Meanwhile the image of the tramp had begun to cast its imaginative spell across a far larger country, Russia. In contrast to America, where the naturalists were the prophets of walking, in Russia that role fell to men who were more concerned with society, and in particular Tolstoy and Gorky. Tolstoy, though not advocating walking for walking's sake, saw it as an essential part of his vision of the simple life, a life where the parasitic rich no longer rode about in carriages. To be happy, a man must exercise all his faculties, his legs as much as his brain. As he ironically wrote, 'By a long series of doubts, searchings, and reflection, I have reached the extraordinary truth that man has eyes in order to see, ears in order to hear, legs in order to walk, and hands and a back to work with, and that if he does not use them for their natural purpose it will be the worse for him.' These precepts were certainly put into practice by Maxim Gorky. When still in his teens he had tramped in the area of the Volga, mixing with all sorts and taking odd jobs; and soon after, in 1891, he spent a whole summer in this way in the Ukraine, Bessarabia, the Crimea and Georgia. This involved substantial spells of walking, in particular along the Black Sea coast, during which he was joined by a plausible young man who claimed to be a Georgian prince but who discreetly disappeared as they approached his supposed territories. For all their radicalism there was a strong element of mysticism in these Russian thinkers which attracted many in the materialistic West: and one who outstripped even Gorky in his tramping in Russia was an Englishman, Stephen Graham.

Stephen Graham was a solicitor's clerk in London who became so fascinated by all things Russian that he resigned his position to go and wander there in the summer of 1910. He had already had articles published in the *Evening Standard* and *Country Life* and reckoned that he could live by writing, on the lines of Hilaire Belloc, and in particular by tramping, as Belloc had done in *The Path to Rome*. First it was in the Caucasus, in which his most ambitious tramp was from Vladikavkaz over the snowy Mamison pass, camping in romantic places such as the cave below the castle of Tamara. On the far side he was arrested as a spy; so, unlike John Dundas Cochrane, he had to retreat from the east and instead elected to tramp in the north, from Archangel southwards up the Dvina river. Here there were no pleasant places for camping out, and it rained continuously; so he had to stay in the houses of peasants or banished revolutionaries. In this manner he reached Moscow, the greater part of the way on foot. As he describes it in his autobiography, *Part of the Wonderful Scene*, 'My boots, which had an intersole of iron, cut into my feet. I took off my boots in an igloo and a peasant plaited a stiff pair of birch bark shoes while I waited – *lapti*. With *lapti* you have to walk on your heels because they put your toes out of action. So for the rest of the way I made a slow stately progress like a priest in a procession. I was slowed down to the pace of a pilgrim.'

This was appropriate, for later Stephen Graham actually became a pilgrim. He began a long tramp from Sebastopol eastwards 'through the majesty of forested hills, glimpsing the foam-crested waves of the sea'. It culminated in a continuous walk of 400 miles along the largely uninhabited shoreline from Novorossisk to Batum, all the way on the sandy beaches or the scrub and stones that divided them. He passed the lonely monasteries of Cape Pitsoonda and New Athos. Other than at these, and during a storm when he took refuge in a barn, he slept out every night as 'nature's guest', and his account of it in *A Tramp's Sketches* is lyrical. He lived off the abundant supply of wild fruit – plums, pears, blackberries, grapes and walnuts – that no one else was around to pick; and he boiled tea in his kettle. He slept in caves, in the forest, on the hillside or in ruined buildings, and learnt how to make a bed of ferns and birch-twigs before lying down. He bathed every morning. As the days went by he felt himself becoming a new man, and a wilder one. As if to assert the change, he would sometimes bark like an animal: this was useful when he was attacked by six mastiffs, which he warded off with his ash-plant. Yet in his haversack he still had his grey tweed Norfolk jacket and a collar and tie, and nearing Batum could still pull weight as the travelling Englishman and pour scorn on a wealthy family who refused him refuge. By now he saw himself as a sort of pilgrim and so it was only natural that early the next year he should join a group of Russian peasant pilgrims to Jerusalem, sailing with them on their voyage between Istanbul and Palestine and tramping with them into the Holy City and down to Jericho for immersion in the Jordan.

Stephen Graham now became a sort of professional tramper, though not a tramp in the sense of a vagrant, for his real profession was

writing and journalism. Although he went off on extended wanderings most years, he lived in London for a lot of the time and was very
much on the literary social scene. His greatest patron was Northcliffe,
owner of *The Times* and *Daily Mail*, who told him, 'Go where you like
and write what you like.' The outbreak of the First World War found
him in Russian Turkestan, and he became a war correspondent, later
joining up as a guardsman in the Scots Guards. After the war, with
Russia now banned to him, he tramped in such places as Georgia 'from
Atlanta to the sea', and Panama 'to a peak in Darien', and eastern
Europe. He also walked for five weeks in the Rockies with the
American poet Vachel Lindsay, from Montana into Canada. They
seem to have had a high old time, with many a scramble and encounter
with the black bears, their steps directed northwards by the
compasses that they wore on their wrists in place of watches.

In *The Gentle Art of Tramping* Graham expounds his philosophy of
the road. By a 'tramp' he does not mean a hobo, beachcomber, casual
labourer or down-and-out: he means 'all true Bohemians, pilgrims,
explorers afoot, walking tourists, and the like'. Walking is certainly an
important component of tramping (coming 'into step with nature')
but not necessarily for the whole way or for any long stages or
continually. The true Bohemian is under no compulsion to keep on
the move: he should stop over at attractive villages and certainly not be
bound by a fixed timetable. Speed in walking is unimportant: the
length and the speed of a day's march will depend on what type you
are, and the two extremes are the 'athletes' and the 'lovers'. For
himself he advocates a stop at midday for a meal followed by a siesta
before resuming. He also prefers mountain walking to road walking;
there is no dust and more variety. But whereas it is permissible to cut
the corners on the walks, camping and sleeping under the stars are
absolutely essential. To enjoy all this with a companion is better than
alone, though it is the ultimate test of friendship. It is also a hard test
for marriage, but despite this he recommends a honeymoon tramp,
though you should be sure to take a double sleeping-bag and not be too
disconcerted if 'the cold wet nose of a hedgehog touching your
beloved's cheek may cause her to rend the air with a shriek'. Graham
stiffens his book with all sorts of practical tips. The tramp should wear
large heavy-duty army boots with nails or metal pads, to which he may
in time feel justifiably sentimental. (J. B. Morton incidentally, nicknamed his own trusty boots Dexter and Sinister.) His clothes should
be of homespun tweed or twill, and his hat of tweed: by dispensing

with waistcoat, collar and tie he escapes from the barriers of class. His knapsack should contain a blanket but not a tent, and in the evening he should light a fire. 'The fire in the rain is a triumph; the night fire in darkness under the stars is the happiest, but it disputes happiness with the dawn fire.' And on the fire he will brew his meal, including good strong tea or coffee. Thus the four 'emblems of tramping' are the Staff, the Knapsack, the Fire and the Coffee-pot. Through all this one senses the joyous and happy personality of Stephen Graham. He had the perfect temperament for a 'tramp' – at ease and at peace with himself, a superb mixer and a commanding personality; and, equally important, with a total disregard for comfort. His attitude is admirably expressed in the lines he so admired:

> Change was his mistress, Chance his counsellor.
> Love could not hold him, Duty forged no claim.
> The wide seas and the mountains called to him,
> And grey dawns saw his camp-fires in the rain.

Very much in line with the precepts of Stephen Graham were the exploits of Walter Starkie, Professor of Spanish at Dublin University. Starkie had his own pet theory about the wandering life, which was that to succeed in it one should travel completely without money and instead rely on some special trick or skill (though he cheated and had a few gold coins at the bottom of his knapsack). He had been impressed, when serving on the Italian front in the First World War, at the way some Hungarian prisoners had knocked up crude violins out of the wood of packing-cases, soothing national animosities with their scratchy music. As he was a violinist himself, he decided that he could play the same game. So in the long vacation of 1929 he left his wife and children in Dublin and took the train to Vienna and the Hungarian border. Starkie answered to the following description: 'A small, stocky man, broad-shouldered and thick about the girth: complexion fresh and hair fair: jaw strong, but his face chubby and double-chinned: eyes blue and in the opinion of the senoritas Nordic: eyebrows short and one twists upwards diabolically: walks with ambling gait, gets easily out of breath, rests often, laughs immoderately, drinks moderately, but prefers red wine to white: has fits of melancholy . . .' Not the recipe for a good walker, obviously. Still, with his fiddle in its case strapped over his shoulder, the plucky fellow proceeded along the highway towards Budapest.

In *Raggle-Taggle* he wrote, 'I walked heavily on my heels without any fixed rhythm and so by the time I had covered eight miles I was footsore and weary. I then remembered how a tramp had once told me that it was much easier to go on for hours and hours if one jogged forward on the point part of the feet in a shuffling gait, always keeping to the same rhythm. "Once you fall into the jog-trot," said he, "you move mechanically and feel no fatigue."' Avoiding the groups of lederhosened Austrian hikers who were also on the road he got to Budapest and continued on to the Hungarian Plain, but despite the good advice about the jog-trot (of course, he didn't mean jogging in its present sense, but a sort of bent-leg shuffle), he was not a happy walker: '. . . my heavy hobnailed boots lacerated my feet, and the weight of my rucksack and fiddle weighed me down as though I was carrying boulders.' Things looked up in the evening, however, once his boots were off. In the local brothel a girl was already dancing for him naked to the sound of his frenzied fiddling when her 'husband' unexpectedly returned and Starkie scuttled out of the window. Fiddle-playing at the local tavern earned him a comfortable billet, for the couple who put him up slept on the floor while he took their bed. Then he met the gypsies. They were a sad disappointment, so different from his romantic notion and from *Romany Rye*. This lot were thieving, filthy and degenerate. Still, he found a young gypsy called Rostas who was prepared to take him to stay in his hovel. This involved a hard walk. 'It was all I could do to keep up with the long stride of Rostas, and at last I insisted on a halt when we had walked ten kilometres.' Some days later, once again on the move, his enthusiasm for tramping was sorely tested. '"A plague on my accursed feet," thought I as I limped along the road on a broiling day feeling that every step I took led me nearer to the infernal regions. I wished I had never left the comparative comfort of Fagares with its taverns for this desert. My feet pained me, for my heavy boots caused blisters to spring up on my big toe. Now I know the reason why the Gypsies bury a good pair of boots with a corpse. They know that the dead must wander many a weary mile over burning plains as I am doing now and well-fitting boots are necessary.' It was soon time for him to resume his responsibilities in Dublin.

But a year or two later he was off again, this time in Spain, walking for most of the way along the Basque coast and then through Castile to Madrid. He took it slowly, with many a stop for a drink or a yarn; and as he walked was wont to conduct imaginary conversations, laughing and gesticulating or shaking his fist and swiping with his stick. When the sacred hour for dinner (i.e. lunch) arrived he was well ensconced in the local tavern tucking into his stew and consuming his carafe of wine, followed by coffee and anisette. This was followed by the sacred siesta, spent lying on a couch in the yard and ogling the buxom servant girls. Afterwards it was quite an effort to resume the walk and, besides, he felt maudlin. 'In the morning when I tramp through the country I feel as hard as steel and as firm a lord over myself as Julius Caesar. But towards evening I become more mellowed and more full of human kindness.' Some of the nights in the open were hell. Once, when he woke at midnight in a heavy downpour, the two sides of his character fell to arguing. The Sancho Panza side was scathing. '"Next time you go vagabonding," said he, "mind you don't forget to buy the Hiker's Annual or 'Tramping without Tears'. Why, any boy scout who has attended a jamboree would laugh you to scorn." But then my Quixotic companion answered: "Out on it, man; get thee behind me, pot-bellied Sancho: the true vagabond is no hiker who has visited Woolworths and brought all the gadgets for his tour. I am a knight-errant: I long for hardship."' And hardship he got, ending with delirium induced by double pneumonia, before he returned to his Celtic homeland.

Laurie Lee, in his book *As I Walked out one Midsummer Morning*, makes no mention of Walter Starkie; but it would be surprising if no whisper of Starkie had reached his ears, because only a few years later, in 1935, he too was off to Spain with a fiddle in his knapsack. He had impeccable qualifications, having in the previous year left his Gloucestershire home and tramped around southern England to London, playing for his supper. He had discovered the sheer pleasure of walking: 'I walked steadily, effortlessly, hour after hour, in a kind of swinging, weightless dream. I was at that age which feels neither strain nor friction, when the body burns magic fuels, so that it seems to glide in warm air, about a foot off the ground, smoothly obeying its intentions.' And he had even fallen in with real professional tramps, such as Alf, who made an annual grand tour of the home counties before holding court in a London doss-house for the winter. He also passed men in shabby coats wandering the roads in search of jobs, 'like a broken army walking away from a war'. Laurie Lee, now aged twenty, landed at Vigo and immediately proceeded on a great tramp, first eastwards to Madrid, then south to Cadiz, then east to Malaga. Initially the heat was terrible but, like a true mad dog of an English-

145

man, he walked on under the midday sun. The hills of Galicia provided some relief, but once he reached the valley of the Douro the contest was unremitting as he plodded along straight white dust roads between prairies of shimmering wheat, the albicant colouring broken only by the scarlet of the poppies. 'I felt I was treading the rim of a burning wheel, kicking it behind me step by step, feet scorched and blistered, yet not advancing an inch, pinned forever at this sweltering spot.' Next day the self-imposed torture was resumed: 'I walked on as though keeping a vow, till I was conscious only of the hot red dust grinding like pepper between my toes.' (He had wisely abandoned his hobnailed boots in Zamora in favour of sandals.) This was the immediate prelude to delirium, and Laurie Lee was fortunate in being lifted on to Valladolid by car. In fact his tramp was punctuated by several lifts in carts or cars, but by far the greater part was walked, and walked strongly. 'At first I'd hobbled, but my blisters had hardened and at last I could walk without pain. I developed a long loping stride which covered some twenty miles a day, an easy monotonous pace – slightly faster than the mule-trains strung along the route, though slower than trotting asses.' By the time he reached the Costa del Sol he was caught up in the skirmishes which preceded the outbreak of the Spanish Civil War.

A whiff of impending political doom could likewise be detected in Germany in 1933 after the Nazi seizure of power, and in December of that year another English boy took a tramp into Europe. Patrick Leigh Fermor had actually been sacked from King's School Canterbury for flirting with the girl in the sweet shop. He was a natural rebel and daredevil, and his life later assumed heroic proportions when as a British agent in Crete he personally kidnapped the general commanding the German occupation force. Sitting morosely in a bed-sitter in Shepherds' Market, he was feeling completely at a loose end when suddenly, reproached by the strains of 'Lazybones' from the gramophone in the room below, he found inspiration: he would walk to Constantinople! This snap decision led him towards a life of adventure and is the subject of his book *A Time of Gifts*, one of the most brilliant descriptions of a journey afoot in the tramping tradition. A common experience of eighteen-year-olds who go on long adventurous journeys is that they start as a boy and end as a man, and this was certainly what Patrick Leigh Fermor found. The whole journey was financed on an initial loan of fifteen pounds and a weekly allowance of one pound, mailed to postes restantes at places such as

Munich and Vienna. From the loan he bought a rucksack and an ash-plant and a passport and was off. The passport described him as a student and this designation opened many doors, easing his way through the Netherlands and Germany. Besides, there still remained a respect for foot-travellers: in many towns, on presenting themselves to the Burgermeister and showing their credentials, they could get a bed for the night and bread and coffee before moving on next morning. Being English also helped on balance, for though there were instances of insult or aggression most Germans had a grudging respect for their island cousins: it was the French they really hated. But none of this would have seen him through had it not been for his personal charm and iron nerve. These led him into lovely situations where he could savour the nuances of German society and character in a way which no English diplomats or journalists of the day could possibly have done. We see him swearing *blutbrüdershaft* with two of the roughest toughest bargees on the Rhine. In the Ruhr he drank with the brownshirts and, when one of them gave him a bed for the night in his family home, saw for himself in simple human terms the basis of the Nazi sweep to power: the communist banners were stacked away in the attic, for the young man had switched to the winning side! On the grander side of the coin he spent two nights with a couple of girls in a smart apartment in Stuttgart when the parents were away and went with them in a chauffeur-driven car to a dinner party wearing his walking clothes, the object of much suspicion. In Bavaria and Austria he was entertained in castles as well as dossing down in cow byres.

Unfortunately Patrick Leigh Fermor does not give detailed information about his actual walking experiences. Apart from when towns are mentioned he doesn't give his daily stages or distances. He admits that he did not walk all the way but did take lifts, besides sailing up the Rhine from Cologne to Coblenz in a barge. However, 'I despised lifts and I had a clear policy about them: to avoid them rigorously, that is, until walking became literally intolerable; and then, to travel no further than a day's march would cover.' This does, of course, slightly beg the question as to what the proposed day's march was pitched at: if lifts were to be accepted towards the end of the day when walking became intolerable one could more readily aim for a town 25 miles off than say 15 miles. Still, by far the greater part of the 2000-mile journey was walked, and indeed if it had not been so and he had merely hitch-hiked an essential element of his odyssey would have been missing: he would not have been quite the authentic figure of a wanderer, and people – rich and poor – would have been less keen to help him. One reason why the author of *A Time of Gifts* is unforthcoming about his muscle-aches and blister-boils and foot-sores and frost-bites is that when he arrived at the Salvation Army hostel in Munich his rucksack, containing all his copious travel notes as well as his passport, was stolen. So was his ash-plant covered with a score of *stocknagels*, the little curved aluminium plaques which pro-vided a proud memento of the towns passed through. Still, we have short glimpses of him on the road. As a scholar and a romantic he had a wide repertoire. 'On straight stretches of road where the scenery changed slowly, singing often came to the rescue; and when songs ran short, poetry.' The Germans could readily appreciate song, but the recitation of poetry was not understood at all. 'Murmuring on the highway caused raised eyebrows and looks of anxious pity. Passages uttered with gestures and sometimes quite loud provoked, if one was caught in the act, stares of alarm.' Between Munich and Vienna he often left the highway when heading for the hospitable castles and walked across the frozen snow-covered countryside. 'I travelled on footpaths and over stiles and across fields and along country roads that ran through dark woods and out again into the white ploughland and pasture . . . I lost my way now and then through misunderstanding instructions at a farm or a cottage; sometimes dialect or lack of teeth or the wind had garbled them.'

After a few weeks of rest and recuperation in Vienna and Prague he was on his way again down the Danube basin. Spring was in the air. 'The dry paths had turned my boots and puttees white with dust. The empty sky was the clear blue of a bird's egg and I was walking in my shirt sleeves for the first time. Slower and slower, however: a nail in one of my boots had mutinied.' The next day, his nail duly knocked back by a cobbler, he proceeded along the Slovakian bank of the Danube by lonely paths through the reeds in 'a world of scales and webbed feet and feathers and wet whiskers'. Night fell, but it was still warm. 'Then I understood, with sudden elation, that my first and longed-for night in the open had arrived.' It was a moment of rapture. 'The notion that I had walked twelve hundred miles since Rotterdam filled me with a legitimate feeling of something achieved.' But hardly was he asleep than he was arrested by border guards on the suspicion of being Black Joseph, a notorious smuggler of, of all things, sac-charin. This slur soon effaced, he crossed next day into Hungary in time to attend the Easter service in the cathedral of Esztergom. A religious curiosity affected Patrick Leigh Fermor, and after he had reached Constantinople he headed for the Orthodox monasteries of Mount Athos: though his winter journey through Europe was by no means a pilgrimage but far more a voyage of liberation, of self-discovery, of joyous wandering, such as we think of when listening to Schubert's song 'Das Wandern'.

Of course, Patrick Leigh Fermor and Laurie Lee were not the only teenage tramps keeping right on to the ends of the roads of Europe in the 1930s. There were several others, though few were capable of describing their journeys interestingly. They tended to be middle-class public- or grammar-school boys making active use of their summer holidays. But they were still something of a rarity, and then the war and national service put strict restraints on their freedom of time and movement. It was only in the 1960s that the Jet Age, coupled with various forms of unemployment – temporary or permanent – released the numberless hordes of youthful backpackers on to airports all over the world. Not all of them are tramps, let alone walkers; but hidden among them are those who are the inheritors of the manner of tramping of Leigh Fermor or Knight. Even now they are wandering around Third-World countries, moving from village to village and staying in the houses of the peasants. They comprise a far wider spectrum of types and attitudes than even Stephen Graham could possibly have imagined, ranging from the inward-looking hirsute hippies to the clean-cut voluntary workers in medicine or agriculture, as well as the straight travellers.

Very much in the tradition of a tramp with a mission, however, and one which Gorky would have well understood, was the walk of Peter Jenkins from the University of Alfred, New York, to New Orleans in 1973–5. Peter Jenkins was a victim of his time. His college marriage had lasted only a few months and he was obsessed by the sense of helplessness felt in post-Vietnam USA. He decided on graduation not to go for a job but to walk across the country in an attempt to find the true heart of America, to meet the people. He would work his way and refuse to accept money as charity. His companion would be his dog, Cooper, an Alaskan Malamite. He took his training seriously for this foot-venture, walking and running for several weeks in a fitness programme, and then he walked out of the campus to the farewells of family and friends. Well, he made it, and *A Walk Across America* became a bestseller. He made it and more: for having trudged every yard of the 1900-odd miles to New Orleans over a period of eighteen months and between a succession of temporary jobs, he met Barbara and, now fortified by a dedicated wife and an evangelistic sense of purpose, walked on with her for 3000 miles more northwestward to the coast of Oregon in 1976–9. But not with Cooper, who got run over in Georgia. By doing it all on foot he was emphasising the need to get back to basics, to forge real human relationships – something which is hard to do from the facile mobility of a car and impossible through the television screen. Though often thought to be a drug-peddling hippy or an undercover agent, and hounded out of Robbinsville, North Carolina, as a hobo, he triumphed over hostility and touched a chord in the hearts of many who had never walked so much as a mile.

Meanwhile many unsung heroes have kept up the great tradition of English eccentricity in suddenly dropping sticks and tramping across the land, and many amusing incidents relate to them. Christopher Bonn, then a lieutenant in the Welsh Guards, decided to tramp across France on a pilgrimage to Rome. He was only a few days out when, seeking a bed for the night, he espied an immense château at the end of a long avenue. Greatly daring, he strode up and rang the bell. Although he refused to give his name and was referred to only as *le pèlerin inconnu* he was received with honour, and when the house party assembled for the formal dinner, served by butler and footmen, they were all dressed in their oldest, tattiest garden clothes so as not to make him feel out of place. Peregrine Eliot, a Cornish landowner, recently trudged in outdated hob-nail boots towards London, his hair close-cropped and his eyes fixed to the ground. Somewhere in Somerset he was overtaken by a gypsy on a horse-drawn cart, who stopped and, handing him fifty pence, confided sympathetically, 'I've been this way too, brother.' For in tramping nowadays the possibilities for curious social encounters are as wide as they ever were in the past. And, amazing as it may seem, there are still people of all sorts in modern life who bear an instinctive respect towards true wanderers, in conformity with the biblical precept: 'Be not forgetful to entertain strangers: for thereby some have entertained angels unawares.'

Ramblers

THE pleasures of cross-country walking, which had been rediscovered by the professional classes, were destined in time to be enjoyed by ever-widening social groups and ever-growing numbers of men and women. One thing they all shared in common, from the don in his quadrangle to the factory-worker in his slum, was that they were urban dwellers whose lives had become divorced from the country-side. Meanwhile those who did live in the country were becoming antipathetic to the age-old habit of walking. Carts, trains, buses and, finally, cars increased their own mobility; and besides, they were suspicious of the strange townsfolk who came to walk over their local footpaths which were otherwise becoming disused in their original function. The farmers felt ever more assertive about the rights of property, and by the end of the last century virtually all the farmland in England had become enclosed. The country gentlemen had admittedly come to recognise in walking an acceptable form of leisure activity but it was only tolerated by them among their friends so long as it in no way threatened their preoccupation with bloodsports – shooting, hunting, as well as fishing. To the average squire the likes of Leslie Stephen were on the whole mistrusted and even despised: they were intellectuals, they were landless, they did not conform to the image of John Bull. To the large landowners the more brilliant of the intellectuals might be acceptable as guests but would have been made to feel very out of place if by some mischance they had been staying during a shooting party. (As did happen once in Norfolk, when the botanist Reginald Farrer, a keen Alpine walker, was so ignored by the other men and so bored by their tedious reminiscences of the day's pheasant-slaughter when sitting lengthily over the port after dinner, that he caused a sensation by leaving the dining-room abruptly and joining the ladies assembled in the drawing-room, announcing lugubriously to his hostess, 'They don't seem to want me in there, so I think I'll be happier in here.')

The inherent conflict between the landed and the landless flared into a series of skirmishes and battles in a war which is not ended yet. From these clashes have emerged a number of folk heroes, of whom two – of utterly differing background and separated by nearly a century – may be briefly cited. The 'Battle of Glen Tilt' occurred when J. H. Balfour, Professor of Botany at Edinburgh University, led seven of his students on a long march of 30 miles from Braemar to Blair Atholl across the Grampians in August 1847. His purpose was to establish the route down Glen Tilt as a right of way by provoking a confrontation with the irascible landowner, the Duke of Atholl, who disputed it. The plan succeeded beautifully for there was a scuffle during which the Duke seized one of them by the collar of his coat and attempted to force him back, refusing to listen to anything he had to say. The party was obliged to wait till nightfall before proceeding down the glen. Balfour's ensuing letter to *The Times* provoked a loud anti-ducal rumble from the Thunderer, and after some litigation the right of way was secured. Eighty-five years later, in April 1932, Bernard Rothman, on behalf of the British Workers Sports Federation, organised a mass trespass on Kinder Scout in Derbyshire along the William Clough path. Several hundred people followed him, and on their return the police arrested Rothman and five others. Rothman was less fortunate than Balfour for he felt the full force of the law with a prison sentence; and indeed public opinion was not behind him, because he was a Communist, and the trespass had been condemned by the Manchester Ramblers' Federation. But the event did at least serve to concentrate attention on the access issue and fifteen years later Kinder Scout, that peaty plateau, was opened to all.

Though Balfour and Rothman shared a common purpose they represented very different attitudes towards walking in the country, exemplified by the disparate numbers who accompanied them on their trespasses. In contrast to the romantics who sought inspiration from their walks or the intellectuals who through walking soothed their souls or sharpened their wits, the new type of walker tended towards using the walk as a means of obtaining good fellowship and camaraderie. There were a number of reasons for this difference in approach. For ordinary men and women life was more restricted: to join a walking club provided a new opening for social contact outside the confines of their immediate family, church or work grouping. They all wanted to go walking at the same time, on a Sunday: even Saturday was difficult until the arrival of the five-day week. Besides, the countryside was fraught with perils for them: how could they find the way on their own, let alone get to the starting point?; how could they respond to angry gamekeepers or officious guardians of the law? Many of them saw the country as if it were a heritage from which they had been dispossessed when their grandfathers had drifted away from the villages towards the dark satanic mills. Rather like the prisoners in Beethoven's opera *Fidelio*, they could be released from their grim confines for a few hours to enjoy the sun. Whilst this image was indeed true in the darkest days of the industrial revolution (for example, it was noted in 1833 that some twenty thousand people used to pass over the river from Liverpool into Cheshire on a Sunday to enjoy a stroll), it was not so relevant to those who, for want of a better description, might be termed lower-middle-class and who, with rather more leisure and surplus energy than they would have enjoyed in previous decades, were the main recruits to the rambling clubs.

At this point it is necessary to note the introduction of the word 'rambler' as denoting a walker in the countryside. We have seen how 'pedestrian' had given way to 'tramp', but both had their special associations. It was all very well for Sir Leslie Stephen or Lord Haldane to call themselves 'tramps' in the sure knowledge that no one would really take them for such, but the likes of Mr Pooter of The

Laurels, Holloway, were haunted by the thought that Farmer Brown might indeed mistake them for vagrants and set the dogs on them. Some fresh word was needed, something which emphasised the respectability of the townsfolk who took to the fields, something which indicated also a certain sense of continuity with the past when people moved more freely across the land. The word was already there: since the seventeenth century 'to ramble' had been in common use as meaning an act of walking without a definite route, for pleasure or recreation. 'Rambler' was additionally distinguished by having been the name of Dr Johnson's periodical, in the context of a wandering discourse. Unfortunately by the twentieth century the word was less commonly used and was being challenged by an import from America – 'hiker'. A hiker had previously meant someone who raises or lifts something, but somehow had got transferred to one who decamps or moves on, and hence to one who walks for pleasure. The Ramblers, in their clubs and associations, never liked being referred to as 'hikers' because they were faithful to the older word and also wanted to distance themselves from the more brash and abrasive types who, as we shall see, began to roam around more independently and were known as hikers. But the press and the public were never much concerned about these niceties and an overlap between the two has continued ever since. It is interesting to speculate on whether some other word would have stuck better than 'rambler'; a word more in common usage, such as 'rover', 'roamer' or 'wanderer'.

It is generally accepted that the first rambling club in England was that founded in 1879 by Leslie Stephen and known as the Sunday Tramps. It may at first seem strange that the cultivated and fastidious Stephen should have wanted to form a rambling club rather than to go for walks alone or with just a single chosen friend: one suspects that at times his solitary nature was sorely bruised by the hearty and jocular banter of his group. The explanation must surely be that any such disadvantages were outweighed by the fascination and satisfaction of planning and executing the route. And besides, he covered himself by being extremely selective in whom he would admit into the circle, for it was not a 'club' in the correct sense of the word, with members who could vote, but merely a list controlled by him and consisting of about sixty gentlemen who were nearly all Oxbridge-educated, distinguished and literary. Each was known by his joining number: for instance Stephen was number 1; Robert Bridges, number 16; and Richard Haldane, number 36. The plan was to go for a walk of 14–20 miles in the country around London every other Sunday for about eight months of the year. When the first group of Sunday Tramps disbanded in 1895 they had held two hundred and fifty-two walks. Until 1891 Stephen was in absolute command. It was he who decided each route and summoned the others by means of cryptic postcards, announcing also the trains on which they would travel after careful study of the Ordnance Survey and Bradshaw's Railway Guide. Usually only about ten turned up but, as may be imagined with such a keen-minded group, conversation was wide-ranging and stimulating and with a heavy emphasis on philosophy. Stephen, known as the 'Chief Guide', often kept his thoughts to himself, interrupting the others only to debunk their theories with some sardonic remark muttered through his beard. But when he chose to talk, preferably alone with one other, he was well worth listening to. They stopped for beer and sandwiches at a pub, though sometimes lunched at the houses of friends. On one such occasion he was observed to remain entirely silent during lunch, only to rise up hurriedly at the end of it and say imperiously to the hostess, 'Come, I must sweep these fellows away', at which they all dutifully filed out to resume their walk. Another host was George Meredith, a great admirer of Stephen who was the inspiration for the character of Vernon Whitford in *The Egoist*; but although a keen walker, he forbore to join the Tramps. The Sunday Tramps' favourite stomping-grounds were the Chilterns and the North Downs and they tried to keep off roads and penetrate public footpaths. They were also prepared to trespass, and to deal with troublesome gamekeepers they memorised the following formula which they would solemnly deliver as if they were a chorus of magistrates: 'We hereby give you notice that we do not, nor doth any of us, claim any right of way or other easement into or over these lands and we tender you this shilling by way of amends.' It sometimes worked.

By the time of the outbreak of the First World War there were scores of rambling clubs in the London area alone. Closely following the formation of the Sunday Tramps there had been the Forest Ramblers Club and the Polytechnic Rambling Club. Then came an ever-growing army, whose names bear a delightful suggestiveness of their special outlooks or interests. As against many church clubs there was the Heathen Rambling Club; and as against the St Pancras Liberal and Radical Rambling Club there was the Harringay Conservative Al-Frescoes. There were the Old Krocks of Honor Oak Park, the Ivy

Ramblers, the Kent Krawlers, and the Rambling Clubs of the Footpads, the Polydipsians and the Twinkling Rinkers; plus many local
photographic and naturalist rambling clubs. Eventually all were
destined to be subsumed under the Southern Federation of Rambling
Clubs, whose *Ramblers' Handbooks* tell us much about these group
walkers. Besides the primary and everlasting involvement in all
aspects of access to the countryside, one of their main preoccupations
was with rail fares, particularly on the issue of cheap day-return
tickets on Sundays which would allow the return from another station
or even another line; and by 1928 most of the railway companies
offered such 'go as you please' tickets, and there was even a Railway
Clearing House Rambling Club.

They were also very concerned about attire. The men were keen to
wear their loose-fitting Norfolk suits with knickerbockers and long
stockings; the ladies, skirts whose lengths retreated progressively
upwards. (Clothing was a real problem for women walkers until the
short skirt became generally acceptable. Long skirts could be managed on level roads or paths, though were always a prey to dirt: as
Mary Mitford had written long before, 'Woe to white gowns! Woe to
black! Drab was your only wear.' But when it came to rough ground or
hill walking, they were a severe handicap. Two devices were used:
one, to wear bloomers and have a light skirt which could be slipped
over when decorum demanded; the other, to have a series of rings and
strings by which the long skirts could be hitched to calf level.) The
men's shoes were usually of stout leather but the ladies often wore
moccasins, shin-high lace-up boots of soft leather. By the 1930s the
universality of leather soles was giving way to rubber, and Phillips
placed this advertisement in the *Ramblers' Handbook*: 'Funnily
enough, it was Sammy – we *used* to call him Sammy the Snail – who
introduced us to Phillip's Soles and Heels. One day, instead of trailing
along behind as usual, he set us all a rare pace, created a new record for
the day's hike, and finished up fresh as paint. Then he showed us his
shoes, fitted with Phillips. Naturally we all wear them now. No more
aching feet! No more waterlogged shoes!' Sticks were also the objects
of much discussion – crook handle versus knob?, ash versus hazel?,
metal- or wooden-tipped?, thick or thin? The clubs also carefully
studied lists of pubs and hotels as hikes of two or more days became
more usual. They began to grade their walks so as to sort out the
stronger from the weaker, for several of the members were there for
the fun rather than the walking and might even have doubted the

wisdom of the aphorism, ''Tis better to have walked and ached than never to have walked at all.'

But more than anything it was social matters that exercised their minds. Should the club accept women members? Should the ramble wait till after the church service on Sunday, or skip church? How to arrange its social evenings? How to relate to the locals at the bar of the country pub? Walking was an activity which brought out surprising facets in people's characters: it robbed the opinionated of their prejudices and ingrained habits, it released the shy from their inhibitions. E. V. Lucas wrote a charming piece fantasising on shoes which took people unwillingly to where they didn't want to go. The vicar is walked to the pub, and held fast to the bar; the publican to the most conspicuous pew in the church; the old spinster to the bachelor's door; and the author himself is portrayed as a recluse who, when he puts on his walking boots, is affected by 'an inability to resist the seductive call of footpaths', those wayward and capricious threads. But the writer who best portrays the social niceties of the Edwardian country walkers is A. H. Sidgwick in his book *Walking Essays*.

Sidgwick is completely unconcerned about the beauties of nature but tortuously agonised about social conventions. In the first place there is the eternal problem of walking and talking. He comes down firmly against any intellectual conversation and will only allow talk that is about the walk itself or things like one's boots, the weather, or places passed. It is his view that by these prosaic themes walkers will really get to know each other better, especially those of the opposite sex. 'They will learn the value of pauses, of silence, of ejaculations, even of grunts. Their bodies will be full occupied, and will shake and settle down the contents of their brains into good solid dogmatisms and prejudices purely spontaneous and characteristic of themselves, the stones on which intimacy can be built.' This healthy intimation of married life seems to him a reason for arguing that a good country walk is the best way for boy meets girl, and he deplores that convention has now abandoned the old country custom of 'walking out' in favour of dances where white-tied men date long-dressed girls with *carnets de bal*. How much better, he feels, if Mrs Y were to give a matchmaking walk instead of a matchmaking dance where everything – the dress, the surrounds, the conversation – is all so artificial and such a false prelude to marriage! In fact he reveals that Mrs Y vented her fury on his friend X when she learnt that the 'previous engagement' that had prevented him from accepting an invitation to tea with her daughters was merely that he had arranged to go for a walk with Sidgwick. All the same, Sidgwick does not advocate walking only for matchmaking. It is also an excellent way for all ages to meet, and on the walk the old should be listened to with respect 'for the sixtieth year is like the eighteenth mile'.

It was a feature of the ramblers that they used frequently to break into song, and if that seems strange nowadays it must be remembered that they had far less received music in their lives. To sing as one walked, especially when beyond the earshot of houses, was quite normal, and not only for the rambling groups. There were echoes of military marches and an established repertoire of old favourites such as 'One Man and his Dog', 'Green Grow the Rushes O', 'Ten Green Bottles', and of course 'John Brown's Body' sung over and over, each time with a note off the end, till at the twenty-first repeat it was completely silent apart from '. . . but his soul goes marching on' – by which time 1344 paces, or around three-quarters of a mile, had been covered. The *Ramblers' Handbooks* contain many rambling songs, such as 'The Foot-Traveller's Song' which begins:

> On foot I gaily make my way,
> > Hurrah!
> O'er mountains bare and meadows gay,
> > Hurrah!
> And he who is not of my mind,
> Another travelling mate may find
> > Hurrah! tra la la la la.

On this aspect of walking Sidgwick is also most illuminating. In his judgement walking has a potent connection with music. 'The theme which sounded hard and obscure takes on a new meaning as it pulsates to the rhythm of the stride: obscurity reveals hidden purposes and possibilities of melody; hardness becomes strength; and the whole sinks gratefully into the minor parts of the walker's consciousness where music abides beside the springs of thought and action.' He has even discovered the quintessential piece of walking music: it is the Allegro of Beethoven's Seventh Symphony. 'There is the song of walking, the sacred music of our craft. The rhythm (♪♫) is the exact measure of the stride, buoyant and elastic, with the uneven note marking the hoist of the outside leg from the hip.' (Here he has hit on a point unnoticed by Ruskin, that 6:8 time can provide an added zest and lilt helpful to walking, as a change from the customary 4:4 time of marching music.) This close association with music also provides Sidgwick with a very effective definition of what constitutes a good walking style. 'A proper stride is not a gift of the gods; it can be cultivated, increased in ease and length, made a more useful servant. There is no little difference at the end of the day between the walker who can move his feet lithely and delicately, making a rhythmic bar of each stride, and the walker who hoists them up anyhow and lets them fall with a bang, like instruments of percussion.' Another question which Sidgwick probes is whether walking for pleasure is a sport or just a recreation. His view is that it is not a sport, mainly because it is not competitive. Generally speaking this still holds good, depending on how you define 'sport' and whether you like to be thought sporty. On the other hand he was anxious to distance himself from what he took to be Wordsworth's 'mystical communion' with the countryside, emphasising that a naturalistic intimacy can only be gained by exhaustive walking. Since Wordsworth walked far faster and further than Sidgwick this slur is unjustified: but the author of *Walking Essays* was not the only twentieth-century person to have misjudged Words-worth as a walker and to think of him vaguely wandering lonely as a cloud whilst never having read the grist and grit of 'The Prelude'.

The formation of rambling clubs was accompanied by the appear-ance of walking guides, a form of literature that has since exploded but was then a tentative novelty. In the days of road walking there had been little need to describe the route, so guidebooks had concentrated on descriptions of places passed. With the shift towards cross-country walking there came a demand for routes across the intricate and enclosed farmland of England, written in as clear and concise a manner as possible. Maps could help a bit, but the old Ordnance Survey inch to the mile did not show footpaths or rights of way. The man who first exploited this demand was Edmund Taylor who issued the earliest of his *Field-Path Rambles* booklets in 1892 under the pseudonym Walker Miles. Taylor was a modest and retiring man with an impediment of speech who devoted his spare hours to this new-found enthusiasm. His technique was to select an area and then methodically walk over all the principal paths so as to choose with confidence long-distance routes of maximum quality, most of them circular. His booklets contained no maps, just text, and the first covered the neighbourhood of Bromley in Kent. Before his death in 1908 he had produced over thirty more, covering areas of Surrey and

Sussex. They were immensely popular with the rambling groups, so much so that at Godstone there was a 'Walker Miles tea house' at a point where half a dozen of his designated walks converged, and copies of his guides could be bought there for sixpence or a shilling. Undoubtedly his dedicated work rescued hundreds of rights of way from disappearance. Those who since his day have written walking guides will be the first to appreciate the tribute to Taylor paid by the inimitable Sidgwick and redolent of scenes in *Pilgrim's Progress*:

> He himself has gone to return no more, and only his works remain. But I like to think that somewhere on the Elysian plain, where prophet and hero and poet tread together down the well-worn paths, a single figure quests somewhat aside, writing words of gold upon an ivory tablet as he goes. 'Continuing on past the Happy Groves take the well-marked track to the right, but at the third clump of asphodel note a grassy track diverging to the left, and follow this until it leads into an open space covered with amarinth and moly.'

North of the Trent, in that other wilder part of England, the characteristics of the ramblers and their clubs earlier this century were predictably different from those in the south. Not merely did the open moors of the Pennines offer a different sort of walking experience from the hedgerows of the home counties, but the men and women who walked on them were, one feels, of an altogether stronger stamp. The early Old Printers' Devils of Glasgow and Edinburgh were soon supplemented by such clubs as the Liverpool Hobnailers, the Birmingham C.H.A. Ramblers and the authoritative Manchester Rambling Club. But the most outstanding were the Sheffield Clarion Ramblers, due to their remarkable founder and all-powerful honorary secretary, G. H. B. Ward. To hear his voice on the subject of walking after listening to Sidgwick is like putting down a book by Jane Austen and picking up one by Charlotte Brontë.

George Herbert Bridges Ward (Bert to his immediate friends but G. H. B. Ward to everyone else) was born in Sheffield in 1876, the son of a mechanic. He was originally set to work as a repair fitter and tool maker on day and night shifts of twelve hours each during which he was never permitted to sit down for as much as ten minutes. However, in his early twenties he was left some money which enabled him to leave his job and he went for a while to the Canary Islands where he learnt Spanish. Back in Sheffield he started a new career as a government officer, labour adviser and socialist leader. In 1900, the year he married, he founded the Sheffield Clarion Ramblers, so called because a local newspaper, the *Sheffield Clarion*, published the initial advertisement, placed in it by Ward entirely on his own behalf, for others to join him for a ramble on Kinder Scout on 3 September. Thirteen turned up (ten men and three ladies) and Ward led them on a route up Jacob's Ladder and by Edale Cross to Hayfield; then over by the head of Ashop Clough to the Snake Inn, where they consumed cakes, boiled ham and tea for one and threepence each. Following this, the club was formed. A description of him about this time reads as follows: 'He had a brown tweed coat and breeches on. A brown sweater – and untidy stockings; thick, strong nailed climbing boots, and his face was unlike his clothing, for it had a sweetness about it that was good to see. His thick black hair was tousled about by wind and rain, the silver streaks in it shone in the bright sunlight that betokened rain in the near future.' He had piercing dark eyes.

In 1910 the first of the club's handbooks appeared: Ward was not only the editor but wrote most of the copy as well, and continued to do so till his death in 1957. His writing reveals him as a born leader and a deep romantic, who was as completely satisfied with ruling the hearts and minds of the Sheffield Clarion Ramblers as was Napoleon with leading the French Army. 'Come walk with me through the black December night; for the wild west wind is blowing clean and through; and the clouds are flying a few feet overhead – but far too fast to spend themselves in tears. And, for once, come and see where the stars have lowered themselves, yea; into the lights of the windows in the valley far below.' A standard notice in all the handbooks under the heading 'Hints to Leaders' made clear that the fixture must take place wet or fine. The leader must wear a distinctive badge and appoint a 'whipper-in'. He must also provide background information, make arrangements for tea, and 'see that some song is sung during the day'. Ward reserved the sterner fixtures for himself, and was quite explicit about who he did and did not want; for example in the notice for the Revellers' Ramble in January 1929:

Train (L. & N.E.): 6.38 a.m. to Glossop; return Bamford 8.27 p.m.
Train fare 3/10
Route: to be decided

Leader: *G. H. B. Ward*

We go, wet or fine, snow or blow, and none but the bravest and fittest must attempt this walk. Those who are unwell, unfit, inexperienced, or insufficiently clad should consult their convenience, and that of their friends, by staying at home. Ladies on this occasion are requested not to attend. The ramble is not estimated by mileage, but by the amount of stamina you possess.

Or take another notice, this time for a Midnight Ramble in 1922:

All ramblers should bring spirit lamp or kettle and provisions sufficient for four hunter's meals. Those who cannot expend an amount of exertion sufficient to cover 35 miles of good walking, without suffering from exhaustion, must stay at home, and only the strongest men and women must attend these rambles.

The January Revellers' Rambles were long remembered. Ward's description for another year tells how twenty-three were gathered, 'including hefty Thorpe and his friend from Barnsley, and hearty Herdman from Manchester', on a 'jolly morn; hard frost, three inches of snow, and a fiery sunrise'. Soon they were up on the watershed 'over the powdery snow and frozen peat and heather; and every lad had a fall some time and a laugh in turn – and sometimes crushed through the ice and gave a bath to his feet.' No lunch was to be had at the Bull or the Rocking Stones, but on they went, eyebrows and moustaches hung with beads of ice, and finally 'conquerors all, we came down the valley, and padded the snow to Lady Bowes and a good meal and a song.' We may be sure that Ward was at the van, leading the way with his regular and relentless long-legged stride, and singing snatches from Schubert *lieder* when the spirit moved him. From the experiences of this sort of day he composed the following:

We are the lads who dare to go through the pelting sleet or the driving snow; and we don't say nay on a Revellers' Day when its over the moors and far away. So we leave our girls in the smoky town and we scamper o'er the moorland brown. Six days with the devil are six days in town, but its one with Heaven on the moorland brown. We steal no grouse, we seek no soil; they've got the land – by work or spoil. But come a day soon or come a day long, the gamekeeper shall sing this song –

Come to the moorland, come with me,
Compass and map is the moorland key;
And the man goes home who cries enough
When he sees a fog, or a peaty grough.

Rambling, for Ward, was a way of life, a 'culture and a craft', which embodied patriotism and humanism. In later years he experienced moods of disillusion, despite the victories of socialism and of access for which he had worked so effectively. He deplored the thought that the fells were becoming full of walkers, even in winter (so different from when he had trudged alone for 60 miles in four days in the snow-covered Lancashire moors one Christmas – encountering absolutely no one on the hills), and that the ordinary people were becoming dependent on motor cars. He could not abide the serious dead-pan approach of the younger members of the club. Resignedly he wrote 'To the Clarion Ramblers' Old Brigade':

We're growing old, and we're going slow,
But we still can face the winds that blow.
And come what may, and, bless that day,
These words to our young men we'll say:
   You number fifty where we were one;
   Your days begin when ours have done.
   Walk hard, work harder, till law has moved,
   A Rambler made is a man improved.

Despite the Harringay Conservative Al-Frescoes the ramblers in both north and south were predominantly of the political left and particularly the Labour Party. So it is appropriate that the first Labour Prime Minister, Ramsay MacDonald, should have been an ardent walker who has left us his thoughts on the subject in his autobiographical *Wanderings and Excursions*. His is very much the same approach as G. H. B. Ward's – warm-hearted, even passionate. 'Have you ever walked on the hills along which the rain wracks scud like mighty regiments of cavalry, whipping, lashing, piercing you to the skin, with the sun following after turning the charge to a rout, the track of which you can follow by the black shadows fleeing across hill and dale, wood and moor? If not, you do not know what it is to live.' Writing at the age of fifty-three he rejoices that he can still do 30 miles a day without feeling it too much, thus proving himself a more powerful walker than

Mr Gladstone at the same age. He recalls walks in the hills around Loch Katrine and the Cairngorms, sometimes with children, sometimes alone, for 'let no man think that he has possessed this happiness to the full till he can walk alone with his own thoughts and songs'. He seems to have taken every possible opportunity to go for walks in the hills; for instance, walking with political colleagues across the moors to a socialist think-tank at Craven, armed with 'walking-sticks, knapsacks, hob-nailed boots and UDC principles and problems'. On another occasion, after addressing a miners' rally, he played truant from his duties at the House of Commons to disappear into the Trossachs for a few energetic days. Of the precious appetite of wanderlust he writes:

> It makes him keep in his cupboard a friendly old suit of comfortable wear that has paled under the fervent eye of the sun, and been matured by dust and mud and rain, and with that, a pair of honest boots nailed like the oak door of an ancient keep which of themselves direct one's way o'er moor and fell and bog and bypath away from the offence and clamour of cars and trains; it saves his soul from being lost in the vain attempt to keep itself alive by indulging in the vices of the smart or the flashy vanities of those to whom the jewels of life are paste or gloss; it keeps his windows open to the winds of heaven and his heart to the song of birds.

All this makes fine reading, but sadly Ramsay MacDonald lost his position as leader of the Parliamentary Labour Party in part by 'indulging in the vices of the smart' and in part because of his romantic and wandering spirit. The reins of power passed to others, but at least there were many who kept up the practice of regularly going for long walks, such as Hugh Dalton and Michael Foot. Besides, it became politically significant, and by the time Labour came to power again in 1945 there was a pent-up demand for reform in the laws of access, resulting in the Act of 1949. Hugh Dalton and Barbara Castle were seen to their political advantage when they stomped sections of the Pennine Way during the Whitsun recess. The political left was additionally fortified by folk memories of walking used for political protest, such as the march of the unemployed from Jarrow to Westminster in 1931, and stretching back in revolutionary tradition to the mass walk of the mob from Paris to Versailles in 1789 to capture the King and Queen.

Mention must also be made of C. E. M. Joad, head of the Department of Philosophy at Birkbeck College and famous for his participation in the wartime radio's Brains Trust. Though not a great walker (his experience was confined to middle-aged rambles in Surrey and Bucks and his loyalty to it was split with riding), he made some percipient points on the subject. *The Untutored Townsman's Invasion of the Country* is a pretty self-explanatory title to a book in which he warns that hordes of hikers will destroy the very thing they love unless they treat it with more tenderness and respect instead of scattering it with litter and shattering it with raucous song. For him, the joys of walking consist in either walking alone 'to heal the ills of the soul', or with a good friend and with occasional talk, not of great issues of philosophy or suchlike, but of 'little things'. During the walk Joad, a convinced atheist, admits surprisingly to twinges of instinctive animism, a suspicion that spirits may lurk around in the stones and trees. He returns from the walk 'I will not say a better and nicer person, but a calmer and quieter, with a replenished fund of energy to tackle one's tasks and duties . . .' (One doubts if Joad returned quite so calmly as this on the occasions when on his walks he indulged in his sport of keeper-baiting. He loved having rows with them – as he did with everyone – and, perhaps in order to make the ultimate battle of words even more awful, kicked off with a variety of artificial approaches: the polite approach, the cringing approach, the brazen approach, the heroic approach, the ironic approach, and so on). Realistic as ever, Joad then goes on to argue that our appreciation of nature is inevitably coloured by the fact that we are not dependent on it, even though we may elect to play at being so for short periods; a point also made, as we have seen, by John Buchan.

Despite the personal predilections of these notables the main effect of the socialist mentality was to encourage group rather than solitary walking, to the extent that a communal experience was considered more desirable than a private one. Anyway, group walking came more naturally to the many who had seen military service. When they trooped across the fields in loose order and under the direction of some friendly leader and in mixed company, they experienced something of the camaraderie they had felt when in khaki, but now shed of its stern disciplines. Many also had been Boy Scouts or Girl Guides, whose activities had included walks, especially when in summer camps. But at no stage did the rambling associations, holiday fellowships or youth groups become agents for political indoctrination, as happened in

Germany. The *Deutsche Gebirge und Wanderverein* had been formed as early as 1883, and then came various youth organisations including the *Wandervogel* who flourished before the First World War. In 1933 the National Socialists took control of all this and set up an insidious indoctrination which attempted all too successfully to equate a love of nature and walking with the doctrine of might is right, as in the pervasive story of the mythical bully-boy Siegfried, himself a forest walker. Today a much higher proportion of ordinary easy-going walkers in both Britain and Germany tend to walk alone or in unorganised groups of friends or family. There are a number of reasons for this, the most obvious being extensive car-ownership, greater and more diverse leisure time, much improved means of route-finding by use of maps and guidebooks, and a more independent outlook.

Of course, group walking still continues to fulfil an essential role; and one area in which it flourishes is in overseas walking holidays and tours. In Europe, these range from simple one-centre stays in small hotels in mountain valleys with easy daily walks, through elaborate walking tours covering a wide variety of scenery each day, to mountain-walking tours involving scrambling and staying in mountain huts. Outside Europe they generally involve a trek (a newish word in the walking vocabulary, this, imported from South Africa and really meaning to travel in an ox-wagon), in which a team of porters or mules carries baggage and equipment each day to a spot where a camp is pitched. The Himalayas are the great pleasure-ground for these and, for Europeans anyway, the Himalayan trek has in a manner of speaking taken the place of the old-fashioned Sunday ramble of a century ago in offering a new dimension to life by getting one completely away from one's immediate environment, and on foot.

What is remarkable about these walking holidays is the diversity of types who go on them. The old rambling clubs by definition were full of the like-minded, similarly aged, professionally associated or politically united. Nowadays it is the great general public which responds to the brochures and ads. The clients of one Himalayan trekking operator recently included an ex-coachman, an ex-priest who at seventy sold long-invested shares to come, an excavator driver, an international telephone operator, a baby of fourteen months and an eighty-year-old, besides the more usual dentists, publishers and lawyers. Some had been lifelong members of the Alpine Club; others had never walked beyond the golf-course boundary. That these apparently incompatible types usually shake down into contented and tolerant companions must in large measure be because the walking expends their surplus energy and erodes their nervous defensiveness. It brings people to respect each other. The sight of anyone panting and sweating and yet jolly well keeping going must inspire some admiration or pity: and to understand all is to forgive all. For one pronounced feature of these modern walking parties is that nearly all the members are prepared – even anxious – to pour out their life story into any sympathetic ear. And, as Sidgwick correctly realised, where better to reveal your innermost self than on a walk? Although certainly interrupted by talk on other things, it is this uninhibited self-exposure which most distinguishes today's group walkers from those of the past. This urge to tell one's own story has been likened to Chaucer's Canterbury Pilgrims, but the comparison is incorrect: his pilgrims each merely told a good story, not their own story. Meanwhile nature is there in awe-inspiring grandeur, and the sights seen on Himalayan treks are never to be forgotten. But behind all the vivid recollections of calls before dawn with tea and hot water, of cooked breakfasts on the trail at mid-morning, of friendly villagers, deodar forests, vast panoramas and meadows of gentians, it is the physical sensation of the walking, exhausting and yet satisfying, which appeals most to the subconscious mind.

I doubt if much subconscious satisfaction rests in the minds of many who pace away on sponsored group walks. So often the course is on hard paved roads. So often the entrants are not properly shod. So often they split their guts to get it all over as quickly as possible. But worst of all, so often they are coerced into doing it unwillingly, or at best as an ordeal, with the result that if they are teenagers they vow never to go for long walks again. The same criticism applies to certain military-sponsored events where the object is to give adventure training. The organisers are so obsessive about not having any casualties that helicopters are constantly circling overhead and Land-Rovers cruising along the tracks: fine if you want to join the army but not if you want to appreciate long-distance walking. Rather different in intention, though similar in result, was the challenge issued by President Kennedy in 1963 to all able-bodied Americans to walk 50 miles over three days, on the lines of an executive order which President Theodore Roosevelt had issued to the marines in 1908. Within a few days tens of thousands of people set out, most of them trying to do it all in one day. Because of the unaccustomed effort few made it, though one who did was, predictably, Robert Kennedy. It was not in this sort of way that the great practitioners of walking began their long distances, but entirely of their own free will.

To conclude on a gentler and happier note, both sides of the Atlantic have recently seen popular nation-wide walks which have helped to boost the social and political respectability of walking. In 1980 the American Hiking Society organised a mass walk across the USA, called Hikanation. At the start several thousand dipped their hands into the Pacific and headed east, and although only a small nucleus of under a hundred walked all the way to Washington, they were constantly joined by others for short stages. The same was true of the Ramblers' Association's Jubilee Walk around England in 1985, a 2000-mile route whose continuity was personified in two admirable walkers, Michael Singleton and Heather Kent.

Backpackers

THE differences between the longer-distance walkers of today and those of the past can be probed by a close examination of the use of the backpack, for the backpack has come to assume a centrality in the walking experience that it seldom had in the past. We have seen how many forms of long-distance walking were undertaken by people who carried very little beyond the clothes they wore. The pedestrian tourers moving from inn to inn typically carried only a change of underclothes, shaving kit and a couple of books, as well as perhaps some food and drink for the day, all stuffed into a small satchel. The ramblers and others on day trips didn't even carry a satchel but just put their gloves and sandwiches into their coat pockets. Englishmen walking in poorer countries or mountainous areas always assumed there would be others to carry their loads for them, and this is how it still is on luxury trekking holidays in the Himalayas or the Andes. But even when walkers did need to carry heavy loads the weight on their back was often peripheral to their general outlook and their expectation of the walk, a burden which had to be borne with the resignation of a mule or a donkey. This was true not only of soldiers but also of various voluntary walkers, such as the tramps of the Stephen Graham tradition or the walkers in mountains and hills who increasingly dispensed with porters and guides. John Ball, the first editor of the *Alpine Guide*, created something of a precedent in the Alps when in the 1840s he strode down the scorching Italian valleys bearing his own pack, and he was followed in time by a geometrical progression of rucksacked figures who found their way into remote places the world over.

The rucksack itself was deemed to be an advance on its predecessors, such as the two-shoulder-strapped knapsacks or haversacks (all words of German origin, incidentally; *haver* is the oats which cavalry carried for their horses, while *knapp* means close fitting and *ruck* means back). It was of Norwegian design and its merits were that it was capacious and framed and belted so that some of the weight was taken off the shoulders and shifted to the waist. Into its canvas cavity the rucksack brigade stowed their extra sweaters, blankets, primus stove and tins of bully-beef, sausages, butter, beans or whatever, and set forth with monstrous loads of 60 lb or more. The type is nicely satirised in Pat McManus's book *A Fine and Pleasant Misery*:

> The rule of thumb for the old backpacking was that the weight of your pack should equal the weight of yourself and the kitchen range combined. Just a casual glance at the full pack sitting on the floor could give you a double hernia and fuse four vertebrae. After carrying the pack all day, you had to remember to tie one leg to a tree before you dropped it. Otherwise you would float off into space. The pack eliminated the need for any special kind of ground-gripping shoes, because your feet would sink a foot and a half into hard-packed earth, two inches into solid rock.

The trouble was that the rucksack, though in some respects an improvement, was not only heavy in itself but was slung right down at the small of the back, thus weighting the body unnaturally and taking no advantage of the line of the backbone. It had quite escaped the attention of these modern men that primitive men and women the world over were accustomed to carry heavy loads either on their heads or at any rate with the use of a tump-line or head-strap, thus bringing into play the powerful muscles of the neck as well as the entire thrust of the spine. But then, the full significance of the backpack had escaped them also.

The heavy-duty backpack, as we now see it, is a symbol of self-sufficiency, and its bearer is proclaiming a message just as explicit as when clothes told of class distinctions. He is saying that he can travel without the help of anyone and, even if he is using his backpack for ordinary travel, at least that he is fit and able to walk when necessary within an urban environment. Once he is out in the country his pack tells us he is prepared for any eventuality – a change in the weather, an unforeseen delay, a sudden accident. The backpack is to the hill walker what the rope or axe is to the climber: a badge of intent, a membership card to a confraternity. At car-parks on the edges of the hills the backpacker is immediately distinguishable from the ordinary rabble of Sunday five-milers and, while they are joking and chattering and slamming the car doors, he is quietly gazing at the hills with a faraway look in his eyes.

He has taken great care what to put in his pack, selecting items with close attention to weight, taking or discarding according to experience in lengthy evening sessions at home with the aid of a check-list and the kitchen scales. He may have ultra-light 'new wave' items such as freeze-dried foods and vapour-barrier clothing, as well as his light-weight down-filled sleeping-bag, hoop tent, mini-stove, first-aid kit and pocket camera; and, as a result, his pack is much lighter than his father's was. But this consciousness of weight, this meticulous prepa-ration, is just what makes the backpack more significant to him. With it he can be entirely alone in the wilderness. No need, as in the past, to live off the land to some extent, to collect brushwood for an open fire, to gather wayside herbs or fruit or fungi – practices that anyway are frowned on in many places. No need, therefore, to go to pre-arranged campsites: the night can be spent anywhere, with water perhaps the only further requirement. No need for companions. He is self-contained, able to be alone with nature though not subject to her. The backpack is his home, as much part of him as the shell of the tortoise. It is like a little house, for inside it are his bedroom, kitchen, clothes-cupboard and all other furniture and housekeeping items. When he leaves it, for example to take a side-trip up some hill, he feels exposed, vulnerable, worried, like a child away from mum. His backpack is smart, brightly coloured and clean-cut. It is cleverly designed and, though not actually on the head or attached to it, lies high above the shoulder-line. It is a source of pride, and all the little day-packs on the backs of the shorter-length walkers pay tribute to it, like small sailing boats saluting a tall-ship ocean racer: every walker feels he must carry at least something on his back. Only in the remoter parts of poorer countries, where to carry a burden on your back is to betray disgraceful poverty, do local people regard the backpacker with the same sort of contempt as was once accorded to the pedestrian tourers.

Whatever the merits of the backpack it brings with it a serious penalty in that the pure physical pleasure of walking is inevitably lessened when one has to carry any extra weight, on one's back or elsewhere. The joy of walking derives from the co-ordinated rhythm of the upright body, unencumbered by dead-weight of burdens, free-flowing and perfectly balanced. Even the lightest of backpacks has the effect of slightly impeding that flow, slightly upsetting that balance. The heavy packs, however well designed, force the body forward so that the head has to be held up to look ahead and the arms dangle in front like those of an ape. The added pressure on the legs tires them unnaturally and forces them down at each pace flatfootedly. Knees, hips and shoulders start to ache prematurely. The walk becomes an ordeal long before it would without the pack, and from the outset it is an exercise in which the legs protest at their handicap instead of rejoicing in their strength. Top-heaviness has to be counter-acted, lack of agility to be anticipated. Footfalls have to be watched extra carefully, slipperiness has to be treated very cautiously. All the same, there is a special sort of satisfaction in walking with a heavy pack, a feeling of superiority over less-burdened walkers. Some hikers put stones into their packs for fitness training, others like to test their maximum weight-carrying capabilities. Volunteers taking summer provisions up to the hiking huts in the White Mountains of New Hampshire boast of carrying loads of over 150 lb for several hours. Besides, there are all the challenges and rewards of camping, the intermissions and destinations of the hike. But none of these are strictly speaking walking pleasures so much as pleasures which involve walking.

The nonchalance and frugality of earlier walkers are now seldom found, and safety first is the order of the day. The dire warnings issued to leaders of youth groups or adventure trainees, which should certainly be absorbed as a matter of course by serious mountain walkers, are often taken in an absurdly exaggerated sense by those just out for a two-hour walk on a sunny afternoon. To get wet is regarded as a dangerous misfortune, a likely prelude to pneumonia, and so everyone is clad in showerproofs or waterproofs often when there isn't a cloud in the sky, and many are the articles and discussions about the qualities of new materials like gore-tex and polypropylenes. Such excessive caution has earned a rebuke from the great populariser of fell walking in Britain, Alan Wainwright. In *Fellwanderer* he writes, 'You are not making a date with death. You are not making a technical excursion into space. You are going for a walk, that's all, no different from all the other walks except that there is more up and down and the way is likely to be rougher.' Another instance of this obsession with safety is the garish colours, the luminous scarlets and oranges, worn in the belief that if lost or stuck the wearer will be more easily found. Already in his mind, one feels, is the vision of the arrival of the mountain rescue team, the summoning of the helicopter, the winching-up of the stretcher, the arrival at the hospital. Sharp in his denunciation of those who make audio intrusions in the wild, whether with transistors or even shouts or singing, he is blind to his own visual intrusion. Such is the typical backpacking walker of today, in some ways so much more sensitive to and appreciative of the wilderness than were his predecessors, in other ways so much more insulated from uncertainty and adventure.

What is dominant in the backpacker's mind as he advances across the moorland or through the forest in insulated self-sufficiency? Like his predecessors he feels the spell of nature, but some aspects of it strike him more forcibly. The silence, for one: in his normal life he is constantly bombarded by sound – speech on the telephone or TV, music on the transistor or car radio. Assuming that he is not one of those who are so hooked on sound that they are plugged into their Walkmans throughout the hike, or unlucky enough to be walking in an area where low-flying aircraft or helicopters are active, the silence will come to him as a shock. The loneliness, for another. Typically, with all the media communication on top of whatever his personal relationships may be, he is never really alone at home. Now he is walking in an area where there is nobody, whether, as in the American national parks, because there never was anyone, or, as in upland Britain, because of agricultural depopulation. The silence and the loneliness will affect him unpredictably, especially if he is away for a few days or more. He may yearn for the city lights or find the thought of them unbearable. He will have to tussle with the problem of which is the 'real' world – the rocks and flowers and streams or the cars and supermarkets and electricity. So far, such problems are shared by all who go off into the wilderness, whether walking or camping or even canoeing or sailing. But for the walker there is a further factor, in that the action of walking induces a state of trance. This soothing calm can take the form of a respite from intellectual pressures and abstract thought coupled with the purely animal satisfaction of placing one foot in front of the other. The reasoning, articulate, part of the brain can be allowed to rest while the subconscious elements come into play, bringing with them the spirituality known long ago to the pilgrims and the intuition recognised by the Romantics, but today categorised as transcendentalism. Techniques which were known to Christian meditatives of the past, such as identification through endlessly repeated phrases, reappear in the form of Zen Buddhism; for instance in the spiritual exercise of walking up and down for fifty paces whilst concentrating entirely on the action of the feet. There can be no doubt that when it comes to meditation, walking is far superior to climbing. An article by Michael Tobias in *Climbing* very effectively demolishes the climbers' claims to be linked to the principles of Zen. The cult of climbing is not truly Zen, he says, because it is a superfluous activity, because it is charged with self-importance and competitiveness, because it is aggressive, and because it plays on acute fear. 'Enraged, almost desperate, the quiet ego maims itself with worry. It can no longer see things. It construes them instead, stacking cairns, falls, piton placements, loose flakes, and storm into a lethal perspective which self-aggravates, and dextro-amphetamizes all beauty.' Hiking, in contrast to climbing's 'vertical landscape of thought', has a 'horizontal perception' (not, by the way, to be confused with 'lateral thinking') and is entirely at ease and unselfconscious. It would also be possible to demonstrate that meditation when running must be inferior to when walking. The furious strain placed on the body, the need to will oneself on at speed, and the much shorter duration must imply that, whilst some sort of forced trance can be induced, it cannot compare to the application of meditative exercises on the tranquillity of mind that emanate from that most natural of all physical exercises – walking.

Another issue to be faced in hill walking today is the extent to which there lingers in it an element of boy-scoutery and male-matery inimical to the feminine temperament. Are hill walkers still trying to re-enact the hunting duties of their forefathers, even though they are not hunting anything? Are the hike and the camp inherently a masculine game, even though females may be persuaded to join them at it? In *The Great Outdoors* an article by Yvonne Bunting suggested something of this kind. She describes a walk on Kinder Scout that went wrong as a result of a sudden turn in the weather. After a sunny start a gale began to blow and the cloud came down. Allan, the leader, was unable to assemble his party and blew his whistle in vain. Light conversation had by this time ceased; feet fell frequently into icy, peaty water. As they pursued their long trudge off Kinder Scout, drenched to the skin and miserably cold, Yvonne and her friend Liz discussed which was more real: this male-dominated physical test, or the tests that they faced in their normal home and professional lives? And what anyway should be the role of the loving wife who wants to be with her husband and share with him his yearning for the wild open spaces, but in her heart feels that the whole thing is a boyish game, even a form of escapism?

Less lucid, but equally relevant, are the thoughts of small children who get taken on to the hills by hiking-loving parents. There is no doubt that even very small children can walk astonishing distances. Three-year-olds regularly walk up Snowdon from the Llanberis pass up the Pig Track: a two-year-old has walked up and down Sale Fell. But they do have to be motivated, and the secret seems to be a series of small and frequent goals. It is no good pointing to the crest of the hill and saying 'Ooh look, do let's get to the top of that lovely big mountain.' A constant succession of minor bribes and half-truths is needed, such as 'Bet you can't reach that rock before mum does', or 'When we get up that zig-zag I'll give you another sweety', or 'It gets much easier round the next corner'. Such constant inducements constitute a labour of love, and don't always work: a carry-pack should always be at hand as an alternative.

Now that so much of the lowlands and cultivated areas are closed to them, and the roads hostile with cars, today's walkers and hikers are more prone to roam in steep and rough places in hills and wilderness in a form of walking which is different from much of the classic walking of the past. Actually, from the strictly pedestrian point of view, the distinction is not so much between 'road' and 'hill' as between 'smooth' and 'rough'. One can stride along a gently graded track or a beaten earth path or a close-cropped ridge with as much automation as on a road; it is the stony rocky path or the boggy tufty ground or the walls and hedges and streams which require concentration, whether they are on the hillside or on the flat. In fact, scrambles on rock ridges can seem tame compared to some of the obstacles that lowland walkers face. All too often the 'public footpath' signs on the verges of roads point straight at dense hedges and (as amusingly described by Richard Wilson in an article in *The Great Outdoors*) the unwary walker who has bravely penetrated the hedge is then 'playfully released by that hedge with just enough momentum to carry him headlong into a ditch whose bottom consists of a six-inch layer of evil smelling slime, and has emerged therefrom to find himself nose-to-nose with an exceptionally fearsome specimen of Hereford bull . . .' Rough walking calls for a balance and co-ordination which are not needed in smooth walking, a skill that is more intuitive and less easy to learn: you either have it or you don't, just as for skiing or rock climbing or dancing. But, whether adept or not, all have to exercise their full attention as they walk along a rough path strewn with disproportionate boulders deceptively wedged and angled, where each step is a potential foot-slide or ankle-breaker, especially towards the end of the day. The ground ahead must be scanned to find the best line of progress, whilst simultaneously each next step is calculated. All this is relatively much more difficult for urban man because in ordinary life all his walking is on even ground and in consequence his ankles are unnaturally weak, despite which, strangely, he has largely abandoned that age-old aid to walking, the staff or stick. It is perhaps this application of the brain to the step that is the greatest difference between rough and smooth walking, for in other ways the same principles of rhythm and continuity apply.

When we look at walking on steep ascents or descents, still further technical aspects come into play. For the ascent, pace assumes an even greater effect on energy consumption than in ordinary walking, and the inexperienced are often astonished at how slowly the seasoned hill-men begin their long climbs. Gearing is the name of the game, the maximising of efficiency, adjusting the length of the stride to the circumstances. Then there is the need to rest the weight of the body on the back foot until the front foot has been placed; the need to put the whole foot down at the same moment and look for heel supports; the skill in accepting slips as they come, without altering the rhythm; the decision to zig-zag or go up straight; the skill in finding the most suitable route. For the descent even more attention is needed and, especially for the backpacked, it is far harder than the ascent. Each step must be used as a gentle brake, and made so that the foot lands in a horizontal position, taking advantage of protruding stones or tufts of grass or flat ledges, and not with the toes pointing downhill. Sometimes the downward steps must be taken sideways, crablike. The knees must be bent, and the kneecap is going to be the first casualty if you get it wrong or land with jarring thumps which may exceed your total body weight by several times (something which joggers are doing all the time, incidentally). You can take short bursts of lots of little fast steps, or you can take some really long strides when the slope eases, to break the monotony; but, these apart, the constraint in holding back and counteracting the gravitational pull is far more tiring than would ever be supposed from the simple idea of 'walking downhill'.

But there comes a point where walking ceases to be walking and becomes something else, though opinions differ on where that boundary lies. If scrambling is defined as where hands are used in addition to feet, it can hardly be considered 'walking' as we understand the term, but is more accurately a facet of climbing. Likewise if someone runs across or down a hill he is palpably not walking. Sliding down on snow is not walking, nor is it when iceaxes or crampons have to be used. But many of these are regular features of wilderness hiking generally and of British fell walking in particular. To this extent the story of mountain walking lies largely outside the scope of this book – which is concerned with Wenders and not Ascenders or Suspenders – and belongs to the history of mountain climbing. There we must place, for instance, Eric Newby's bestselling account of his attempt to scale Mir Samir in Afghanistan, which he ironically called *A Short Walk in the Hindu Kush*. (From the purely pedestrian viewpoint, the most remarkable occurrence in the book is that when, after endless difficulties, they finally arrived by vehicle at the start of their foot journey, Newby hadn't walked for more than three hours before his feet were bleeding severely from sores induced by his specially made Italian boots.) Besides, as is also the case with camping, the walking has often not been central to the achievement: the accounts of mountain walkers tell us little about their legs and feet, rather, they dwell on their climbs; their sense of achievement lies in the conquest of a peak rather than the length of a walk, on the glory of the mountain rather than the satiation of the body.

Despite these limitations British fell walking provides some interesting examples of pedestrian prowess during the nineteenth century from when the Wordsworths first climbed the Lakeland peaks. Three Anglican clergymen led the way over the hills in the 1860s and 70s, the first unfortunately nameless but commemorated by the appellation of the fine rock-snout on Cwm Glas in Snowdonia as 'The Parson's Nose'. All we know is that this enthusiast, a tall thin man of middle age, was wont to 'follow the skyline' of the hills, usually alone and in all weathers. Although he kept going for up to twelve hours a day he was remarkable in taking nothing to eat or drink with him but, as an antidote to thirst, he carried a small pebble in his mouth. When he got down to his base at the Pen-y-Gwryd inn, drenched with perspiration, he would continue to pace up and down, staff in hand, like a racehorse after exercise, so as to cool down gradually: and his abstemiousness extended into the evening, during which he never smoked, and drank at the most a couple of glasses of sherry. Meanwhile the Reverend Julius Elliott had sparked off the 'Lake District Round', and in 1864 covered 15 miles plus 6500 feet of ascent in eight and a half hours. But perhaps the most eccentric was the Reverend James Jackson, an unlikely cleric if ever there was one, having only taken holy orders after a military career and, when he had done so, devoting his energies to mountain scrambling. As a pedestrian, when aged sixty-nine he walked 46 miles in fourteen and a half hours, following this up two days later with 56 miles in eighteen hours and, after another two days, 66 miles in under twenty hours. 'Steeple' Jackson died at the age of eighty-two, having fallen 300 feet in an attempt to repeat his ascent of the Pillar in the Lake District three years previously. Then there was Frederick Bowring, another Lakeland figure, who walked with great vigour and precision until nearly sixty and, scorning the new-fangled Norfolk jacket, wore an old-fashioned tail coat into the copious pockets of which he stuffed his maps, compass, string, field-glasses, sandwiches, gloves, woollen scarf, several books, pipe and tobacco, and an immense blue kerchief whose purpose was to secure his wide-brimmed felt hat to his head in windy weather.

Moving on towards the turn of the century we find the excitements of hill walking enthusiastically discovered by Ernest Baker, a leading rock climber of his day. Writing later in *The Highlands with Rope and Rucksack* he describes an adventurous hike in the Grampians at the end of June 1897, in company with one Hamish Roy. They set off from the railway station at Blair Atholl each with rucksacks weighing around 25 lb and containing all sorts of tinned provisions, though no tent. Rather than walking straight up Glen Tilt they first headed up across moorland on to the long ridge of Ben Aghlo, ascending some 3000 feet; they mistook their way in the mist and so, instead of traversing the summit, reverted back into the glen, drenched with rain and dripping bracken and heather. From here they walked by the rough track over the pass into the top of Deeside, wading through flooded burns, till at evening they reached the forester's cottage at Bynack Lodge, where they slept in front of a peat fire. Next day it was clear that climbing was out of the question as the weather was worse than ever, so they decided to outflank the Cairngorms by proceeding westwards up the Geldie burn and over the watershed into Glen Feshie. On the way up there was no path, just a dreary morass, a desolate featureless waste that had to be navigated as if at sea. This was succeeded by 'the most formidable stretch of quaking bogs, unfathomable moss-hags, and miry pools that we had ever seen'. Eventually they reached the Feshie, but soon found their way along it blocked by the swollen Eidart burn, thundering down with tons of floodwater. They had to go up it for some distance before they could cross it, only to discover that they were on the wrong bank of the Feshie at a point where it enters a ravine. So they had to ford that too, holding each other's hands and probing with their sticks. Hamish now showed signs of exhaustion and his legs slipped frequently into bog-holes or over stones. Down the glen they trudged along a narrow path, shaggy braes looming up on either side, birches and alders waving over the stream. At Feshie Lodge they were offered drams of whisky and then they were off again, now in darkness, for four more hours until eventually they found the inn at Insh just before midnight. On the map they had only covered some 35 miles in the two days, on the ground perhaps 50: but in hill walking miles are meaningless and it was their thirty or so hours on the move that gives a better indication of their achievement. Nor was this all, for next day saw them walking up through the Rothiemurchus forest in early afternoon (having ridden in the train for the short distance to Aviemore), picking up logs and sticks for a camp fire, right up the Larig Ghru and over to the Shelter Stone above Loch Avon in the grim fastness between Cairn Gorm and Ben McDui, a walk of at least 12 miles and ascent of some 2600 feet, much of it extremely rough. Once again they reached destination around midnight. On the fourth and final day, after a breakfast of sardines, tomatoes, bacon and oatcakes, Hamish opted out down the Larig Ghru whilst the indomitable E. A. Baker, having scaled Cairn Lochan, proceeded to walk down to the Pools of Dee and then up the slopes of Braeriach, round the ridge to Cairn Toul, back to Einich Cairn, and then steeply down to Glen Einich for the long walk back to Aviemore, a day of some further 25 miles and cumulative ascent of some 3300 feet.

In this classic account of fell walking we can see one of its greatest attractions in strictly pedestrian terms – its variety. In the course of a single day one may typically cover sections of ground which are rough or easy, hard or soft, steep or level, grass or stone, path or untrodden, firm or slippery. On such a walk the correct calculation of energy expenditure becomes far more subtle than for the same number of hours spent walking along a constant road, a matter of judgement based on a mixture of experience, map-reading and visual apprecia-tion. Facile rules of thumb, such as Naismith's formula (one hour for every three miles plus an additional hour for each 2000 feet of ascent), will be treated very cautiously indeed. It is pointless to set a standard pace or speed, since constant adjustments are necessary. At the same time, underlying rhythm and continuity must be maintained so that each section remains part of the whole. In some ways it may be compared to riding a horse; only *you* are the horse, for *you* are Shanks's Pony (or, as the Germans have it, *Schusters Rappon*, cobbler's stallion; or the Italians, more spiritually, *Il Cavallo di San Francisco*, St Francis's horse). And just as an unruly horse must be broken in and reined, so must the will control the physical instinct of the leg muscles to stride ahead at the start of a long day's hike or to run downhill in sheer exuberance when there is still a further 10 miles to be done. Indeed, this ability to maintain a walk and resist a run, so as to cover really long distances most efficiently, distinguishes man from all the other mammals.

More recently a main preoccupation in fell walking has been the breaking of speed records in competitive events which, because they mostly involve extensive running, are not of prime interest here, nor relevant to the chapter on walking athletes. However, there is one great non-competitive challenge which permanently awaits Scottish fell walkers. This is the honour and achievement of having scaled all the two hundred seventy-six currently designated peaks of at least 3000 feet in the country. Those who do so are known as Munro Baggers or Munroists because Sir Hugh Munro was the first to compile a list of such peaks. The first recorded Munro Bagger was the

Reverend A. E. Robertson, who completed the task in 1901. The most notable recent Bagger is Martin Moran, who did them all within a three-month period in the winter of 1984–5.

Trail walking should by definition be easier than fell walking, but its ultimate challenge is sheer length, nowhere more so than on the Appalachian Trail, the longest marked footpath in the world. It runs for 2034 miles through a total of fourteen eastern States, from Georgia to Maine, alone a series of mountain ridges which basically constitute the watershed between the eastern seaboard and the central plains, and along which lay the Great Indian Warpath at the time that the settlers were still hacking their way inland. The highest point on the trail is only 6650 feet (Clingman's Dome), but this understates the severity of the total route, which is mostly on rough paths and through an endless succession of forests up and down an infinite series of humpy hills. The weather is often violent, as are various predators, both animal and human, that hang around the trail. It crosses highways at intervals, but often at obscure places without houses or shops. In effect, it is a hidden hikers' highway offering a unique alternative experience to anyone rash or bold enough to walk it from end to end. In 1975 a book edited by James R. Hare and entitled *Hiking the Appalachian Trail* was published; it is most instructive because it gives the personal accounts of nearly forty people who did so. Here we have an in-depth sample of super-hikers, veterans of the trail whose views must be of far greater import than any theorising by us lesser mortals; a group of often contradictory conclusions, from which one may assay a consensus whose value may be greater than the views of any particular marathon walker.

Of the forty-odd accounts there are twenty-nine by those who did the whole length consecutively in one direction or the other: that is to say, they did it without a break, though some may have rested for the odd day en route. Three of them give accounts of a second full hike along the trail, making thirty-two recorded times. If we exclude one which was done very slowly over nine months through a winter, with snow and storm a severe impediment, the remaining thirty-one records give an average timing of a hundred and thirty-nine days, which in its turn implies an average day's hike of just under 15 miles. The slowest was two hundred and eight days and the fastest, by Branley Owen, was seventy-three days: his backpack weighed 28 lb (Branley Owen's time is not the record for the trail, however: that is held by Warren Doyle of Shelton, Connecticut, who made it in sixty-seven days without a pack). Most of them had already had considerable hiking experience but at least four had never hiked before. When they were asked their main reason for deciding to hike the entire Appalachian Trail, their answers were various. Some cited personal problems at home, such as being bored with high school or suffering a bereavement. Several saw it as a challenge, one of them quoting the famous reply of Mallory as to why he wanted to climb Everest – 'Because it is there.' Another main theme was the desire to see nature in the wild and experience the simple life. Finally, there were at least two who started off without intending to do the whole thing but just kept going: one said it was like the lure of a good book, and that moving from state to state was like reading from chapter to chapter. When asked whether they would hike the trail again, given the opportunity, the majority not surprisingly said 'yes'; but it was in response to another question that their views are of greater interest. This was whether, were they to do it again, they would prefer to be alone or with a companion. Of the twenty-four who answered this question, fifteen had in fact hiked alone. Now, reflecting on the issue, only nine would want to do so – eight of them people who had hiked alone and one who had not. This response by people who had walked for four or five months on end is indeed an authoritative indicator of the balance that exists between people of varying temperaments on the age-old question that had vexed the minds of the essayists such as Hazlitt or Stevenson. It must be said that the fifteen who wanted companionship expressed some very restrictive reservations, such as that the companion should remain silent during the walk and only talk when in camp, or that he/she must be a proven friend beforehand. As for the loners, their replies included such caustic remarks as 'to become tied down to marching to some other piper's tune from the outset is an appalling prospect', or the spartan Andrew Giger's comment, 'Maybe he would have snored.'

At the time he decided to walk the Appalachian Trail Andrew Giger was an extremely fit man of middle age who had already hiked extensively in several American national parks and scaled a number of Californian peaks. He was also a man of exceptional precision and laid his plans with meticulous attention to detail as might an engineer or a scientist set up an intricate computer programme or a co-ordinator at Cape Kennedy get an astronaut onto the moon, as indeed did happen when he was on the trail. Armed with guidebooks and maps he determined the locations for thirteen 'caches', or boxes of provisions, which were to await him at post offices. These were between 106 and 195 miles apart. He then calculated the number of days between caches, taking account of terrain, and this varied between six and eight days, for he was to cover over 20 miles a day on average. Now he devised his trail menus, to be supplemented by periodic meals in restaurants, and spent much thought on how to prune the weight of his backpack and eliminate non-essentials. Bearing in mind the sequence of trail shelters he carried no tent, just a sleeping-bag and poncho. His kit also included a miniature gas stove, knife, torch and camera. The total loaded weight exclusive of food was only 14 lb. He wore a T-shirt and shorts and, as for his boots, he started with conventional Wolverines with vibram soles but had to change during the walk to a pair of close-fitting Georgia boots and later to a pair of Dunham Tyroleans: inside them was just a single pair of woollen socks. Mount Katahdin in Maine was his destined 'moonfall', programmed by him for a hundred days. He made it in ninety-eight, blasting off up Springer Mountain in Georgia on 12 May 1969.

Even in the first week he was made aware of how tough the hike would be. It rained unceasingly for four days; he was among trees with hardly any views for hundreds of miles; and he was all alone on the trail. And worse, he soon developed foot troubles – a blister, and then a torn heel tendon which 'swells to nearly twice its normal width' and 'protests the steady clomp, clomp, clomp with a shocking surge of pain that requires an immediate stop': meanwhile his knee played up, specially downhill. But none of these ailments prevented Andrew Giger from keeping to schedule, and after some days they all righted themselves. On he went through the Great Smoky National Park, the haunt of the black bears, where at night trail hikers are bolted behind the wire-mesh frontages of the wooden lean-tos like animals at the zoo, while the bears scavenge around the campsite like hikers. Other bothersome features included an electric storm, rattlesnakes, an aggressive Dobermann Pinscher, and gnats from which he soon got some protection by using a leafy branch as a whisk. When he reached the entrance to the Shenandoah National Park, 734 miles from his starting point, he found he had lost 17½ lb which he sought to put right by gobbling down an enormous dinner and breakfast at the hotel. This proved a mistake, for next day on the march he suffered from stomach pains and a form of gastritis. His energy fell away and his ability to hike was 'gone like last year's leaves'. He became so depressed that he decided to give up the whole expedition and turn back to the road. As if to ratify this decision, he sat down to rest. But then 'the sunshine filtered through the leaves. A bird sang. It was a nice day, but the trip was over for me. The bird's song repeated, repeated. It's crazy, but to me the bird's song sounded like a word: *"Premature, premature."*' Thus did Andrew Giger receive support from birdsong, a charming and recurrent feature of man's relationship to the natural world and known to history and legend through the stories of characters as diverse as Siegfried and St Francis. He went on slowly and after some days the gastritis had eased, though he still had the sensation of walking mesmerised, as in a dream.

Now he came to an area frequented by hikers, campers and trippers. At least this meant more restaurant meals and an occasional laundromat, but it also meant that the shelters were often full of noisy scout groups or sometimes unsympathetic big-city motor cyclists. He noted wryly how many people, after their initial astonishment at his hike, announced with almost religious fervour that they too would go and walk the Appalachian Trail! By now it was getting really hot; he had no hat, and there were several long sections of road. These were followed by a gigantic roller-coaster as the trail led straight up and over and down a series of rounded mountains; and here Andrew Giger gives us a marvellously graphic account of his ordeal:

> Frequently there are merciless climbs up the steepest part of the slope, no grading, no switchbacks. Everything has to be put in low-low gear for these. Breath comes in deep gasps, my heart pounds like a pile driver. Step after step up, up. And it's a long one, no top in view. Ages seem to drag by, but it's only five minutes. You can keep it up, can't you? You're supposed to be in great condition. It'll take an hour, maybe. An hour, ugh! Stepping, stepping, leg muscles weary with the load, but you force them to go on up, up, up. Eons pass by, a glimmer of blue through the trees! A flattening! A false top! You're not half there yet! Only 30 minutes have passed.

He was obsessed with the idea that the trail blazers here had made it all needlessly difficult and that somewhere through the trees there would be an easier path. He devised mental games to keep his mind off the pain: how many steps would he take on the entire trail? (answer, four million); how long would a snail take to do the trail? (answer, two hundred thousand years). But there was no let-up. 'Rocks! they fill the trail. No avenue over or along it is not paved with these anvils of torture. Your feet never touch a level place. Bend, twist, wrench, turn; your feet keep step on the rocks by slipping, arching, squeezing, sliding forward, sideways, backways, and around them. This is a murderous footway.' By this time his feet were swelling and his boots felt constricting and his toes hurt: 'How can a little toe hurt so much? it's like toothache.' Worse, his tendons were playing up again: 'Have to take it easy on my feet there are no spares.'

Through the states of New Jersey and New York Andrew Giger plodded on. Once the rain had died out the going was good and his main concern was with insects and reptiles. Mosquitoes and deerflies were extremely active, puff adders and blacksnakes slithered across the path, spiders together with worms and toads crept over him at night. He had to watch out for angry ground-hogs and fierce dogs, and saw porcupines and racoons. It became wet again: 'Boots squish with water, bubbles come through the seams.' After this the Appalachian Trail led for the first time across long stretches of open country above the forest and with wide views when fine, but then it was back in the endless trees and alone in the wet. 'Boots slog through the murky black decay of vegetation and stumble against roots raised as if in hope of escaping the mire themselves. Footsteps are caught in the vacuum of the oozing quagmire.' Though at times he sang or whistled to himself his mood was by now one of uncaring resignation: he felt no elation at approaching the end, merely a conditioned reflex to keep on going. On Old Speck he encountered ice and snow; moose and bears crashed off into thick undergrowth as he approached; a swirling river was crossed by the use of two cables suspended across it; and at last he made it to Mount Katahdin in dark thick cloud and howling wind. The ordeal over, Andrew Giger reflected: 'What has it been like? It's been wet, wet water; flies; beds of boards; mosquitoes; pulsing aching feet; uncut brush; greenbriars; poison ivy; waterless stretches; un-graded trail; enervating heat; rocks that macerate your feet; gnawing hunger; loneliness that had you talking to yourself.' And his advice to those who would like to walk the Appalachian Trail was 'Don't do it!'

Two other trail walkers deserve mention – the oldest and the youngest. Emma Gatewood was a month short of her seventieth birthday when she last hiked the entire trail in 1957, and that wasn't the end of her walking, for she did the Oregon Tail two years later and the Sherborne Pass to Rainbow Lake section of the Appalachian Trail

five years after that. The 1957 walk was a repeat of her previous
through-trail hike two years earlier, during which she sprang to
national fame. She was known to the public affectionately as Grandma
Gatewood, but the remarkable thing about her was not that she was a
granny but that she was the mother of eleven children. Besides an
indomitable will and a placid temperament, Emma Gatewood had two
personal habits which undoubtedly helped her powerfully on her way:
she walked extremely slowly, and she ate no hot food but just cold
snacks. Her pack weighed around 20 lb on her first walk but less on
her second, and contained only the most basic things such as first-aid
kit, knife, water-bottle, cape and hat, as well as some food such as
chipped beef, raisins, peanuts, powdered milk and salt. She wore
sneakers, not boots. Thus equipped she set forth up Mount
Oglethorpe in Georgia and she hadn't been going for more than a few
hours before she encountered a black bear. As the gap between them
narrowed, Grandma let go with what she called 'my best holler'.
'"Dig," I hollered, and he dug.' Emma Gatewood is no more, but her
ghost haunts the Appalachian Trail, and sightings of her are reported
at remote shelters or plodding along the long green tunnel.

At the other end of the scale we find Eric Ryback, who hiked the
trail from north to south in a very creditable eighty days in 1969. At
the time Eric was only seventeen and still at school. He resolved to do
it during his summer vacation without realising what he was in for,
having never hiked before. (He subsequently kept up his hiking,
however, and has walked both the Pacific Crest Trail and the Continental Divide.) He started off up Mount Katahdin at a tremendous
pace, so much so that at the end of the first day he stumbled and fell
and 'I was too exhausted to rise; I went to sleep right where I lay. The
thought of never waking occurred to me and it was almost pleasant.'
Heaving his monstrously heavy 60 lb pack he forced himself over the
exposed summit of the mountain in a storm and the hostility of the
terrain and adversity of the weather beat so hard against his will that
he found tears streaming down his face. After the initial days, during
which he got lost more than once, he adjusted his walking to a slower
pace though still keeping up his mileages, for instance doing 34 miles
in a day to Monson so as to telephone home. His boots got singed by a
camp fire, he capsized when being ferried by canoe over the Caratunk,
the blackflies were so bad that his shirt was stuck to his skin by dried
blood, but 'my rewards for the punishment I was taking were in the
beautiful scenery and the good feeling of using my body to its limit

every day.' Once into New Hampshire he found things easier but, as a result, loneliness became more oppressive. So he arranged for his fifteen-year-old brother to join him; but after four days the brother found the going too tough and Eric realised he would have to combat his loneliness himself. On he went, through a great heat with snakes coiled around on every rock, and then a great rain where slippery stones lay in wait for faulty foot-falls. Here he often fell, and cut his boot, struggling ahead in a trance till at the end of the day he collapsed on the mountainside. Ironically, at the next town he came to he was cold-shouldered by the citizens because he hadn't watched the moon-walk ('one small step for a man, one giant leap for mankind') on TV! In Virginia his parents came by car to meet him and arranged to transport his pack to another road crossing 48 miles ahead along the trail so that he could make it in just one day. He did make it, at first tripping over his feet due to the unaccustomed lightness, jog-trotting for 18 miles and then slowing to a walk. Further vicissitudes included stomach pains, broken backpack straps, violent storms and prowling bears: also stumbles in the dark when he adopted night walking to avoid the heat of the day. Towards the end Eric Ryback spent a night up in a fire-observation tower, and when dawn came the scene was so unutterably beautiful that he wept. 'I reflected back to the boy I had been when I started and the man I now thought I was.'

Nowhere is the contrast between age and youth better exemplified than in the utterly different attitudes of Grandma Gatewood and Eric Ryback as they hiked along that identical trail, albeit in opposite directions. Grandma represents the obstinacy of age, the dogged guts that we have seen in the likes of Borrow, Cooper, Burroughs and, above all, Hutton. One can hardly imagine that any of these tough old birds would have wept to see the sunrise or seen life in a new way as a result of their walks. Eric is in the tradition of Rousseau, Heine, Belloc and Lee when they first set out on their journeys, wide-eyed and ripe for romance. To them tears did not appear shameful, and each fresh impression was vividly absorbed. Their walks were in a manner of speaking a forty days in the wilderness, a period of withdrawal from the worldly world by which their spiritual powers were enriched. Wordsworth, who walked so extensively from adolescence to old age, experienced a gradual deadening of the emotions and expressed what many come at length to realise when he wrote in 'Intimations of Immortality' that he could no longer perceive nature with 'the glory and the freshness of a dream'.

Even when youths undertake great walks they often do not write about them until long afterwards: and since long-distance walking is usually a solitary and even secret affair, idiosyncratic and undramatic, the mass media generally ignore it except for those few exploits which they have themselves sponsored (and inevitably overkilled, the well-oiled support team in close attendance). Thus the heroic figures of walking – even of race-walking – are seldom young when they become heroes. Although some of them have walked extensively ever since they were young, others only take it up later in life. In this latter group is John Hillaby, the most influential writer on the subject of walking in Britain today. Already aged fifty when he strode to fame in his *Journey through Britain* nearly twenty years ago, he still dominates the scene and is accepted as the guardian of the mysteries though, like the legendary Priest of the Golden Bough, he is always liable to be toppled by some younger challenger. Hillaby owes his success not only to being a formidable walker but to interpreting the craft intellectually and in contemporary terms. He employs the method of walking to investigate what is really going on in the countries through which he travels, making full use of his skills as a newspaperman in drawing people out in passing conversations or long drinking sessions. His books are loaded with all sorts of curious facts, historical, sociological, scientific or whatever, dug up to decorate his story and laced with irreverent jocularity.

Stripped of all these, what is the essence of his message about walking itself? In the first place, he is basically a loner who believes there is a mystical quality in walking alone and in communion with the countryside. To this end he feels that the discerning walker should wear discreet colours – dark greens and browns – and should, so far as possible, blend into the physical and social scene: he should appear neither as a scarecrow nor a tramp but rather as the questing citizen who happens to be on foot. Secondly, he believes in walking fast, and finds that once in overdrive he can stay there for a long while in a motion which is akin to gliding. He sees himself as a 'light footman', as opposed to the 'crashers' and 'plodders' who are less nifty with their feet; something of a dancer, even, in that he is quite prepared to skirt around muddy patches in his lightweight boots. Interestingly, his favourite piece of mental music is the second movement of Beethoven's fifth symphony. 'The clarinet skips along pursued by the bass. The footfalls are light and irresistible. They contain the very stuff of motion, of controlled unrest. There is a gait, a going-forwardness in every phase.' (Despite this description, it must be conceded that this *andante con moto* bears a distinctly slower tempo than does the *allegro* that had been selected by Sidgwick as the optimal walking music.) But it is not merely for these precepts that John Hillaby is admired. For, though a 'light footman', he is in no way a pale imitator of the pedestrian tourers of the past. For one thing, he tents and dosses down without much regard for comfort. For another, he ranges over a full spectrum of terrain, from the post-industrial wastelands of Lancashire or Brabant at one extreme, to the snow-covered heights of the Maritime Alps or the Pindus Mountains at the other, and he makes both seem equally interesting. Most of all, though, he describes the processes by which walking came to be for him a means of self-discovery, particularly following the death of his wife. On his two greatest walks, those through Britain and Europe, he had constantly rejected easy options and walked the whole way. But then, with personal tragedy so close, he cast about for new ventures, some of which he failed to undertake in full. From a consequent realisation of human frailty came a new love and marriage to a lady who shares his passion for walking. It seems that the crucial turning point in this mental progress took place on the Appalachian Trail, which John Hillaby set out to walk from the northern end, as described in *Journey through Love*. There came a point when he pondered whether he still retained his former zest for walking alone. Previously he had always been able to conquer loneliness by asking himself whether he would really prefer to be anywhere else (a mental trick that had also been used by Belloc): but this time the answer was unclear. After he had taken his decision to call it a day and leave the trail at a point in New Hampshire, he reflected:

Journeys undertaken alone have a life of their own. Each one is different. One common factor among many in my previous walks had been elation at successful accomplishment. I strode to my goals with the pride of Lucifer, imagining myself the conqueror of yet another portion of the earth. Whole orchestras played for me. Given time, I thought, I could walk anywhere. In between times, during those unavoidable dull stretches which are to be found everywhere, I either jingled the light chains of memory or foresaw more walks to make parts of a personal mosaic more of a whole. On this jaunt I thought, wrongly, I could foresee the outcome of solitude. In fact my comfort, my drive to reach one brief shelter after another, came largely from the good companions I met on the way. Could it be that, like all good egoists, I could not bear to be alone for long?

To observe him in his prime, one should read *Journey through Britain*, in which his distinctive walking style is clearly seen. The walk from one end of Britain to the other is harder than it used to be. If you stick to the roads you are at the mercy of traffic; if you leave them the going is rougher. John Hillaby intended to keep off roads completely, but was forced to compromise and went on lanes and sometimes busy roads for part of his walk. Even so his route involved about 1100 miles, mostly over rough ground, which he covered in fifty-five walking days over a period of about two months. His backpack weighed 35 lb loaded and contained a small double-lined tent, sleeping-bag, maps (inch to the mile), two compasses, knife, purse, camera, binoculars, notebooks, several paperbacks and minimal spare clothing. He had a light anorak, windproof but not truly waterproof, and wore Italian lightweight walking shoes. He had no logistical support but took money to buy food and accommodation when needed. In fact he slept in inns or houses for about half the nights, the remainder mostly in his tent but once (unusually) in a children's tree-house and once (romantically) in a turret of the Roman Wall. As for hot meals, he took them when he could, finding them best value either at transport cafés or large hotels rather than in genteel boarding houses. He began the day with coffee and sandwiches, and drank three pints of liquid at midday and the same in the evening.

Kicking off from Land's End he scuttled rapidly through the West Country, but as he approached Bristol he became painfully aware that something was seriously wrong with his feet and calf muscles. He had been walking too fast; and so, after a few days of complete rest, he continued at a rather less frenetic pace. But this did not preclude bursts of speed, as for instance when he marched for a while with a platoon of commandos training in the Black Mountains, or when he walked through the grizzly Scottish industrial belt as fast as he could: and generally he bustled along as a good 'light footman' should, head held high and arms swung across the chest. He tells of the torture of walking along a railway line with its maddeningly short-spaced sleepers, and the joy of walking naked through the conifer plantations of the Forestry Commission. Also of a succession of minor setbacks, such as getting lost on Dartmoor, or taking a nasty tumble off a wall and bruising his ribs at the end of a 25-mile slog in the Pennines. But more severe tests awaited him in the north of Scotland, the wildest part of Britain. After a week of real adventure, losing his way twice and traversing ground so rough that it was 'painful even to recall', he experienced a sense of lassitude and was thankful to be guided for two days by a climbing instructor: 'I had become tired of path-finding. All the pleasures of pioneering had drained away; I wanted nothing more than to conserve what little energy and enthusiasm I had for the one remaining obstacle ahead, the crossing of the Assynt.' Assynt was indeed the ultimate test. In this wild, rocky, scree-sloped maze of knobby peaks he slipped to the edge of a precipice, the soles of his shoes came loose, he got lost in cloud, and he came down the wrong side and had to trudge for hours across boggy land till he reached a shepherd's house near midnight after nearly eighteen hours on the move. Throughout there are references to his habit of singing – padding over Penhale Sands 'I sang as loud as a man can sing on his own', and there were sing-songs in the pubs of Derbyshire and choruses with the marching commandos. So it is not surprising to learn that when he was lost in the mountains in mist for the night, he found himself singing psalms. In this way he reached John o'Groats, that sad counterpart to Land's End; reflecting on his journey he concludes that the most satisfying aspect was the 'sense of gradual transition from one place to another'.

In America the prophet is Colin Fletcher, and his *Complete Walker* has been called the 'Hiker's Bible'. His influence thus comes not so much from accounts of his own hikes (though he has written about them, too) as from his six hundred-odd pages of fascinating detail on everything one needs to know about backpacking. Now in his sixties, he hit the hiking scene when he walked from Mexico to Oregon across the deserts and mountains of California nearly thirty years ago; and later he became the first man known to have walked up the length of the Grand Canyon within the rim. For him the paramount objective for the walker is to be fit and able to penetrate into the green world of the wilderness. So far as the actual action of walking on rough ground is concerned, he gives the following advice: 'A delicate sense of balance is vital to good walking, day or night. And it's not just a matter of being able to cross steep slopes without tightening up. Your body should always be poised and relaxed so that you just put down your feet, whatever your size and whatever your load, with something close to daintiness.' He has no problems with loneliness: 'Mostly, I find that everything takes care of itself. My mind soars or grubs along or meanders halfway in between, according to the sun or cloud, the wind or rain, the state of my metabolism, the demands of the hour or other elements beyond my control.' Of course, in reality he leaves very little to chance; but it is an element of the greatness of his book that he warns against obsession with dogma in terms of walking rules. On the contrary, he feels, walkers should adjust to the peculiar circumstances of physique and terrain, and not agonise over planning or equipment. However, he has nothing against an obsession with walking itself, which he commends wholeheartedly as 'a delectable madness, very good for sanity'.

Fletcher doesn't elucidate on this paradox, but perhaps we can dissect it more closely. To walk extensively, habitually and determinedly is excellent so long as it is having a beneficial effect over the mind as well as the body. In this context it is not an obsession – though it may appear so to others – but an act of sanity. But walking, though always beneficial to the body, can in some instances act against the psyche. When this happens it can be considered as obsessive, and even a mild form of madness. Such is the case when those who have enjoyed walking triumphs in the past feel they must continue because it is expected of them and not because they want to. It is true also of those who, though once able to endure solitude, now find it almost intolerable, but wouldn't dare admit this to anyone else. Again, it applies to those who use walking as a means of escapism, an excuse for shirking harder personal problems which they ought to face (though not to those who are frustrated in their desires by inexorable external forces). The trance-like effect of walking can be used by some to avoid constructive and logical thought, an aspect well understood by drill sergeants. If this applies to several of the characters in this book, so be it. For walking itself cannot bring contentment, it can merely assist. To suggest that long walks are a prerequisite for happiness is to say that only the fit and healthy can be happy. Happiness in life is far more than keeping the body in good trim or getting into the countryside. In effect, in writing about walking just as much as in actually walking, it is essential to keep one's feet – or one of them at least – firmly on the ground.

Appendix
Warriors

THE Poor Bloody Infantry has been the most basic element in all armies from time immemorial and, by whatever name it has been known, foot-slogging has been its inescapable lot – that is, until modern times and the use of mechanised transport. (The only exceptions to this generalisation were certain foot-soldiers in history who moved about on horseback but fought on foot, such as the Anglo-Saxon *housecarles* who lost the battle of Hastings.) Unlike ordinary pedestrians who were always in an obvious way inferior to horse-riders, the infantry has at various times enjoyed a decided battlefield superiority over cavalry. This was particularly true in classical times when the discipline of the Greek phalanx and the Roman legion in tight formation could ward off and destroy any of the horsemen that might be set against them; and then, after a thousand years of domination by cavalry, came the specialised uses of long bows, pikes, muskets and rifles, which re-established the foot-soldiers as decisive in the field until the arrival of machine-guns and tanks, aeroplanes and bombs. The Roman Imperial Army made use of a marching pace which must have been a quickstep. From a late-fourth-century source we learn that the legionaries were taught by continuous practice to march quickly and in time, and were sent on training marches covering 20 miles at 3 miles to the hour (in terms of our present 'miles' and 'hours') inclusive of a short halt each hour, and with a heavy load of over 60 lb. They wore sandals, but in cold weather lined them with fur; and they marched in columns of ten. We also know that the centurions at any rate were in the habit of occupying themselves on idle days in camp by going on walks simply for the exercise. Iberian tribesmen, on first observing this, supposed they must be mad and offered to show them the way back to their tents.

After the collapse of the legionary system there were only two ways in which foot-soldiers marched long distances. Either they walked out of step in loose formation, each to his own pace; or else they marched in unison, using a slow pace with little or no arm swinging. But then, from the time of the Renaissance, there came the introduction of more artificial steps for manoeuvring in the face of the enemy, also demonstrated at ceremonial parades. Machiavelli in *The Art of War* (written in 1520) says: 'The soldiers, then, are to observe the motions of their ensigns, and the ensigns are to observe the beat of the drum: for when that beat is rightly managed, it is a direction to the whole army which acts and moves in a certain measure and pace according to the different notes and sounds so that the army may know how to keep due time and order.' The present slow march of the British Army at 75 paces to the minute derives from this, and from the later days when the battalions would hold their fire till they could see the whites of their enemies' eyes, even waiting till the enemy fired first. Prussian generals disputed whether 75 or 78 to the minute was more efficient. Then the French Revolutionary Army kicked over the traces of these conventions and manoeuvred at a faster pace with electric results. The slow march was now relegated to ceremonial parades and drills, becoming a more formalised affair, with a pause of the leg as it moves forward, and contact with the ground on the whole foot at once. The German Army also adopted a quickstep parade march – the 'goose step' – still retained in Eastern Europe. The effort of kicking the leg stiff and straight ahead before bringing it flat-footedly to the ground is so great that the goose step can only be sustained for a few hundred feet at a time, but quite long enough to give a splendid martial image to the saluting stand and to all the cameras which record it, even though to democratic eyes it smacks of Prussian militarism.

The use of quicksteps for route marching increased with the development of a specialised form of light infantry in the late eighteenth century. In England, General Sir John Moore established a pace of 160 to the minute. This didn't mean that the light infantry always marched at this pace, but that it could be used in bouts if needed. Later, in Italy, the Bersaglieri established what must be the fastest marching pace by means of either alternate quick or double marching or by an unvarying jog-trot. Meanwhile the regular pace for normal infantry in modern armies hovers around 120 to the minute. There is something mathematically precise, pleasing to the military mind, about two paces to the second, but it is certainly a fast rate for covering 15 miles or so. At 30 inches to each pace (doubtless checked from time to time by some obsessive drill sergeant with a pacing stick) it means 3½ miles to the hour. The arm swinging that went with it on parades – arm swung up to shoulder level, fist closed, thumb upward – was usually abandoned as soon as the barracks were out of sight, and the troops marched for most of the way 'at ease'. This speeding up of the route march was the result of changing factors in military logistics, including the general improvement of roads, the use of transport for provisions and better organisation of large formations. In any unit of marching men a slight check at the front or an obstacle always causes a concertina effect, with the rear at first stationary then desperately trying to catch up. With large bodies of troops the contingents get spread out, the last arriving long after the first. Even without checks thirty thousand men marching three abreast is reckoned to take up at least 5 miles of road. Strict discipline is needed to achieve even this, such as keeping to the side of the road so that mounted men or civilian traffic can pass. Incidentally, the reason why in continental Europe people keep to the right is thought to derive from the time of the Napoleonic Wars when civilian traffic was ordered to do so on trunk roads and get off to the side when oncoming military units approached. To walk on the right is unnatural and contrary to normal custom which has always been to tend to pass to the left, thus keeping the whip hand, or sword hand, on guard against potential impact or attack. Recently, Napoleonic practice has been revived in codes of conduct for pedestrians to face oncoming traffic.

Based on these march patterns military science derived all sorts of rules and theories, as a few quotations from the master of that science – Clausewitz – will show. 'For our modern armies it has long been settled that a march of fifteen miles should be the usual day's work which, on long distances, may be set down as an average distance of ten miles per day, allowing for the necessary rest days, to make such repairs of all kinds as may be required.' Bearing in mind the move-ments to and from camps or billets and the staggering of the line of march: 'We see, therefore, that the fatigue endured by a soldier loaded with his pack for ten or twelve hours is not to be judged by that of an ordinary journey of fifteen miles on foot which a person, on tolerable roads, might easily get over in five hours.' For a Division of eight thousand men it takes eight to ten hours on tolerable roads, or ten to twelve hours in hilly country, to cover the 15 miles. But Clausewitz is at pains to point out that all these calculations are merely yardsticks against which to place all manner of unforeseen circumstances such as the state of the roads, terrain, weather, and the condition and morale of the troops.

Nevertheless there were some remarkable achievements in the movements of infantry by marching. For example, in the Seven Years War in 1760, the Prussian General Lascy marched a corps of fifteen thousand men 225 miles in ten days, an average of 22 miles a day, from Schweidwitz to the relief of Berlin. Earlier in the century the Anglo-German army under Marlborough had marched to the Danube before Blenheim at the average rate of about 10 miles a day, despite bad roads and a lack of parallel roads, and with diversions for billeting. But the greatest achievements were those of the French. In the Italian campaign of 1796 the divisions of Augerau and Massena in the course of one week each marched over 100 miles as well as fighting two engagements. Then came the biggest advance of all. The Grand Army, from its camp at Boulogne threatening England, in 1805 marched to the Rhine at over 18 miles a day. In September it advanced into Bavaria, and over eleven days of sustained marching Soult's corps covered 275 miles. Finally Davout's corps arrived at the field of Austerlitz after doing 70 miles in little over forty-eight hours. Napoleon's troops carried their rifles and pack-loads of 65 lb. They wore mass-produced leather boots that were glued and pegged, not stitched. At night they bivouacked around a fire (Napoleon had dispensed with tents) and slept under their greatcoats, feet towards the fire. They were issued with rations and brandy, which were usually eaten too soon, and which they kept in a canteen, and part of the success of these long marches was that the commissariat was there to feed them each evening, for there was no time for foraging: the maxim was 'the army marches on its stomach.'

It also marched through its ears, for behind the leather-aproned pioneers with felling axes at the head of the column came the drum-major, drummers and musicians, with the band divided into sections. Even if the men could only hear the fife and drum, the sound would send the well-known march tunes reverberating through their minds, stirring hymns by composers such as Mehul or Rouget de Lisle, played with natural harmonics. Of these the most remarkable was the Cripples March in which the drumstick claps and silent beats evoke the agony of tired feet and an ironic attitude to military pomp and ceremony. For marching has from the earliest times been helped by music. The drum beat has instilled its mesmeric spell into the minds of marching men for thousands of years, as they trod in rhythm and unison. From it has developed the full panoply of the military band with its drums, trombones, trumpets, cornets, bassoons, saxophones, clarinets and piccolos, and its four-square music. Nowadays the band is confined to concerts and ceremonial parades, but in the past it actually played on long route marches and was a powerful aid to the achievement of those Napoleonic armies.

But despite the stirring sights and sounds it has to be conceded that a body of marching men inevitably expresses a restrictive uniformity in which there is no liberty or artistry. Soldiers are not willing walkers, and though some of the most amazing feats of walking have been done by soldiers, these are more a measure of the achievements of their commanders, and of the extent to which the commanders have grasped the principles of men such as Clausewitz. Communal discipline is not so admirable as self-discipline, and our main sentiment in contemplating those marching thousands may be not so much approval as wonder and perhaps pity for the individuals who composed even the most terrifying fighting forces, whose fortitude was often tested on route and forced marches, and whose humanity was sometimes suddenly exposed when things went wrong and they had to endure a chaotic retreat, as these two brief but graphic references will remind us. First, the testimony of Captain von Borcke, from Magdeburg, of what it was like to walk in the retreat from Moscow in 1812:

Gloomy, silent, and with downcast gaze, this rabble of dying men walked from Orsha to the Berezina like a funeral procession. Preoccupied only with oneself, feeling the seeds of death in one's enfeebled body, and only reminded that one was a human being through one's instinct for self-preservation, one was no longer capable of conversation, of communicating to companions and friends about what was going on and what was of common interest.

And second, going back into the dawn of history, these words of Xenophon in his classic account of the heroic retreat of the Ten Thousand Greeks across Armenia in 401–400 BC:

Some of the soldiers likewise were falling behind – those whose eyes had been blinded by the snow, or whose toes had rotted off by reason of the cold. It was a protection to the eyes against the snow if a man marched with something black in front of him, and a protection to the feet if one kept moving and never quiet, and if he took off his shoes for the night; but in all cases where men slept with their shoes on, the straps sunk into their flesh and the shoes froze on their feet; for what they were wearing, since their old shoes had given out, were brogues made of freshly flaged ox-hides.

Index

199

201